THE ONLY BOOK OF ITS KIND

all about the miracle substances that have revolutionized modern gardening—

---

gibberellic acid—the growth stimulator
that makes plants grow bigger, stronger, more luxuriant

foliar feeding—with your garden hose you
can feed your plants quickly and directly through their leaves

chelated iron—the magic element that fights
burnt patches in your lawn, helps keep it bright and green

soil conditioners—they keep the earth
loose, receptive to moisture, perfect for healthy root spread

2-3-5 triodobenzoic acid—the hormone
treatment that speeds up flowering by 10 to 20 days

demeton, schradon—the systemic insect slayers
that stay in the plant to far outlast old-fashioned insecticides

pre-emergence weed killers—
use them before you plant, goodbye weeds!

frit—the magic "glass" chips for those important
trace elements, boron, manganese, copper, zinc, molybdenum

**and hundreds and hundreds of other
important FACTS on the new, modern methods and formulations
developed by science for your garden**

Books by Samm Sinclair Baker

❦ MIRACLE GARDENING

❦ SAMM BAKER'S CLEAR AND SIMPLE GARDENING
  HANDBOOK

❦ Published by Bantam Books

MIRACLE GARDENING

•

BY SAMM SINCLAIR BAKER

•

BANTAM BOOKS
TORONTO · NEW YORK · LONDON

MIRACLE GARDENING

A Bantam Book / published March 1958
2nd printing ....April 1958   4th printing ....March 1960
3rd printing ....March 1960   5th printing ....April 1960
Bantam Gardening Guide edition published March 1966

Cover photograph courtesy of Oregon Bulb Farms
Text drawings by Lillian Chestney
Insert drawings by John Floherty, Jr.

Library of Congress Catalog Card Number: 66-14719

Bantam Books are published by Bantam Books, Inc., a subsidiary
of Grosset & Dunlap, Inc. Its trade-mark, consisting of the words
"Bantam Books" and the portrayal of a bantam, is registered in the
United States Patent Office and in other countries. Marca Registrada.
Bantam Books, Inc., 271 Madison Avenue, New York, N. Y. 10016.

PRINTED IN THE UNITED STATES OF AMERICA

CONTENTS

MIRACLES FOR <u>YOUR</u> GARDEN

This is the age of "miracles" in gardening— and lucky you, you're a living part of it!

Exciting new formulations in fertilizers, soil conditioners, insect sprays, weed killers and other miracle workers have been developed and are being created daily. Use them right, and they'll help you produce mammoth blooms such as were hardly even dreamed of not long ago.

But that's only one side of the new gardening miracle. You can not only boost growth, but also you can often control and inhibit growth as you wish. In fighting garden enemies now, you can eliminate many harmful insects. And you can help others to thrive which aid your garden to grow.

Truly a revolution in gardening has taken place. All you have to do is *take advantage of it*. The pages that follow will tell you how.

Hundreds of Miracle Tips for You

In addition to helping you use the miracle chemicals and formulations available now, this book is filled with special tips, hints, short cuts, bright and new suggestions that other gardeners, scientists and professionals have found to be miracle growth boosters.

The points detailed here will help you grow bigger blooms, hardier plants, more exquisite varieties, exceptional species, prized giant tomatoes, the sweetest berries in the neighborhood—in short, this book aims to help you get something special, something extra out of your garden.

If you love to experiment, if you thrill to unique gardening triumphs, if you want to grow something a little or a lot better than your neighbor—then this book is written for you. It will help you have more fun and get more enjoyment from the thrill of creativeness and "discovery."

And even if you only read, and don't actually put these suggestions into practice, I hope and trust that the pages which follow will nevertheless increase your joy of living.

Now, as to what this book is not: It's not a complete manual or detailed gardening guide; there are plenty of such compendiums, a number of good ones.

This is a collection of "miracle gardening" instructions and tips based on miracle developments in the field. It will help you in dozens upon dozens of practical and inspirational ways to add to your gardening triumphs and achievements, with actual thrilling miracle results.

If you're a long-experienced gardener, you may be aware of many of the points noted here. But if you find only one truly valuable new suggestion, or a vital reminder—or a dozen, or fifty or a hundred helps—then you'll find this book worth your while.

I've been interested and immersed in gardening for years, as a gardener and as an anonymous professional and business writer and investigator in the field. One of my most warming satisfactions from life is that I've helped hundreds of thousands of people to greater enjoyment from gardening, and that means—from *living*. It's my fervent wish, and sincere conviction, that this book will do more of the same for you.

In order to maintain absolute impartiality for you, no brand names are mentioned in these pages. As a reader of newspapers and magazines, as a visitor to stores selling gardening supplies and a reviewer of mail-order offerings, you'll be able to get the materials described; the brands are your own choice.

Now *dig in!*

The Basic Secret of Gardening

In preparing this book, I checked every possible source I could find for really helpful information, tips, hints and instructions for you. In addition, I talked with hundreds upon hundreds of especially successful gardeners.

I met one lovely lady, well into her seventies, whose garden was one of the most exquisite and flourishing I've ever seen. I asked her, "How do you do it?"

"Well, for one thing, I work at it," she replied. "I keep up to date, trying all the new miracle products. I test the soil carefully, I fertilize properly, I plant according to the way you're supposed to do it, going by the instructions. I spray a lot . . ." She paused, smiled slightly and remarked, ". . . and then I add my special secret."

"What's your secret?" I begged.

She answered slowly and seriously, "Well, after I do all those other things, then . . . I add *a touch of love!*"

Perhaps that's the most vital ingredient in growing any living things—*a touch of love.*

Taking Advantage of the Gardening Revolution

The day when you in your garden and the farmer on his arid acres had to work hard and bitterly, then wait and hope helplessly for results—that's gone. I've traveled the farms recently in many states, as I did when I lived among farmers years ago. What a difference I've seen!

Today I find a generation of alert, educated, scientifically minded men on the farms who add the miracles of the laboratory to the miracles of Nature. As a result, they harvest rich, abundant, more dependable crops such as were not possible less than a generation ago.

Every day new miracles are occurring to help you. Scientists working on wonder drugs discover by-products that help promote exciting growth. From the laboratory to you come new aids to produce expanses of greener, lusher lawns, and riotous improved flowers, vegetables, fruits and other growth in your garden. Yes, this is the new miracle age in gardening, with many new elements ready to revolutionize your gardening procedures and results.

But that doesn't mean that the fun of working at your garden is over. Far from it! You, personally, are still the most important partner of Nature. Your co-operation is vital. How carefully, enthusiastically and industriously you apply your abilities still makes the difference between success and failure.

So read on and then apply yourself. To paraphrase a familiar saying . . . the extraordinary can be accomplished immediately, miracles still take a little longer. But they're right at hand for you.

Don't Expect It to Be Too Easy

Is gardening really for you? As one wit remarked, "A garden is something that some men prefer to turn over only in their minds!" Here's one thought you might apply for self-analysis:

There was a new fertilizer which advertised along these lines: "A child of six could grow a magnificent garden with Fertilizer X, it makes gardening so easy. Just spray on X through your garden hose, then lie back in a hammock and watch your garden grow!"

The ad practically promised that results were so fast and easy, you could almost *hear* your garden grow.

The company went out of business after a few seasons. I'm convinced that the "child-of-six" approach was one of the reasons. Because, first, it rendered the entire ad unbelievable, even though the product was basically good. Obviously a child of six in a spotless white organdy dress, as illustrated, merely spraying on Fertilizer X, couldn't grow a magnificent garden.

And, second, while a gardener doesn't want to break his back and wear down his fingers to the nubs, he doesn't want to shirk all work either. You want the enjoyment of application, leading to the ultimate thrill—*accomplishment!*

It's like working out a crossword puzzle. If all that the millions of fans had to do was fill in the squares as fast as they could write, there'd be no challenge and thus no triumph over obstacles. It would be more satisfactory to simply draw circles on paper and at least improve your penmanship.

We all want the challenge and *sweet victory* that is found nowhere more than in successful growing, whether it's a simple little house plant or banks of flowers, orchards of fruits or any live, growing things.

So if you expect gardening to be as easy as the proverbial rolling off a log, you're not really a gardener, friend. You'd better get your avocational pleasures some other way.

But if you're willing and eager to do some work, the new *miracle developments* will help you achieve the thrilling and constantly renewing triumph of collaborating in Nature's miracle of growth.

Important Warning on Miracle Gardening!

Through connections with some leading plant and soil scientists, agricultural colleges and fine commercial companies in the field, I've been fortunate enough to be in at the very beginnings of some of the miracle compounds that have revolutionized gardening. *And I've seen many of these miracles lost and wasted in home gardens by lack of understanding on the part of gardeners*.

You and you and you are often at fault when you try something new and then, disgusted at your failures, complain that the claims are fraudulent. Admittedly, there are some commercial opportunists who promise you the impossible. But if you'll be guided by long-established, reputable companies whose success is based on your *repeat business,* you'll find that most often if you've failed, it's simply because you haven't read and followed the printed instructions.

Abe Lincoln once said, in referring to liquor, that the trouble was not in the use of a bad thing, but in the abuse of a good thing. And that applies to the new miracle products. Use the good things well and correctly, and you'll enjoy miraculous rewards from gardening.

Each Miracle Element Has Its Own Function

Read the labels, study the instructions, to know what to expect from the new miracle workers. For example, a soil conditioner doesn't *feed* your plants . . . it functions by *conditioning* the soil, by affecting the *texture and structure* of the soil and not the soil's content. A fertilizer or plant food *feeds* your plants.

As a comparison, the function of baking soda in making a cake is not to supply nutrients but to affect the structure of the cake, to make it rise, to give it an airy, tender texture; thus, baking soda doesn't replace flour or butter or eggs or milk.

Face it: Have you been guilty of counting on a soil conditioner to also fertilize your plants? In spite of the failures many gardeners report, soil conditioners can accomplish miracles in many cases to give you a better lawn, more abundant fruits, vegetables and flowers. More details on the how-to of soil conditioners on later pages.

The Place of the Wondrous Gibberellins

Another example of proper use or improper abuse: the new *gibberellins* are clearly offered as *stimulating* the growth of plant life, not as fertilizing the plants. The literature on just one of the gibberellic acid products states clearly that it is *"not* a hormone or fertilizer, but a new type of plant growth stimulant."

It goes on to elaborate that this product stimulates plants to make more efficient use of the plant foods available to it. Primarily the product works by increasing the size of the plant's cells and opening more surfaces for Nature's own processes of digestion and growth to take place.

The instructions make it clear that gibberellins are comparable to something that might increase your body's *efficiency* in utilizing the food you eat—*but you still have to eat the right food*. Yet, most gardeners I've talked with who bought and applied gibberellins thought that they were providing their plants with *food!*

Heed this warning: Read instructions carefully on every miracle product you buy, and you'll usually get the exceptional

Gibberellin spray boosts growth of geraniums dramatically.

results you want. For instance, let's see exactly what the amazing gibberellins—a by-product of the manufacture of one of humanity's greatest wonder drugs—can do for you in your garden.

Using Gibberellic Acid, the Miracle Growth Stimulator

I've seen it in my own garden . . . one tulip towering twice as tall as its neighbors, with petals stretching as wide as a melon! Yet this mammoth tulip was the same species as the others of normal growth, planted in the same area, fed the same selected fertilizer. The difference—a few seconds of spraying with the miracle chemical, *gibberellic acid*.

I was in on the beginnings of garden application with this fantastic element, using a commercially packed powder. I must emphasize that at this writing, gibberellic acid is still in the testing stage, but you can buy it and have lots of fun testing it in your own garden. Used right, you'll achieve astounding growth that will make your neighbors' eyes pop.

Spraying gibberellic acid doubled size of leaves in 3 days.

Some of the Miracles with Magical "G"

You simply spray the proper solution of gibberellic acid on plants, and remarkable things happen, sometimes overnight. Follow instructions on the package you buy. Exactly what happens organically is not even clear yet to the chemists working on it, but basically this growth stimulator *increases the size of the plants' cells*.

Gibberellic acid appears to spur Nature's own process of photosynthesis. That is, it accelerates the process by which a plant uses water, sunlight, carbon dioxide and other elements to produce healthy green growth. The plant seems to have an increased "appetite," and utilizes plant foods more rapidly and efficiently.

The result is quicker growth, longer stems, more buds per stem, bigger leaves, larger blooms and fruit—heavier, sturdier, *more energetic* plants. I've seen tomato seedlings burst into flower four to five times faster than usual, beating untreated seedlings by a week to ten days.

My roses treated with gibberellic acid produced blooms up to two weeks earlier than untreated bushes in the same garden area. And what blooms—larger, gloriously radiant, and with long long stems, the kind that cost dollars more in a florist shop!

I've checked carefully controlled tests at universities which show that spraying with gibberellic acid makes dwarf corn grow as big as normal corn. Sugar beets speeded up and produced seed the first year instead of the second, gaining a full year! Barley and peanut seedlings grew up to three times faster when treated with gibberellic acid. Flowers such as asters and cyclamen bloomed days earlier than others which were unsprayed, even though planted only a foot away.

But . . . caution! Lettuce sprayed with gibberellic acid shot up like Jack's beanstalk, set seed a month sooner than untreated plants, and lost their heads completely—so they were practically useless for your delicious salads.

Your Use of Gibberellic Acid

Bearing in mind that this wonder element is still in the testing stage, you'll certainly want to get some. Stores now have several for you to use and enjoy. As an alert and adventurous gardener, let yourself go, have fun.

Simply use the solution as detailed on the package. In the case of a powder, stir a little gibberellic acid powder in water, pour into a sprayer, and you're all set. Or, simplest of all, use the new aerosol bombs as directed on the can.

Spray one bush, leave the next one untreated. Do the same with flowers, fruits, vegetables. At least one good packaged gibberellic acid powder tells you exactly what plants are apt to respond well, and which you should leave alone.

I've seen African violets respond enthusiastically with double and triple the number of blooms, and with larger and more lush leaves.

I held in my hand two leaves from an indoor-blooming orange tree, one double the size of the normal leaf *within three days* after being sprayed with gibberellic acid. And the treated leaf was heavier, healthier, glossier.

I lined up three geranium plants, analyzing a test. One plant was normal size, untreated. The second plant had been sprayed with one-part-per-million solution of gibberellic acid, and was *double* the size of number one. The third plant, a magnificent giant, was *three* times the size of the normal geranium, after being sprayed with a ten-part-per-million solution of gibberellic acid! Similar results can be yours.

How Lawns Respond in a Hurry

Experiments indicate that some grasses also benefit miraculously from gibberellic acid. You'll find this product particularly useful in covering "problem" spots in your lawn.

Here's how: Feed the grass normally, then spray on some solution of this wonder-working element—or reverse the procedure.

In my own tests, I attacked a barren patch of spindly grass that had always given me trouble. I sprayed on the gibberellic acid solution, then followed by sprinkling on a miracle liquid fertilizer (a packaged 15-30-15 solution fortified with trace elements). Within a short time, this bad spot was the greenest, lushest area on my lawn.

I must emphasize again that gibberellic acid increases a plant's appetite but doesn't feed the plant any nutrients. So you must provide plenty of plant food to satisfy the plant's greater hunger. Your abundant, thrilling results will reward you many times over for the little extra work and care.

Another happy angle is that this wonder element doesn't seem harmful to humans in any way, according to all the tests I've noted.

Right now, you can spray your way to new miracle results with gibberellic acid. Follow directions on the package you buy. Mix each solution fresh, and go to work. You'll feel as you push that plunger or press the areosol button that you're a functioning part of a whole new era being born in horticulture!

Here's How to Grow a "Miracle," or Not

Here's some necessary advice, since the big purpose of this book is to help you grow *exceptional* plants, grass, trees, whatever you want to grow, rather than just ordinary and often below-ordinary blooms.

Everything you do, or don't do, from selecting the plant on, contributes to the final results you'll get in your garden. There can be a tremendous difference in your personal joy, and in the compliments from your family, friends and neighbors.

A good example is the roses you grow. Will they be "just roses"—a few commonplace blooms (if a rose can ever really be commonplace)—or an abundance of exquisite, ravishing beauties? It's up to you, from planting to picking. What you put into growing roses will govern what you get out of this richly rewarding pursuit called gardening.

Let's start right at the beginning, when you select the variety you'll plant. I advise you to buy from a good, established company, store or nursery, with a proved reputation. And beware of plants that cost amazingly little, or are offered at very low prices as "sensational bargains."

Of course, on occasion, there are some unusual values offered. But, for the most part, you get only what you pay for. Low prices usually mean that you get very young plants, or those grown on a mass basis without the care in selection, breeding and growing provided in finest nurseries.

It takes a lot of time, effort and money to develop a good strain of roses and plants, and it only makes sense that this must be reflected in the initial cost to you. Since you're going to lavish time, effort and cost of fertilization, sprays, etc., on the plants you buy, you'll want to make your selections carefully and sensibly—if you want "miracle" blooms.

Each Step Influences Results

After you've selected a good rose plant, how you plant becomes mighty important, as affecting final results. Select the proper site, with enough sunshine. Prepare the soil well, because even today's miracle products cannot grow miracle plants from cementlike earth.

Be sure you plant deeply enough, giving the roots plenty of room, aerating the soil well with a good chemical soil conditioner, peat moss or other recommended material. Water well. Fertilize properly right away.

As the rose bush "takes" and grows, continue to water sufficiently, keep feeding with a good water-soluble plant food or other effective fertilizer. Spray or dust as required with the excellent insect killers and disease fighters. Keep the soil well watered and weeded, by hand or using a modern weed killer carefully.

On some of the bushes, experiment with a few of the new scientific wonder workers—for example, spray on a good gibberellin product, so that you may produce some breathtaking long-stemmed roses such as are rarely seen in home gardens.

The "Impossible" Takes a Little Longer

All this may seem like a lot of time and work involved, but actually the hours required are fewer than you think. And working hand in hand with nature this way, step by step, gives you constant rewards—you see your accomplishments growing and flourishing week after week.

And finally, you *will* be able to see and enjoy and even boast of your glorious "miracle" roses, thrilling in their perfection of form, color and size.

Yes, garden miracles are all yours, with this special attention and application—with roses or any other plant life. Many tips

Liquid plant food makes big difference in growth of plants.

in this book and elsewhere will help you, but it's up to you to follow them, not just read about them. You'll have a few failures, but so many heartening successes.

Above all, it's deeply worthwhile!

Definitions Made Easy

In talking about this gardening book while writing it and gathering experiences from gardeners everywhere, so many people have asked me to explain the basic differences between "annuals," "perennials" and other common terms that I believe it's worth a brief review here, even though you probably know all the answers. In any case, you can refresh your own knowledge.

An *annual* is basically a plant that grows from seed to full flowering, and then dies—in one season. It's true that some so-called annuals could live two or even more years. But since they're varieties that are usually winter-killed if left outdoors, in most areas of the country, they're still referred to as annuals.

The *perennial* usually survives each winter and goes on and on—not quite forever, but for at least a few years unless killed by lack of nutrition, by neglect or disease. When you plant a perennial, you can count on it returning for a number of growing seasons, with reasonable care.

Another large class is the *biennial*. This is primarily a two-season plant, which gets started the first year without producing its best blooms. It comes back the second year in full flowering glory, if well cared for—then fades and dies away generally. Some popular varieties generally regarded as biennials are: canterbury bells, foxglove, hollyhock, pansy, sweet william and forget-me-not.

There's some confusion about variations in the class of growth commonly referred to as "bulbs." It may be helpful to clarify this group.

A *bulb*, such as a tulip bulb, is formed by a series of tightly overlapping "leaves," and is sometimes referred to as a "swollen stem"—a term I don't consider very flattering to the exotic blooms that emerge. In a bulb, the roots develop from its base, while the flower stem arises from the top.

A *corm* is very much like a bulb, but is usually much more compact and smoother, without the overlapping formation. The gladiolus, for example, grows from a corm.

A *tuber* is more generally an underground stem, having overlapping leaves like a bulb, but also with buds, sometimes referred to as "eyes," on the surface. In addition to the very popular tuberous begonias, potatoes are tubers and so are dahlias. No, ma'am, you're not correct when you refer to dahlia "bulbs"—but the blooms are just as exquisite if you tend them properly, whether you call them bulbs or tubers.

Just to make it more complicated, a *rhizome* is another variety of underground stem, often confused with tubers. Your favorite perfumed lily-of-the-valley and anemones are some of the gorgeous plants that grow from rhizomes—which aren't much more or less than thickened roots.

Perhaps this brief clarification will help you to distinguish between varieties better. Then you may have greatest success in choosing exactly what you want featured in your garden, and following correct planting and care instructions. That's the whole purpose of this book—to help you produce and enjoy better and more beautiful growth in your garden.

LAWNS

---

6 "Miracle Points" for Beautiful Lawns:

It may seem as elementary to you as A-B-C, but unless you keep checking on and acting on the following 6 basic points, you can't have and maintain a beautiful lawn year after year . . . the kind of lush, rich green grass that enhances your property and your pride and enjoyment in the looks of your home.

What's more, you won't deserve the velvety lawn you want. In our civilization now, Nature helps you best when you help Nature correctly. No matter how able or experienced a gardener you are, keep this check list constantly in mind:

1. Soil must be prepared with good fertilization and texture, and kept well aerated. Grass won't grow luxuriously in cement-like soil.

2. Start with good seed, and use fine quality seed for any necessary reseeding and renovation (yes, even the best lawn will usually develop some spots that require repair).

3. Deep watering is a "must" in dry weather.

4. Fertilize regularly or grass won't keep its glorious green color.

5. Use the wonderful new insecticides, fungicides and weed-control products to overcome the harmful insects and weeds that constantly invade your lawn.

6. *Don't let up for a single season in your lawn-maintenance program!*

A Constant Battle to Win

Just like in the Western movies, the "bads" are always trying to overcome and defeat the "goods" in regard to your lawn. It's up to you to help keep the balance on the side of "good."

Harmful insect life and weeds attack over and over again, and you have to repel the marauders. Your grass eats up nourishment and you have to replace it with good fertilizers, just as surely as you have to restock your own cupboard. When your lawn needs a drink, you must supply it—and properly— or the grass will shrivel and weaken and die, even as you and I.

Common-sense "Miracles"

The 6 steps aren't actually "miracles," are they? Just common-sense procedures, but "miracle lawns" only grow when you apply them all, and *continuously*. It's not difficult—simply that you can't let up.

Much easier than keeping yourself in top condition, isn't it?

With today's marvelous aids, it's a cinch and a certainty to have a lovely lawn—if you just prepare it right and tend it and deserve it.

Marvelous Modern Way to Start a New Lawn or Renovate an Old Lawn

Because of the amazing chemical calcium cyanamid, especially compounded for lawns and gardens—which you can now buy most anywhere—the work of lawnmaking has been cut way down. I've seen gardeners bursting with pride as they point to their luxurious lawns produced by this modern short-cut method.

Traditionally, the way to make a new lawn, or renovate an old lawn, has been to dig up the ground to a considerable depth, mix in peat moss and humus or other aerating materials, add topsoil, then scatter seed.

This is still effective, but is far more costly and time-consuming than the new way—and if your expensive topsoil is loaded with weed seeds, as happens all too often, you may find yourself growing a fine lawn of weeds.

No one claims that the modern cyanamid method is the *only* way to grow or renovate a lawn, but it is certainly an excellent one—and usually produces wonderful results.

In most areas, you must start about the middle of August, as there's a three-week interval between applying the cyanamid and sowing grass seed. About the middle of September is the best time in most places to start seeding, for the best start in lawn life. It's true that some gardeners have had success in early spring with this method. Fall is best, but it's up to you.

First Step . . . Test the Soil

You'll find details elsewhere about testing your soil. If you learn that your earth is woefully deficient in some element, then this should be corrected. If the soil is hard and badly compacted, it must be loosened well to a depth of several inches and aerated. But under average conditions, requiring normal fertilization, here's the step by step cyanamid process. (If the product you buy gives other directions, and different proportions, follow the instructions on the package—in careful detail!)

Poorly rooted neglected grass.

Way to a Luxurious Lawn

1. Mow your lawn right down tight to the ground if there is any growth.

2. Take a tough iron rake and remove the old growth, scratching hard and deep into the surface of the soil to loosen it and scar it well. Don't worry about harming any good grass because you're going to kill it—yes, kill it before you sow new seed.

There's no point at all in saving any clumps or patches of good grass. This is a drastic clean-out process. You say good-by to the old, bad and good alike.

3. Water the area thoroughly to a depth of 4 inches. That means 4 inches, not 1, 2 or 3 inches. Dig down in place after place to make sure the water has penetrated that deeply.

4. When the soil surface isn't mud, scatter the cyanamid over the area evenly at the rate of 5 pounds for every hundred square feet of surface (unless the product you buy recommends

application at a different rate—then follow that rate carefully and accurately).

5. Now go over the entire area slowly and diligently with the same hard iron rake, working the cyanamid thoroughly into the soil, where it will exert its powerful action. Don't grumble about the hard work, which it is, because it's not nearly as difficult as digging up the entire area and adding expensive topsoil.

Well fertilized and watered
— deep roots and strong turf.

6. Now forget about your cyanamided lawn area for three weeks, except for light watering about once a week to keep the soil moistened, helping the chemical action. Since it will probably rain during that time, you probably won't even have to water. You can just loll around and let your muscles loosen from their previous considerable exertions.

While you rest, the chemical is working wondrously. When the cyanamid is in the soil and moistened, what is known as "free" cyanamid forms. This kills all growing plants and seeds in the area, including any good grass that may remain.

And now another astonishing process takes place. The "free" killer changes character. It breaks down and is transformed by Nature from villain to hero, producing nitrate nitrogen and ammonia which will help feed your new grass seeds.

7. After the three-week annihilation period, fertilize the soil well—in addition to the plant food now being provided by the cyanamid.

PURSLANE

CRABGRASS

BUCKHORN

CHICKWEED

PLANTAIN

SORREL

DANDELION

KNOTWEED

MORE CRABGRASS

Common lawn weeds.

Apply a good 5-10-5 dry fertilizer over the area, in quantity as directed on the particular package you buy. Or, for even better results, water in a good complete water-soluble plant food, such as an excellent 15-30-15 formula which contains chelated iron and many trace elements as well; this is more costly but will give you faster and thicker growth.

8. In either case, with liquid or dry fertilizer, wet the soil thoroughly again, to a depth of 4 inches.

9. While the soil is still damp, but not muddy, scatter your grass seed, applying in quantity according to the seed you buy. Choose a seed that's particularly suited to your local growing conditions. In most areas, you can't do better than the excellent mixture of about 40 per cent Merion bluegrass and 60 per cent Pennlawn fescue, which is costly. Ask your local dealer's advice.

Rake in the seed lightly, and bring it in close contact with the soil, by tapping in with a flat board contraption or light roller. But *don't roll heavily* lest you pack the soil too solidly and make it difficult for the young grass to fight its way through the surface!

10. If it doesn't rain, water thoroughly about once a week to a depth of about 4 inches, to help the grass become established sturdily.

11. This is the most delightful instruction of all: Just keep checking after the first week and thrill to the first tender green growth, and then the deepening luxurious thick emerald color and texture as your lawn grows healthfully and vigorously.

But don't just forget about lawn care from here on; don't expect your lawn to maintain itself year after year. You must help Nature keep a favorable balance against the enemies of grass.

You must feed your grass well each season, as it uses up valuable nutrients in the soil. Water *deeply, deeply, deeply* to keep your grass roots plunging down deeply and not just growing on the surface to get moisture existing only on the top.

Keep on guard against weeds, infestation and harmful insects. Use the modern materials described in this book—to conquer these villains in the early stages *before they get a foothold* and thus tip the balance of power against your grass.

With constant vigilance, and not too much effort, you'll enjoy the rich rewards of a lush lawn, season after happy season.

Quick-patch Bad Lawn Spots!

There isn't much you can do about a shabby, worn spot in carpeting without replacing the whole area, but you can patch up lawn spots now with very little work. And you'll find the patch filled in beautifully in just a few weeks, with just a few minutes' work, using quick-acting modern liquid fertilizer.

Best time to patch a lawn is in the fall, but actually we've done it at other times during the year, with excellent results. It's only human that you can give a small patch more attention and care than a large area—and so your results are bound to be at least a little better.

Here's how to go about it:

1. Take a long-pronged, tough hand tool such as a small cultivator. Pull out the patches of dead grass and dig into the soil, loosening it thoroughly at least 2 inches in depth.

2. Add some peat moss to help keep the soil loose and airy— a few handfuls or more, depending on the extent of the area you're patching. If you have some good topsoil to mix in, all the better. Smooth the surface without firming it.

3. Sow the seed by hand, scattering it lightly and not too densely. You can afford to use an excellent lawn seed for such small areas—such as 60 per cent Pennlawn fescue and 40 per cent Merion bluegrass. Tap the earth down lightly, with the palm of your hand or a flat board. Be sure not to make the top surface hard or compact.

4. Water in the area gently, waiting to apply more until each dowsing soaks in, then add more until the soil is soaked thoroughly. For watering, use a solution made with a good water-soluble plant food, in proportion as directed on the package (usually a tablespoonful per gallon of water). *This is the modern trick that gives the seed a quick start to catch up fast with the rest of the lawn!*

5. Set up a stick with a rag tied to it, in the center of the patch, or protect the area from traffic with stakes and string. Water the area gently but thoroughly at least every other day.

You'll see grass spouting within a very short time, in as little as a week. Don't mow that spot until grass is two inches high or more. Apply more liquid plant food three to four weeks after sowing seed.

Bare and scraggly patches in your lawn can ruin the whole appearance, as you'll see when you correct it. A little patching work this speedy way will beautify your lawn tremendously.

Long-lasting "Greening," with Natural Organic

You want the "something new" in organic fertilization, not old messy manures and such! There's no disputing the value of natural organic fertilization, with good nitrogen content, for grass. But gardeners have long resisted using animal manures extensively, or sewage by-products packaged as natural organic fertilizers. No wonder: Who likes odorous, messy application in the garden?

But now science comes to your rescue with another garden miracle, now available to you at garden stores—packaged 100 per cent natural organic plant food, containing over 7 per cent nitrogen, but *no animal manure, no sewage by-products*—clean, odor-free and pleasant to handle. In dry form, it flows freely through your lawn feeder.

When you apply this 100 per cent natural organic plant food, you help build up valuable nitrogen in the soil. This feeds your grass the vital coloring and enriching element over a period of months, also is a valuable booster for your garden. Applied correctly, it won't burn grass, whatever season it's put down.

You'll find that this fine fertilizer helps keep grass greener all winter too, and promotes a better start in spring. It also helps build healthier root growth for turf, and makes it more resistant to insect pests and disease.

The dry organic won't give you results as quickly and dramatically as a good nitrogen concentrate that you spray on grass. And remember, it's a supplementary feeding, not a complete feeding for your grass and garden. But it's worth keeping in mind as a "natural" (not synthetic) aid particularly toward building the *exceptional* lawn you want!

"48-hour Green" Miracle for Lawns!

I've sprayed spots in my lawn which were brown, dried up, thoroughly discouraging, with a miracle nitrogen compound which started the grass turning a lively, lovely green within 48 hours!

This compound is a special nitrogen concentrate, almost 50 per cent nitrogen. And nitrogen is the element which is so vital to produce rich, green color in grass. Also, nitrogen is very quickly used up by grass, and thus usually needed by the average soil. It's also so essential for the development of chlorophyll in grass.

So no wonder a "miracle boost" like this produces amazing

new green, revivifying color in the lawn almost overnight. You can buy a commercially packaged clean white powder concentrate, which you mix with water according to instructions. It's easy to spray it on through a hose attachment—one pound makes as much as fifteen gallons of spray, enough to treat about one thousand square feet of lawn.

Spray on this nitrogen boost once or twice in late spring, and about once a month during summer months. It's a great help as an addition to general fertilization of your lawn. Dry nitrogen fertilizers are also available which work well and have longer-lasting effect. However, there's lots more work applying them, and you don't get quite the thrilling quick boost that the concentrate to be applied with water gives you.

Why does this nitrogen boost work so magically? Because, almost as soon as it enters the soil in its liquid solution, it breaks down into various forms of nitrogen, all readily usable by the grass. Some are taken up by the grass so quickly that "presto-change-o" in color shows up in 48 hours or less. Other parts of the nitrogen are slower acting, furnishing the precious element over a period of weeks.

Many country clubs use concentrated forms of nitrogen to give their greens that velvety rich, deep color that so many gardeners envy. You can do likewise. Particularly if your grass goes brown during a hot dry spell, you'll startle your neighbors and delight yourself with nitrogen's "48-hour green" miracle on your lawn.

Liquid Lawn Feeding Made Easy

Once you've tried it, you'll see the evidence with your own eyes that feeding your lawn and gardens with a good liquid fertilizer can produce "miracles" of growth within a week, even in days, because of quick absorption of the nutrients by plants. *Modern devices* now make it quick and easy for you to give your plant life the benefits of this complete feeding.

Now you can choose from a variety of effective "automatic" feeding attachments. I've gotten excellent results personally from devices that attach to the water faucet directly, or at the nozzle end of the hose; the concentrated water-soluble plant food is mixed in correct proportion by the water passing through the compact container. Insecticides too can be used, following directions and precautions carefully.

Such devices, and others, also provide "automatic" feeding with the concentrated fertilizers through various sprinkler systems.

However you do it, don't fail to give your plant life the

complete fertilization that's absolutely essential to lush, luxurious growth.

New Wondrous Lawn Seed

From experiment stations, universities and home owners come enthusiastic reports about a comparatively new lawn seed mixture which is rich in color, luxurious in texture and coverage, and vigorous in growth.

This highly recommended grass is a mixture of 60 per cent Pennlawn fescue developed by a state agricultural station . . . and 40 per cent of lush Merion bluegrass. Unlike some other touted "new" grasses which are not really grasses at all, this Pennlawn-Merion mixture produces a lush turf which rates in beauty with most any other grass.

This combination is now being used more and more for home lawns, golf fairways, parks—most anywhere that hardy, luxurious growth is needed and appreciated. It is more resistant to many common grass diseases, grows faster and produces denser growth.

The disadvantage in planting over a large area is that the 60 per cent Pennlawn/40 per cent Merion mixture is more costly than other grasses (although a considerable saving over 100 per cent fine Merion bluegrass). But you can certainly use it for renovating and reseeding bad spots in your lawn.

Properly fertilized, and with minimum spraying against insects and disease, the Pennlawn/Merion seed mixture will provide an enchanting green carpetry to enrich your home for years and years.

Criss-cross Lawn Seeding

When you sow lawn seed by hand, you'll get a little better result usually if you use the criss-cross method. Simply divide the seed ahead of time into two separate little piles, according to amount needed for the area to be covered.

Now sow one of the piles of seed *criss* in one direction, scattering as evenly as possible. Then sow the other pile of seed *cross* in the opposite area, in tic-tac-toe fashion. Of course, be sure the earth is very loose, with well-defined rake furrows or other over-all indentations, to hold the grass seed.

Best way to cover a large area with lawn seed is to use a lawn spreader, which you can set for proper dispersal of seed. Generally, 3 pounds of good seed will cover 1,000 square feet—but go by instructions given with the specific seed you purchase.

If you're using the good old-fashioned hand method (don't those seeds feel pleasant against your palm and fingers?), remember—criss, cross, and away you sow!

Lawn-seeding Warning!

I stopped to watch one of my neighbors seeding a new lawn.

He beamed at me and said, "I'm going to have the thickest, lushest grass in this whole town. I'm laying in plenty of seed—plenty."

I remarked, "You're putting in too much seed. By planting too much grass seed, you'll get overcrowded growth. Because each grass plant will have to fight for survival, you'll get thin, weak plants."

"But," he protested, "by putting in lawn seed extra heavy, I figure I'll get extra-thick grass that'll crowd out weeds, and keep my lawn free of weeds."

"Not so," I explained, "you'll get weak, frail grass that won't be able to overcome weeds, and that won't be able to resist common lawn diseases."

"Well," my neighbor said, "I've already seeded half my lawn heavy. I'll lay down a normal quantity of the seed on the other half. We'll see what happens."

We watched, week after week. The grass with *more* seed had *less* thick, healthy growth, turned out clearly inferior to the normally seeded, carefully tended section.

Were you listening?

Seed as You Weed

A fine old gentleman of over seventy who was a master gardener for years taught my wife a neat little weeding-seeding trick.

Every few weeks, she'll rove the lawn to pounce on any dandelions, plantain, crabgrass or other weeds that rear their ugly bodies. First, she yanks them out thoroughly, roots and all.

Then she reaches into a pocket where she hides a choice combination of grass seeds. As she scoops out a weed, she fills in the dirt and drops in a few seeds.

When finished with her search, she prepares a sprinkling can with water and a water-soluble 15-30-15 fertilizer. Then she goes from spot to spot and waters in the new seed with the mixture.

Sensible, easy and very effective in keeping a lawn thick with rich green grass and under constant control.

Zoysia "Grass"—Miracle or Mess?

To read some of the claims about zoysia, you might think it's today's answer to all lawn problems—that at last here's a grass that resists the ravages of severe drought, and overcomes the pesky problem of crabgrass. True or false?

First, it certainly seems true that zoysia stands up far better than the usual grass in living through intense drought and still retaining green color in summer. Also, zoysia does squelch and smother and crowd out crabgrass so you do wind up with a crabgrass-free lawn. Sounds heavenly, doesn't it?

But, looking at the negatives, many gardeners have told me that they don't really consider zoysia to be a true grass at all! They say that zoysia is in effect a kind of glamorized weed— and that *it doesn't compare in beauty with a fine, true, velvety green grass*.

It's a fact that during the cold months, zoysia goes dormant and turns a yellowish-brown color, staying that way until it comes back to green growth in the spring. And, in cooler areas, you often wait and wait, and don't see that wanted *green* appear until late spring, sometimes not until May—a great disappointment when your neighbor is pridefully pointing to his rich green grass!

Those who like zoysia say they prefer its dormant brownish color to the drab, grayish color of other grass, particularly when infested with crabgrass. As a home owner and an independent spirit, the choice is up to you.

It's generally conceded that the best way to plant zoysia is with plugs, placed right in the middle of barren areas, or on worn spots in your lawn. It's most effective in barren areas where it spreads out and provides a ground cover within a year or more. Planted in your lawn, it will not only smother out crabgrass, but will also usually overcome other types of grass growing near it—varieties which many consider far more beautiful than zoysia.

If you do plant zoysia, you'll find that the plugging is a lot of hard work, but many consider it worth while when they report that they have a green lawn during the hottest, driest months. However, when planting, be sure that you water often and thoroughly until the new zoysia is established. And feed it plentifully with a complete fertilizer, liquid or dry.

The zoysia debate finally boils down to this, as I see it from a very practical and impartial viewpoint: zoysia is a lot better than bare, barren ground, providing a fairly attractive green cover except during the cold months. But if you want a lush, velvety lawn of great beauty, that will be your own pride and the envy of your neighbors, then zoysia is *not* a lawn miracle for you!

You Can't Be Sloppy on Slopes!

"I need a miracle to grow grass on the slope of my lawn!" I heard a gardener sigh. I told him he could enjoy the miracle of growth on that slope, but only if he prepared with a little work, like this:

The best way to start grass on a slope is with sodding, but that's also the most expensive—and you *can* do it from seed. Just prepare your soil by digging in a little humus, adding some plant food, then raking smooth. Now seed and cover the slope with burlap. Peg down the burlap at reasonable intervals with wire that you can bend into short hairpin hooks with about 3-inch shafts that will hold to the ground.

Keep the burlap moist as much of the time as possible. You'll soon be rewarded by seeing spears of new grass poking through the mesh. Then remove the burlap gently.

Your grass now has an excellent start, but you must keep it moist with *gentle watering*, not drenching! Best way is to water through a length of porous canvas hose (available at stores), and which you lay across the top half of the slope. You'll appreciate the difference as you note the water oozing through the canvas in large droplets that sink into the ground and don't wash the soil away.

Just one more tip: water deeply instead of just a quick, shallow top-watering. That way the roots will grow downward instead of sideways. That's your best way to develop a deep mass of roots which will balk and survive any soil erosion.

You'll be proud of results—no more ragged, bedraggled sloppy slopes for you!

Gone But Not Forgotten

A proud gardener, saddened by the condition of his grass which had turned sparse and brown during a drought, placed this sign in the center of the area: *LAWN LONG AGO.*

Clobbering Crabgrass Problems

One murky dawn I was awakened by a voice mumbling, "I hate crabgrass! I hate crabgrass!" After a few dizzy minutes, I realized that my wife was talking in her sleep.

When she arose later, she said, "I'm all worn out. I've been dreaming all night of inching around our lawn on my hands and knees, gnashing my teeth as I pulled out that blankety blank crabgrass by the roots . . . just as I did all day yesterday!"

That was some years ago. Today you have plenty of excellent miracle chemicals to help you control and get rid of this ugly invader of your lawn, if you'll only use them correctly and often. You can't let up, because even after almost fatal attacks against it, crabgrass has a nasty habit of reseeding itself and trying again—and succeeding unless you clobber the new growth once more.

Best way to conquer crabgrass is through a combination of chemical attack and good cultural practices, not relying upon pulling out clumps on your hands and knees. That alone won't work.

And you must keep up the persistent attack against crabgrass season after season, eliminating it more effectively each season until your lawn is finally free of this persistent weed. Even then, you must be on guard, ready to attack once more if crabgrass rears its ugly growth again.

It's important to understand that crabgrass loves warmth and sunlight to thrive and sprout plenty of seed. Therefore, if you mow your lawn too closely, you help the sun and warmth to come through and benefit the crabgrass. That's true especially during late spring and summer when the weed is at its peak germination period. So it's best at this time to mow your lawn high—as much as two or three inches high; this tends to shade the ground, inhibiting the crabgrass seed and helping the good grass to choke out the invader.

Also, certain neglect of your lawn tends to help the crabgrass and hurt your fine, desirable grass. If you don't rake up leaves well in the fall, you'll find that the leaves often smother patches of good grass. Then the crabgrass, which has "gone underground," takes over in those patches and thrives disgustingly.

When you see the crabgrass seedheads ripening, rake up your lawn thoroughly so that the seedheads will stand erect instead of cuddling to the ground and hiding. Then mow the lawn thoroughly, but be sure to put a catcher on the mower, and get rid of those blasted seedheads.

As crabgrass goes dormant with the first frost of autumn, take a strong iron rake and rake out the plants. This requires a strong back and will, because you're bound to rake up some good grass at the same time—and when you dig up the patches of crabgrass, you'll be left with some bare ground.

But that's an excellent time to sow good new grass seed. Also in the fall, give your good grass a boost by applying a complete fertilizer. That'll help greatly to give greater vigor and health to your grass, and will keep down the crabgrass crop that would ordinarily be forthcoming in the spring. This fall fertilizing is one of the most vital steps to building a good lawn, for that's when crabgrass and other weeds are at their weakest. Early spring and early fall fertilizing should be "musts" to promote a rich, healthy lawn.

However, you don't have to rely on good cultivating practices alone any more. Use the miracle chemicals that are now available to you. Three effective compounds are at hand for you in a variety of commercial products. Look for them on labels: potassium cyanate . . . phenyl mercuric acetate . . . and one of the newest, and considered best by many, *disodium methyl arsonate.*

Use one of these products in late summer and fall for best results, when the crabgrass is firmly established. You'll be delighted to see that a single application of a good product based on disodium methyl arsonate will kill small crabgrass plants. A second application about a week later will kill the larger plants.

This powerful chemical won't just spank the crabgrass, it'll really clobber and kill the plants. You'll see the effects with your own eyes, as the crabgrass starts to die in a few days, and is completely expired in a couple of weeks.

Apply this crabgrass killer, or any other, *exactly as directed* on the package you buy—whether through a sprinkling can, sprayer or other methods. Rigid care is so important because otherwise the chemicals may do some damage to your good grass also—but, if you don't overdose, your good grass will recover while you gratefully sigh "Good riddance!" to the unwelcome weed.

In spring, watch for any seedlings that may sprout from seeds that may have escaped the fall extermination. At that time, apply a good 2,4-D crabgrass killer which works wonders in conquering the seedlings at this period. Again, follow directions to the letter, and you'll conquer the new crabgrass with several repeated applications.

As science scores new advances, there's now a promising new crabgrass killer available to you. It kills crabgrass *seeds.* You apply this dry arsenical formula to established (not new!) lawns, with a fertilizer spreader—when most of the seed is in the ground. In general, that's from late September up to April.

Exhaustive testing proves that this new product kills crabgrass seeds on contact, and may be effective for a year or more! Universities report over 95 per cent elimination of crabgrass with proper usage.

In addition, this new miracle killer contains some aluminum

sulphate to provide some helpful nitrogen. And it also has some chlordane to help fight unwanted lawn insects. It's available in stores now; as with all the wonder chemicals, apply exactly as directed on the package.

All these crabgrass control methods may seem a lot of work to you, and it is, although science has given you excellent eradicators now, and fairly easy devices for applying them. It's all worth it to get rid of those crabgrass nightmares, to stop crabbing about crabgrass, and start admiring your own rich, green, velvety lawn unmarred by the ugly weed!

Modern Fungicides Overcome Lawn Fungus!

Many gardeners have become panic-stricken in the past when they see spots in front of their eyes on the lawn. That is, when they see irregularly shaped brown spots, anywhere from an inch to several feet in diameter, marring the green grass.

If that happens to you, look closely and if you see a dark "smoke-ring" appearance around the outside edges, you can diagnose the disease as brown patch fungus. This unpleasant infection is most apt to set in during periods of high humidity, when there are severe temperature drops during the night, with heavy dew and fog in the mornings.

But now you needn't be too concerned about brown patch. First, cut down on nitrogen feeding during the period that the fungus is present. Second, apply immediately one of the excellent fungicides now available; look for these names on the labels: acti-dione, calocure or calo-clor.

You'll have more fun watching the evidence of fungus disease disappear!

Dollarspot Doomed!

As the "doctor" in charge of keeping your lawn free of diseases, watch out for the appearance of straw-colored spots about the size of a silver dollar. You can usually diagnose this as a fungus disease aptly named dollarspot.

Better treat your lawn in a hurry, otherwise inflation may set in, and the dollar-size spots may spread to form large, irregularly shaped patches of ugly damage. This fungus is most likely to appear in spring and fall, encouraged by cold nights and humid days.

Effective miracle-workers are at hand to destroy dollarspot. Apply the powerful herbicide PMA, or acti-dione, calocure or calo-clor. Here's one kind of "dollar" spot you'll be happy to see disappear in a hurry.

Clues to Causes of Lawn Browning

Comparable to the pleasures of looking out on a blue, blue sea or lake is the gardener's joy in surveying his unmarred expanse of green, green grass. Let a brown spot appear and you're out of your comfortable glider like a thunderbolt to find out what caused the browning and to correct it so that you'll have a completely beautiful green lawn again.

This check list will help you to diagnose, correct and even prevent the unsightly browning; here are the common causes:
- —Fungus diseases; how to take effective counter-action is told in this book.
- —Burning with chemical fertilizers, usually due to too liberal application, exceeding directions on the package.
- —Burning by too heavy application of chemical weed killers. (Don't be too upset when careful use of weed killers and herbicides seems to injure healthy grass and turn it brown, because the green generally returns in a few weeks, richer than ever.)
- —Dog damage; whatever you do about this is up to you, your conscience and relations with your neighbors. One method is to apply, with care and discretion, available dog-repellent products which help keep dogs away from the areas you wish to protect.
- —Smothering grass by carelessly letting pillows, mats, rugs, tools, table tops, etc. lie on the lawn too long. This occurs more often than you might think; for example, if you have one or more heavy gliders or lawn chairs, keep moving them about lest they keep sun and rain away from one spot which will be weakened and will invite browning and infestation.

Keep in mind that Nature is rich in its rewards when you take proper care of your lawn. But there's a delicate balance between the good and bad in Nature. If you're careless or inefficient in tending your precious grass, the evil invaders tend to take over. Winning this battle is part of the fun of gardening and growth.

No Mess from Moss on Lawns

If moss develops on your lawn, nine times out of ten you can blame yourself for not fertilizing the soil sufficiently. Some of the other common faults may also permit moss to develop—high soil acidity, poor drainage of the area, improper watering, lack of aeration in the earth, or a number of these ills combining against the good health of your grass.

What to do? You can remove the moss by careful hand raking, and then correct the condition that caused it to appear in the first place. Usually, applying a good fertilizer will promote growth of the grass and keep moss away.

For more drastic measures, apply a light solution of copper sulphate in water. This will also get rid of *algae*, which sometimes grows in moist areas under trees and large bushes, and may be mistaken for moss.

You'll profit most if you regard the appearance of moss as a warning that your lawn needs fertilizing and adequate drainage—otherwise the moss will return later to haunt you!

Making Slime Molds Scram!

During periods of wet weather, you're liable to step out on your lawn some morning and be appalled by the sight of black, bluish gray or yellowish masses of gluey slime molds. Aside from the unsightly aspects, these may also smother and kill your grass if you don't do something about it quickly.

Fortunately what you can do now is simple, speedy and effective.

First, seize an old garden broom and sweep apart the masses, breaking them up with thrusts of the bristles. Of course, be careful that you don't uproot any of the grass by too vicious an attack. After this counteraction, the masses of slime molds will usually disappear when the lawn dries out.

If the slime molds persist after a few days, turn to one of the excellent modern antidotes available to you. Dust lightly with sulfur or a copper fungicide, which you can get at garden supply shops.

You'll prevent serious damage to your grass, and it'll be a delight for you to see your lawn bright green and unmatted once more, thanks to your careful detecting and efficient action.

Chickweed Succumbs to Chemical Combination

One of the toughest lawn villains, unattractive chickweed, can now be conquered by watchful applications. When much of your garden work is done, in late fall or winter, and your good grasses are dormant, chickweed is growing actively and exultantly.

That's when you have your best chance to wipe out this muscled weed. Get a good herbicide that combines powerful 2,4-D and 2,4,5-T (ask your garden shop people, or check the labels). Apply it, and in a matter of days you'll see the thriving, proud chickweed start to wilt and fade and die. Since the weed is so strong, further applications may be necessary.

Again: be careful to follow directions exactly. Just stay on your toes, get set to apply when the chickweed shows—you'll be a most effective sharpshooter, a modern miracle gardener, and you'll dominate this obnoxious lawn weed instead of having it make life miserable for you!

Now Bomb Away Broadleaf Lawn Weeds!

Say good-by to most of your troubles with the broadleaf lawn weeds—the obnoxious dandelions (fine in salads but not helpful to lawn beauty), plantain, buckhorn and such. Just your fingertip pressure applying a good 2,4-D aerosol bomb will spray away this ugly growth, often in one application. Or, you can apply 2,4-D in a spray, watering can, or even in dry form—though the liquid is usually faster in action and more effective.

Best seasons for application are in early spring and early fall, the peak periods for germination and growth of these broadleaf weeds. You'll usually see them die completely within two to four weeks. Sometimes it may be necessary to apply for a second time six to eight weeks later. In any case, you'll kill the weeds, without too much effort, with 2,4-D.

Here are a few special tips for you in using this miraculous weed killer. Watch your weather reports and apply when you're informed there won't be any rain to wash away the chemical for at least 12 hours. Then, avoid mowing your lawn for at least four days after applying the weed killer.

To improve your lawn fast, apply fertilizer to the lawn a few days after using the weed killer. That will stimulate growth of good grass so that it will help fill in bare spots left by the dead weeds. If the weeds have been so plentiful that many bare spots show up, seed in with grass at the next proper seeding season.

As with most all effective chemicals, here are some vital precautions for you. Be careful not to get any of the 2,4-D on flowers, shrubs, vegetables, trees or other desirable growth, as it may produce severe injury or even death to such plants. Therefore, don't spray carelessly and never spray the weed killer on windy days!

Also, it's better not to use this powerful chemical on lawn

seedings that are less than six months old, or less than two inches high. Follow instructions on the product to the letter—don't overdose.

If you use 2,4-D in a sprayer, that's fine, but be sure to clean out the sprayer with soap and water. Then leave in a strong solution of household ammonia for several days, and rinse out once more, and you're ready to use the sprayer for other purposes on vegetables, shrubs, flowers or other tender plants.

Don't be afraid to use wonder-working 2,4-D, and don't let the safety measures discourage you. Actually this fine product is easy to use, and worth using, just keeping in mind the few simple precautions. And now that science has given you the aerosol bombing method, it's easier than ever.

Just take aim—fire! It's almost as simple as saying "Boo!" to those unwanted broadleaf weeds.

Important! Light-fingered Leaf Raking

Fall planting of a new lawn, and reseeding of bad spots, pose a problem that calls for a light touch on your part.

On the one hand, fall lawn planting is excellent because it enables the new grass to dig in roots down deep . . . and your fertilizing doesn't feed dormant weeds so much. But, on the other hand, when autumn leaves settle on the earth they tend to stifle the new grass and even smother out life unless you remove the leaves.

Yet, when you rake up leaves, you're likely to dig up, damage and even ruin the tender new grass seedlings. What to do?

You must remove the leaves, but try to pick dry days, so your feet won't impact the wet soil and crush out new growth more readily, and because the leaves will be easier to lift away without digging in. And, above all, use a very light-fingered leaf rake, handled with as feathery a touch as you can manage.

As one of my gardening friends puts it—this is a time for true TLC (tender loving care)!

"Miracles" That Retard and Regulate Growth!

Only a single mowing per season needed on your lawn! Your grass growing luxuriously and beautifully, yet just about as slowly as you want it to grow!

All that isn't just a dream any more. You can now buy a

number of products containing an exciting wonder chemical called *maleic hydrazide* which is performing marvelously in retarding and regulating various growth—without being harmful to the health of the plant life. (For brevity, I'll refer to the chemical as mh from now on.)

Controlling Lawn Growth

If you wish to cause your grass to grow at a much slower rate in height, and thus require mowing much less frequently, simply get a good growth-regulating product for lawns, *containing mh*. Spray it on your lawn at the specific rate instructed on the package you buy. If applied properly, you won't hurt the grass but you will save your back muscles with much less pushing of the mower across your lawn.

For best results, don't apply during the summer, but either in April when the best growing season starts, or in the fall when the grass is still green but hasn't yet entered its dormant period.

Within a day after you've applied it, it will have been absorbed by the green grass. The wonder chemical works down through the grass, slowing up normal division of the plant cells, and holding back stem growth—but without injuring the plant visibly.

Then you see the miracle happen! Usually within a few weeks, you notice that the grass is as green and vigorous as ever, but it's not growing as tall, and doesn't need the usual repeated mowing.

It's as amazing as though a man's hair stayed thick and normal, yet grew so much slower in length that a haircut was required only once every few months rather than every few weeks! (No, don't spray mh on your hair; for one thing, your barber wouldn't approve.)

Where to Use mh

Mh is very practical in application on lawns which are well established and where foot traffic isn't too great.

However, in areas where children are constantly at play, or where wear and tear is heavy for any reason, it's better not to use mh because the hammering down of the grass by foot traffic alone retards growth anyway. Under those tough conditions, grass has a difficult time maintaining thick growth without being held back further by mh.

You'll want to use wonder-working mh particularly in hard-to-mow places where there's seldom much foot traffic. For example, along fences, around the edges of the lawn, under a grove of small trees—mh will help you as nothing else can.

I have a grove of eight lovely old lilac bushes, tall as small trees, and have always had difficulty mowing the grass areas between the trees. Now, with mh application, I still have the attractive green grass under the lilacs, but rarely have to twist my way through there with the mower to keep the grass from growing tall and looking ragged and unsightly.

Mh Is Safe, but Use with Caution

One of the excellent qualities of mh is that it seems quite harmless to humans and animals, as shown by extensive testing. You don't have to worry about the spray drifting and harming most other growth, as may occur with many of the strong insecticides and weed killers.

The primary cautions are simple to follow. Don't dose with mh excessively or your grass may turn brown for a while, though it usually grows green again after a period of anxiety for you. Don't use more than twice a season, and usually not more than once over a short season, no matter how strong and healthy your lawn may appear.

And, it's worth repeating, don't use mh on a newly planted lawn, or on grass that is weak or struggling for sturdy life in any way. Give that young or weak grass every possible chance to grow as much as it wants to, then enjoy the benefits of mh after the grass is thoroughly established.

Remember, a good gardener requires patience, which is most always rewarded eventually!

Give Your Hedge Clippers Less Work!

Tired of clipping your privet hedges every couple of weeks, or even more often? Let mh give those clippers, and your muscles, a very welcome rest. Spray on the mh solution, as instructed on the package. Your hedges will be just as beautiful, but you'll only have to clip a few times per season.

Of course, mh won't *shape* your hedges for you—but you don't mind that artistic light snipping so long as mh relieves you of much of the muscle-straining heavy clipping.

Don't overlook this wonderful modern gardening aid!

Water Miracles with Sprinkler Systems

New, long-lasting plastic pipes now make it possible for you to install your own sprinkler system on the lawn without too much work, and for long-lasting utility. *This is positively one of the best steps you can take to assure having a beautiful lawn.*

In addition, you'll save yourself the tedious work of directing water over your lawn with a hose, or remembering to move a sprinkler around at frequent intervals.

With your own sprinkler system, you'll be far more likely to water your lawn as it should be watered—soaking in the water six to eight inches deep, instead of just giving a totally inadequate surface watering through a hose.

Installation is actually simple, and doesn't take nearly as much time or expenditure as you might think offhand. New plastic pipe materials are amazingly resistant to rotting, cracking and corrosion.

Installing Your Sprinkler System

Your local dealer will help you plan exactly how much plastic pipe you need, and how many metal sprinklers you require for the size of your lawn. To install the flexible pipe, you dig a series of narrow six-inch-deep channels, as many as needed for the lawn area.

Durable, simple metal sprinklers are quickly and easily attached to the hose, at proper intervals. You cut lengths of hose rapidly with an ordinary saw.

Since the modern sprinkler heads are readily placed flush with the lawn, there's no mowing problem. And, as no water is flowing through the hose in winter, you don't have to fear freezing troubles.

Simple Operation

After installation, simply attach the end of the hose to your outdoor water tap, turn it on—and with this one twist of the wrist, watering of your entire lawn area begins, all at the same time, no spots neglected in favor of others.

With this modern do-it-yourself miracle, there's no unsightly hose or connections to mar the beauty of the lawn, no hose to wind up after each watering. And your lawn won't suffer during drought because watering will be deep and thorough, and even infrequent sprinkling will keep sufficient moisture in the soil over a long period.

Also, in some areas, when use of public water systems for lawns and gardens is restricted to after dark, you can turn on your sprinkling system and give your grass a good long drink. Ordinarily you wouldn't care to stay up to hold a hose or drag around a portable sprinkler during the wee small hours of the night.

"Musts" about Mowing Your Lawn

There's very great pleasure in the beautiful even symmetry of a freshly mowed lawn. But there's danger too if you mow too low. Don't ever mow new grass until it's at least two and one-half inches high. Don't mow any grass at any time any less than one and one-half to two inches high.

You may think you like a close, crew-cut lawn much more, but you'll find that grass mowed smoothly at a height of one and one-half inches has an even more graceful beauty. And it's much healthier for your grass.

You see, the blade areas of the grass plant have much to do with manufacture of usable food by the entire plant. When you chop off much of the grass blade, you cut down its vigor, its resistance to drought, disease and wear—and you leave it weakened for attack by weeds and other enemies.

So don't mow too low, and you won't mow the life out of your lawn!

New Trimming Materials Trim Your Lawn

Your nerves get frazzled at times when you see hard-to-trim frazzled grass edges on your lawn and flower beds. But all that can be a trouble of the past, when you use new trimming materials. New corrugated aluminum which comes in rolls and strips handles almost as easily as heavy cardboard . . . almost.

Have you built your flower beds or foundation plantings with a trench around them to separate them from the grass? Does the trench become a muddy ditch when you water? Does the grass grow straggly against your walks, driveway and sidewalk? Correct all that now with easy-to-handle aluminum stripping.

Snip . . . Bend . . . Hammer . . . Done!

Special garden aluminum stripping is available to you right now. It's light in weight but sturdy, corrugated for extra strength. And it won't rust or corrode, so it should last the proverbial lifetime.

Here's how easy it is to use the stripping. Most practical size is four inches wide. Use it from the roll, or strips will serve just as well. Simply cut the stripping to lengths you desire, using an ordinary heavy household scissors.

Place the stripping in the ground where the edge of the lawn meets a flower bed, next to a driveway, around a tree, around shrub areas—most anywhere that the grass grows straggly and becomes hard to cut.

Make a slit in the soil with a spade or any other such instrument, if the earth is hard—then hammer in the stripping with a hammer or mallet, until it's even with the top of the ground. If the earth is soft, you may even be able to pound the stripping directly into the ground without a preparatory slit.

You can bend this marvelous new stripping to most any contour you like, including a complete circle around a tree, for instance.

Functional . . . Attractive . . . Saves Work

Once the stripping is in the earth at soil level, it's practically invisible. You run your lawn mower right over the edge, because the strip has stopped the grass from growing past its prescribed boundary.

And there's no need for a ditch around your flower beds. The stripping keeps the water where you want it, while it prevents grass from invading the other plant areas. The underground barrier keeps grass roots from spreading where they're not wanted . . . makes weeding and application of weed killers easier too.

Your lawn, flower beds and other areas around your home will have a much neater, well cared for look, once you strip for garden maintenance this modern way!

FERTILIZERS

The Miracle of Concentrated Liquid Fertilizers

Along with the trend in modern living to get better results faster, a great boost to gardening in the past few years has been the great upsurge in concentrated liquid fertilizers. And no wonder! Within less than a week after applying a good liquid fertilizer, you actually start to see results in speeded-up growth, healthier foliage, bigger blooms faster.

Those *results* are what you want, so that's reason enough for you to use the concentrated water-soluble plant food. But perhaps you also want to know why such foods work faster than the traditional fertilizers.

Growth Elements Combined for "Instant Action"

Instead of lugging around heavy bags of dry fertilizer, then working the fertilizer into the soil with hands and tools, you simply spray on the liquid fertilizer through watering cans, or through your garden hose with special attachments which are now available.

Let me straighten you out on one point first. There's still an important place for the dry fertilizers. They work effectively. They feed the soil, lawn and plants over a longer period. They are less costly. They have these advantages, and it's up to you to decide whether to use dry fertilizer, concentrated water-soluble plant foods, or both.

But you'll certainly want to try and then decide—the basis of all good gardening. And, without question, you'll be thrilled with your results from a good water-soluble plant food. The one I've used for miracle results is a 15-30-15 formula, available in most places where garden products are sold. Those figures mean, of course, that the plant food contains 15 per cent nitrogen, 30 per cent phosphorus and 15 per cent potash, the basic needed elements for healthy growth. In addition, this plant food contains important trace elements: magnesium, manganese, iron, copper, zinc, boron, molybdenum and other elements. That's mighty good and essential eating for your plants and lawn!

Open the package and you find a clean, odorless, pleasant-to-handle powder. You simply follow package directions, in this case mixing just one level tablespoon to one gallon of water. Sprinkle the solution on and around each plant, and on grass—wetting the soil just as you would water plants. For larger areas, you can purchase and use special attachments which fit your hose and measure out the fertilizer solution into the water stream automatically.

It's a great thrill to know that, as the liquid fertilizer reaches your plants, it goes to work to feed these vital elements to roots and foliage instantly.

Astounding Radioactive Isotope Tests Prove Instant Feeding

A tremendous boost to use of the concentrated liquid fertilizers was provided by tests made at a leading university. Scientists added radioactive isotopes—a product of atomic research—to experimental batches of the concentrated plant food in its water solution. These radioactive plant foods, especially prepared for the test purposes only, were then used in extensive experiments. Results were astonishing!

The radioactive plant food in solution was then applied to the roots of a plant by ordinary methods, just as you might water your plants. A leaf was then cut from the plant within 15 minutes after fertilizing. The leaf was then photographed against radiosensitive film. The resulting film, called a radio-autograph, looking something like an x-ray film, showed positive and considerable traces of the fertilizer nutriments already throughout the leaf—only minutes after the solution was applied to the roots!

In another growing plant, a Geiger counter was used for the test. The fertilizer solution was again fed to the roots. Upper leaves and the upper stems of the living plant were then tested with the Geiger counter—and positive traces of the radioactive matter mixed with the liquid plant food registered on the counter. This proved without doubt that the solution worked throughout the plant, feeding it *within minutes* after application.

Another test involved a large, growing 6-foot-high rose bush. Within sixty minutes after the bush was fed with radioactive liquid plant food, traces of life-giving food were found within the entire bush.

No wonder you'll actually see miracle growth in your plants, lawn and garden within a week after using a good concentrated water-soluble plant food.

Getting These "Instant Results" in Your Garden

Simply apply the plant food according to instructions on the package. As I've noted, these water-soluble plant foods are more costly than dry fertilizers. But there's no question that they're pleasanter and easier to handle, safe, and give you quicker results. Also, I find the liquid fertilizers not as expensive as might seem at first.

For example, the product I use is highly concentrated, so that a five-pound package makes 200 gallons of fertilizing solution (one level tablespoonful per gallon of water). This feeds many plants and shrubs, or up to 5,000 square feet of lawn.

With most garden flowers, berries and vegetables, you feed every two weeks, shrubs twice a season, lawns every two weeks. House plants also respond beautifully to regular feeding with a concentrated water-soluble plant food.

You'll See Glorious New Garden Beauty

I've had tomato plants growing twice as large as my neighbors', loaded with two to three times as many big, luscious tomatoes—up to two pounds each—thanks in part to regular feeding with concentrated water-soluble plant food.

My initials "written" in part of my lawn with a sprinkling can containing the liquid fertilizer, have stood out all season long in rich, green clarity against the surrounding unfed grass. In other areas, where I applied the liquid fertilizer regularly and watered faithfully, I've had lush carpets of thick green grass that others envied—yet this can be yours just as readily!

I've seen an entire garden perk up almost instantly after feeding with the liquid fertilizer, with growth and flowers showing new energy and beauty overnight. *All these miracles are yours for the using.*

Look for Special Penetrant in Fertilizer

Within the past few years, one of the important strides in chemistry is the production of special penetrants which result in faster absorption of food by the plants. Check the package of the water-soluble plant food you buy for this benefit.

When the plant food contains a good agricultural penetrant,

Complete liquid plant food feeds fast through soil, foliage.

it penetrates the soil even faster and spreads farther. Thus, it saturates wider areas and reaches the deepest roots more readily, going more quickly where it's needed most. Even hard-baked problem soils are penetrated more quickly and thoroughly.

The penetrant also helps the entire plant, branches and leaves to absorb the plant food faster and more completely, all helping to promote better and quicker growth.

You want to give your garden all the miracle benefits science makes possible, and so this is one advance you don't want to miss.

Quick Results with Foliage Feeding

The radioactive tests made in the laboratory proved dramatically that plants absorb the liquid plant food right through the leaves also. So there's a double benefit for your plants. Apply the solution to the soil, and in addition to the foliage. You'll be delighted by faster, healthier and more beautiful growth through this double boost.

As a word of caution, check the plant food package to make sure the product is recommended for foliar feeding. Otherwise it may be too strong. However, any such fertilizer which is safe for feeding foliage is definitely safe for application to the soil.

Important Preventive of Transplanting Loss

When you transplant tender young plants, such as tomato and vegetable plants, and perennial flowering plants, apply the same solution of concentrated water-soluble plant food immediately. Don't "flood" the plants or soil, but apply plenty gently and easily, soaking the soil thoroughly.

This mild solution, loaded with vital nutrients, will help pick up the plants, avoiding that unsightly weakening and wilting that you often see upon transplanting. You'll find that the tender plants perk up faster, often thriving vigorously the same day, because the nutrients are going to work almost instantly in the soil both above and below the hungry, shocked roots.

Don't pass up this vital feeding upon transplanting, if you're to get the healthful growth miracles you want.

Starting Seeds Better

Yes, seeds themselves, the very "elements of life," will benefit greatly from your application of a good concentrated water-soluble plant food.

Just plant the seeds as instructed on the seed package. Then, before covering over with soil, apply the fertilizer solution slowly and easily, so you won't wash out any of the seeds.

Now, cover over the seeds with soil, adding another soaking with the solution. You'll have given the seeds a great start in life, and they'll reward you accordingly!

A Life-saver for "Dying" Plants

There are many ills that can kill plants, but sometimes plants that have the look of dying are simply starving to death. If that's the case, you'll see miracles of life-saving in a hurry by applying a good concentrated water-soluble plant food.

The plant will start "coming to life" in a hurry, almost right before your eyes, frequently within hours, because the nutrients are carried to the roots and throughout the plant so fast. For an extra-fast boost, apply the solution to the foliage as well as to the soil for root-feeding.

This life-giving miracle can apply to your flowers, vegetables, shrubs and even to trees. In the case of trees, there are no holes to dig, no ground to plow up; simply apply plenty of the fertilizer solution to the roots through the soil, soaking in thoroughly, and spray on as much of the tree's foliage as possible.

You'll find that one of the prime gardening thrills is to bring seemingly dead plants "back to life." It won't always work, of course, but it's certainly worth trying, and even if you only save a percentage of your plants, shrubs and trees, you'll experience the joy of seeming to work miracles.

Miracle Key Unlocks Iron!

Suppose your system were starving for vitamin C, and a bowl of luscious oranges, rich in the healthful vitamin, was only a few inches away. You'd still be starving for vitamin C, if the oranges were locked in a heavy mesh cage so you couldn't use them!

That's what frequently happens with plants that are starving for iron. There may be some iron in the soil, or even in the fertilizer you apply, but if that iron isn't in the form that the plants can readily take up and assimilate in their systems, it might just as well be—and in effect is—locked away from them.

And that's why science has performed seeming miracles in turning yellowing plants that needed iron, into lush green beauty and health, by creating wonder-working *chelated iron*. This is iron in a form that plants assimilate and use quickly and easily, so you see marvelous results in a few days or weeks, sometimes almost overnight.

Now you can buy chelated iron either in dry form to be spread on the soil, or in water-soluble concentrates which you water on soil and foliage. The liquid application works faster because the plants absorb the nutrients more rapidly.

Of course, yellowing of plants is sometimes due to harmful fungus or insect infestation, and to other soil deficiencies. But usually, in acid or lime soils, your troubles in that direction are due to a woeful lack of usable iron.

Most effective application is usually with a water-soluble or other plant food which contains *chelated iron* along with other balanced elements and nutrients. Not only your broadleaf evergreens and other acid-loving plants, shrubs and trees, will benefit amazingly from *chelated iron* feeding, but also many vegetables—when foliage starts to yellow and wither. You'll see a thrilling improvement in color and health with cabbage, celery, radishes, tomatoes, etc. (However, it's better not to spray with chelated iron products when such plants are in blossom or in fruit.)

Test and see how miracle products boost plant growth.

Yes, chelated iron (pronounced key-lated) is a wondrous key provided by science to unlock and correct specific iron deficiencies in soil and plants. It helps you, as never possible before, to be a garden magician—changing unsightly yellowing to glorious rich green for much of your precious garden growth!

Sugar Sweetens Foliar Feeding!

Yes, just common ordinary cane sugar, right out of the sugar bowl on your dining table, can improve the effectiveness of foliar feeding in your garden. That's been tested and proved at a noted university.

When you spray liquid fertilizer on the leaves of your plants, add about a teaspoonful of sugar per gallon of fertilizer solution. Closely controlled studies prove that the nutrients will enter the leaves more thoroughly, feeding your plants more effectively.

It was also proved that the sweetened spray is even absorbed efficiently by leaves after dark. That's when activity of plants, like man, is usually at its lowest point.

So, "sweeten up" the foliar feeding of your plants, and they'll repay you with lovelier, sweeter blooms and foliage than you've had before!

Safety Test for Foliar Feeding

Are all concentrated plant foods, which you mix with water, safe for spraying right on foliage for foliar feeding? No! Check the instructions on the package you buy. It must state "safe (or recommended) for foliar feeding," otherwise use the product only on the earth for root feeding.

If a spray is too strong, it will often harm the foliage. However, you can be sure that if a spray is mild enough for foliar feeding, it's also safe for feeding the roots.

Urea-form—New Nitrogen Miracle!

Science has done it again: accomplished another laboratory "miracle" for the greater glory of your garden! For many years, scientists have been trying to produce nitrogen—principal source of life-giving "green" for nature's growth—in special synthetic, easily applied form. Now they've done it.

The aim has long been to take magical urea, produce it synthetically and *control* it, so that it would be possible to provide nitrogen to plants both rapidly and slowly. Purpose would be not only to feed nitrogen to plants quickly, but also to feed the magical element over a long two- to three-year spacing.

After thousands of unsuccessful attempts, in many laboratories all over the country, the key which has unlocked the obstinate door turns out to be a combination of urea and formaldehydes—now commonly called urea-form. This dramatic substance provides nitrogen to plants safely, at a controlled uniform pace. What's more, urea-form feeds plants the nitrogen over a much longer period of time than has been possible even with most excellent natural organic fertilizers!

So, tip your wide gardening hat again to science for a major step forward. With urea-form, you can stop worrying that the precious nitrogen that you apply will disappear rapidly from soils, particularly after an extended period of heavy rains.

When you use one of the new urea-form fertilizers properly, you're in effect rationing out the wondrous nitrogen to your plants little by little, instead of giving your lawn and garden a boost for a few weeks and then having much of the effectiveness of the nitrogen dissipated.

I don't mean to promise you that you simply apply urea-form once and then figure that your soil is supplied with nitrogen for as long as two or three years. Nature's growth loves nitrogen, so for the "miracle results" you want, I recommend that you feed urea-form two or three times a year. Thus you give your grass and plants a rich, muscle-building feast regularly, instead of just providing a sustenance diet.

You'll be delighted to know also that the urea-form fertilizers are odorless and very pleasant to handle. And—of top importance—when applied exactly as directed on each package, they're very safe in use, won't "burn" your plants!

I know that many of you have been shocked after feeding a high-nitrogen dry fertilizer to your grass, without precise care, to see your beloved grass wilt, turn brown, and then realize to your horror that you've "burned" the lawn. That won't happen with the urea-form fertilizers—unless you're extremely careless or overfeed.

But—feed the urea-form fertilizers exactly as instructed on the package you buy. Don't be too liberal, don't overdose, and your properly seeded lawn, and plants, should respond beautifully.

Don't be too upset at the comparative high cost of urea-form fertilizers now. Undoubtedly the prices will come down as production increases and manufacturing methods are improved. After all, you don't have to use urea-form fertilizers on your entire lawn or garden if you don't want to.

Experiment with a small package if you prefer; that seeking and trying and finding out from actual usage is a big part of the creative thrill of gardening. You want to keep trying many approaches and products and methods. And, as you note from the many tips in this book, there are a number of different ways to get the "miracle results" that make your lawn and garden extraordinary instead of commonplace. In fact, as explained elsewhere, a high-nitrogen fertilizer concentrate mixed and applied with water will usually give your lawn a quicker green boost than urea-form.

But certainly you want to know about all the modern-day miracles that can make your thumb greener and your eyes brighter as you gaze pridefully at your garden glory. And a good urea-form fertilizer can definitely help to boost and keep your garden in top form!

To Lime or Not to Lime?

Whether or not to lime your soil is a very acid question—literally. If your soil is not acid, you can harm it by adding lime. If your soil is acid, you'll improve plant growth wonderfully by adding lime and bringing the earth into proper balance for best growing conditions.

So . . . here's one case where you positively need a soil test to guide you. When you've taken soil samples, as described elsewhere in this book, and found that your soil has a pH of six or less, then it's acid and needs lime. Proper application will make a remarkable improvement in your gardening success.

Many Advantages from Liming

Although far from being a new material, good lime can work wonders in improving your soil—as you'll undoubtedly find out from soil test results. *However, it does not take the place of proper fertilization . . . you still should use a complete fertilizer in addition to improve your soil.*

You'll get many benefits from liming. In addition to counteracting soil acidity, and bringing the degree of "sweetness" or "sourness" of your soil back to desirable neutral range, liming adds calcium and magnesium, helpful plant nutrients.

Also, liming acts to improve the actual structure and texture of the soil. Roots can grow more easily in the looser soil. And the earth will retain moisture for a longer period.

Here's How to Get in Lime

1. Be sure you don't use just any kind of lime, but the best agricultural lime, which is made from finely pulverized dolomite limestone. Don't stint by purchasing a cheaper grade, because your results will be far inferior. The fine agricultural lime isn't caustic, it does add plant nutrients, and it's not dissolved out easily by rainfall.

2. Many gardeners get good results by using lime most any time during the year, but the best period is in the fall. During the winter, the lime is carried way down deep in the earth, where its "sweetening" action is needed most. So apply in September or October if convenient for you.

3. The results of the soil test will instruct you on determining what quantity of lime to apply. It should never be applied at more than 70 pounds per 1,000 square feet of ground in any single season, for safety. If your soil test shows that you need even more liming, apply the balance the following year. Lime stays in the soil for many years.

4. Always apply lime with a spreader, unless the area is very small, than you can apply by hand, using garden gloves. Spread

the lime in criss-cross fashion—half the quantity criss, and the other half cross, for most effective distribution.

The same spreader can be used for seeding and feeding with dry fertilizers, if you wish—you can even do the two or three operations the same day.

Some simple precautions to follow: Wear garden gloves. Keep the lime away from your eyes, ears, nose and mouth, and from any open cuts or wounds in your skin. Don't apply lime on a windy day. Keep it away from the soil around evergreens, which love an acid soil condition.

In addition to your delight over seeing improved growth from well limed soil, you'll be pleased to know you've accomplished good for a long long time and are usually finished with this operation for many fruitful seasons.

Miracles Can Come from Compost

No garden seems complete without a good compost heap—at least once during every gardening career. Compost is simply a "waste" pile, composed properly and decaying thoroughly. It's certainly not a necessary element in gardening, but a good compost heap does provide excellent organic matter to help your garden grow miracles of beautiful blooms.

After it's properly seasoned, you use the compost to mix in with the soil for good texture for growing things. It's also beneficial as a top mulch to hold water to and in the soil better, around growing plants.

How to Make a Good Compost Heap

Select a corner of the plot that's as remote as possible from your and your neighbor's view, as a compost pile is not a decorative spot.

Now simply start piling on, day by day, leaves from your property, waste grass after mowing, vegetable (not meat) garbage, and waste vegetable matter such as foliage.

It's desirable to keep the pile fairly flat on top, as the materials accumulate. This way, rain—which is an important element in helping decay—soaks into the pile more uniformly instead of running off.

Every time you've added about six inches to your compost heap, it's desirable to water down with a good liquid plant food, to help bacterial decomposition. This isn't essential, but it's helpful in having a *better* compost for your garden.

Come spring, about six months later, you should have a well-rotted compost heap. Apply it to the soil, several inches deep, then turn under through the soil, mixing it thoroughly with the earth. Use it also as a mulch, a use described elsewhere in this book.

Much Controversy about Composts

You'll feel that you're really getting back to Nature, more as an active partner, by building a compost heap and watching it grow day by day, week by week. And this natural organic matter will do your soil plenty of good. *But don't count on it to replace proper fertilization.* Use your compost, mixing it right into the soil, and using it as a mulch, in order to benefit your soil. But fertilize also.

These paragraphs don't begin to tell you the whole story of compost heaps. Hundreds and even thousands of pages have been written on the fascinating subject. You can build simple or elaborate bins and other setups. You can vary your compost heaping and treating, in dozens of ways. Just a very simple but effective form of compost heap is described here to help you get started, if you're so minded.

Yes, miracles can come from compost. But if you're at all finicky, it's one garden miracle you can get along without—in spite of some claims to the contrary.

Miracles in Manure?

There's not much question that farm manure, properly applied, is an excellent fertilizer. But, if you don't own a farm, or a lot of animals producing manure for you, it's rather costly paying out for the manure. In fact, considering the lack of joy in handling manure, it's hardly worth handling for gardeners, at any price.

Commercial fertilizers today, scientifically made and dependably balanced, are more efficient and effective than manure. So why bother?

So the answer is: outside of price if manure is free to you, there are no special miracles in manure that you can't get in commercial fertilizers. Furthermore, when it comes to handling for your garden, no matter how you figure it—it's still manure!

SOIL CONDITIONERS AND GROWTH BOOSTERS

Synthetic Soil Conditioners . . . Miracles or Murder?

A few years ago, sensational articles appeared in magazines raving about new synthetic soil conditioners that would revolutionize gardening. Miraculous results in improving all kinds of farm and garden growth were described—with photographs to prove it.

A mess of soil conditioners, and many were a real mess, hit the market. Many gardeners rushed to the stores, cast the conditioners on the soil . . . and found themselves with shocking lawns and gardens of "cement"!

The word went around that synthetic soil conditioners were a fake and a fraud, a miracle gone sour. What's the truth?

I was in on the early beginnings of synthetic soil conditioners, and spent days in research at one of the world's finest laboratories. I saw miracles happen almost before my eyes. Side by side, I saw two potted plants grown in the same soil, both soils enriched with plant food, but the soil in only one pot treated with the synthetic conditioner.

The plants in the pots where the soil was treated with synthetic conditioner *were two to three times as high and lush and healthy as the others;* with so many more blooms that the results were almost unbelievable. No fake. No fraud. A breath-taking wonderment.

Why did this happen? You can realize why quickly and easily. Visualize a soil that's become almost as hard and dense as cement; you know how difficult and almost impossible it is for roots to breathe and feed and fight their way through. Now, if you loosen that soil, you help temporarily, but soon the earth becomes hard again, and once more the roots and plants have to fight to spread and survive, let alone thrive.

Here's how the synthetic soil conditioner works: when you loosen and crumble up that soil, mixing in the soil conditioner,

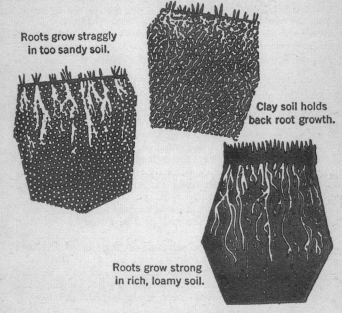

Roots grow straggly in too sandy soil.

Clay soil holds back root growth.

Roots grow strong in rich, loamy soil.

the conditioner *fixes the soil in that state for years*—keeping it loose and airy, helping the roots to feed and spread and thrive. I repeat: the synthetic soil conditioner fixes the soil in the state it's in when applied.

So, if you crumble up the soil into a loose airy texture, the conditioner keeps it that way, almost as if you applied a permanent plastic coating to each individual crumb of soil. *But* when gardeners applied the synthetic condition to a hard soil, the action tended to harden it even further; no wonder many unhappy souls complained about "fields of cement."

Yes, you can work miracles in your soil's texture with a good synthetic soil conditioner, but you must use the greatest care to apply it properly.

It's easy to judge if your soil needs conditioning: take a handful of soil and add just a few drops of water, just enough for the slightest moistening, not dampening. Now close your fist tight, then open it. If the soil has formed a tight clod, it needs conditioning; if the soil breaks apart completely, it's in good shape texture-wise.

I advise most emphatically that you apply synthetic soil conditioners to only one area of your lawn and garden for experimentation. If used properly, your results will probably inspire you to condition other areas the following year. For, as I've explained, synthetic soil conditioners can work wonders in helping your plants and grass to grow. And since the soil will stay in wonderfully loose condition for years, the cost is not as great as you might think at first.

But number one—you must first break the soil into the loose, tiny particles you want, even if you do it by hand, because that's the way the synthetic soil conditioner will keep them. If you apply the conditioner to large, hard lumps, you'll have a soil made of large, hard lumps from then on. And be sure you loosen the soil deep enough, because the conditioner won't loosen the earth any further than you've done by tools or by hand. Follow directions exactly with the conditioner you buy—applying no more than the quantity instructed—and watering right away, lightly only, as instructed.

But number two—your conditioner only fixes the texture of the soil, it doesn't feed the soil, as I've stated emphatically elsewhere.

The combination of good soil conditioning and good fertilizing produces thrilling miracles of growth, because the food is more readily available to seeds and roots, and the well-fed roots don't have to fight the soil in order to grow. Tender young plants become established much more quickly and flourish more rapidly and healthfully.

I sincerely hope that all the negative conditions I've stressed about synthetic soil conditioners won't scare you away from trying them. Actually you can accomplish the miracle of fixing soil in just the condition you wish, and knowing it'll stay that way for three or four years or even more.

I recommend that you try one patch in your garden, and judge the results for yourself.

Now—"Bacteriaerated" Peat Moss!

"Bacteriaerated" is my own word to describe the double action of an old friend of the soil, peat moss—now available in improved form to help you grow healthier plants—faster!

Thus, improved, modern peat moss performs two primary functions. First, it helps condition and *aerate* the soil to ease root spread for plants. Second, it introduces *more* friendly bacteria into the soil to help speed up the mysterious process by which nutrients are made available to plants most efficiently and effectively.

Feel the "Aging" Process

To give your plants a speedier boost, this peat moss is "aged" by special scientifically improved process. Growth of friendly bacteria is so accelerated during the processing that the peat moss actually gives off steam that can be seen with the naked eye!

Even when you buy the package of improved peat moss, make this simple test to tell the difference. Thrust your hand deep into the package and you'll feel a special warmth caused by the thriving bacterial activity. This translates into faster action when the substance is combined with your soil.

Helps Most All Plant Life

Although you necessarily use peat moss in limited quantity because of its costliness when applied to a large area, it will help your flowers, vegetables, shrubs, fruits—most all plant life—grow healthier and more beautiful season after season. The effect is long-lasting.

When you apply peat moss to sandy soil, you help bind the soil together so that plant foods and nutrients don't wash out in a hurry. In clayey soils, the peat moss helps loosen the hard-packed earth, so roots work through and spread much better. And the peat moss helps keep moisture in the soil, a tremendous benefit during drought periods.

And now, as you improve your soil with peat, you'll be an even more successful gardener if you take advantage of this special "plus"—and apply the peat moss teaming with extra multitudes of friendly bacteria, ready to apply their microscopic muscles for better plant growth in your garden.

Conditioning Soil with Wood Chips:

University scientists report very encouraging results for gardeners through treating soil with wood chips. Yes, these are the same inexpensive or free wood chips that are by-products of a number of different industries that employ woodworking in their operations.

In carefully controlled experiments, soil treated with wood chips turned out to contain up to *ten times as much organic matter* as the same soil without wood chips.

How to Use Chips

Recommended procedure is to work the wood chips into the soil along with regular fertilization just before planting season. The "chips off the old block" not only help enrich the earth, but more to the point, they condition the soil so that it stays in a looser, better aerated texture that promotes faster, healthier growth of plants.

As a result, the chip-treated soil resists baking and hardening that inhibits plant growth, and helps prevent erosion on banks and other steep surfaces.

With all these advantages, here's a new soil "miracle" that's worth trying in at least one area of your garden or lawn to gauge the benefits for you.

Where to Get Chips

Local lumber yards, woodworking factories, industries which use wood in manufacture, are often more than willing for you to remove piles of wood chips at no cost, or sell them to you at very low cost.

If your town is advanced, they may have a chipping truck or machine which converts branches of trees that they remove regularly into excellent chips for soil conditioning; they may be only too glad to give you this produce if you phone the local authorities.

Once you get "in the chips," you'll surely gain new excitement and possibly magnificent improved growth in your garden.

Astounding Flowering Speed-up

Experiments at a Western university now show that flowering of some popular varieties can be speeded up as much as three weeks ahead of normal flowering time!

Using a wonder-working hormone material known as *2-3-5 triodobenzoic acid*, some petunias and zinnias were treated while other plants of exactly the same varieties in the batch were left untreated.

Results were breathtaking. The treated plants burst into flower from ten days to three weeks ahead of the similar untreated plants. In fact, some of the treated petunias to which the wonder-working hormone was applied flowered and set new seed even before nearby untreated petunias began to flower!

Watch for products containing 2-3-5 triodobenzoic acid and experiment with it. You'll soon be able to point with pride to the speediest-growing flowers in your neighborhood.

"Ground Glass" Corrects Minor-elements Lack!

Imagine mixing ground glass with your earth? Doesn't sound very beneficial, does it? Yet there's a new compound, made of tiny pieces of specially prepared "glass" which feeds plants needed minor elements: iron, boron, manganese, copper, zinc and molybdenum.

This dramatic material consists of "fritted trace elements," also referred to simply as agricultural frit. It's now packaged commercially for your use.

I've seen exciting results with use of the fritted trace elements when they were mixed in deficient soil. Blooms were richer, lusher, bigger than in untreated areas. But, while you can increase growth wonderfully with agricultural frit, there's a big "but" attached.

First, these tiny bits of specially treated "glass" must be mixed in the soil thoroughly, because roots must have close contact with the particles of frit in order to benefit fully. So don't think you can just scatter the material on the ground haphazardly; that won't help your plants.

Second, you must use a complete fertilizer, in addition to frit, because while the minor elements are desirable and even essential, they're not enough to feed plants thoroughly for the miracle results you want.

So, while you'll get excellent results using a complete fertilizer plus frit, you can get exceptional results in your garden also by using a good complete fertilizer that *already contains the important minor elements*. Check the labels of good fertilizers available now, to save you time, effort and money. This tip alone can make a big difference in whether you get ordinary results or "miracle results" in your garden!

More Miracles in the Making

Even as you read these words, scientists, agriculturists, nurserymen, gardening experts are all working to make gardening life better and more beautiful for you.

Imagine, for example, a new soil mixture which is almost ready for your use at this writing. It's made of new materials based on "lava rock." When you start seeds, cuttings and young plants in this material, they won't become waterlogged and ruined as may happen now without real care.

This wonder "earth" actually holds four times its weight in water without becoming sodden—then gets rid of any excess water. And this exciting material is amazingly light, so it's particularly good for potted plants that you move around and carry indoors and out. Something to look forward to!

Products of the Atomic Age in Gardening

And scientists at one of the Atomic Energy Commission's great laboratories announce new steps forward in solving problems of photosynthesis, which is one of life's most exciting mysteries. That's the process by which plant life may make its own protein food directly through a combination of water, carbon dioxide absorbed right from the air, and the energy of sunlight.

These new discoveries may provide direct methods for the production of protein through *light* energy in plant cells. Such a development in all forms of plant life is too big to even grasp fully at this point—but it indicates a whole new world of wonders of growth, as never possible before.

Keep Looking Ahead

It all adds up to this: As wonderful as gardening was yesterday, and is today, you always have so much more to look forward to! So keep alert, reading about and trying the new "miracles" in your garden, for always increasing rewards and pleasures from the good earth.

INSECTICIDES AND FUNGICIDES

"All-purpose" Insecticides— a Modern Miracle?

Can you count on a true, complete miracle in your garden in respect to insect and fungus control, using just one dust or spray to do the entire job? Paradoxically, you can, and you cannot—it all boils down to this:

There's no question that some of the "all-purpose" or "multi-purpose" pesticides available now are quite effective in killing and controlling many of the common garden pests. Such products make life much easier for you, since you buy, store and apply only one dust or spray instead of a whole shelf full. The label will generally list a combination of insecticides, fungicides and inert materials as carriers for even distribution and application of the active ingredients.

But it's also true that no one product can control all garden pests completely. In your case, you may find that an "all-purpose" product protects your plants adequately and keeps pests under control sufficiently. If so, you've saved yourself a lot of time and work.

Special Controls Usually Necessary

However, after using an "all-purpose" product, you'd better keep examining your garden closely and regularly for any evidence of further infestation and destruction.

In case of invasion by some one or several species of pests

which your pesticide application has failed to stop, get one of the miracle workers described in this book, for special control.

In your case, one good "all-purpose" product, and one or two special materials, may be all you need to keep your garden and lawn growing beautifully. But keep watching carefully for signs of infestation, lest you overlook a destructive invasion, through overconfidence in one "all-purpose" killer.

Read the Label—Again and Again and Again!

The same modern insecticides, pesticides and fungicides that can produce miracles in killing insects and controlling diseases in your garden—as never possible before in past years—can also cause damage to growth if not handled correctly. Also, a product that will work wonders for one species of plant may ruin another.

The greatest proportion of damage is generally due to careless handling, measuring and application by the gardener. So the choice between "miracles" or "murder" in your garden is usually up to you.

Let the label be your guide! Insecticides and such products are under strict government control. Every word on the label must be checked and passed by government authorities before the manufacturer can finally print the label and market the product.

Furthermore, reputable manufacturers are eager to comply with regulations and have you follow instructions and claims on the label to the letter. Remember that the manufacturer counts on your satisfaction and *repeat purchase* to build his business year after year.

So, rely on the label, and don't experiment lavishly by using an insecticide on an unspecified variety of plants just because the product has performed well for plants listed on the label. Remember that a powerful modern insecticide on your hands is an instrument of life or death for plant life, depending almost entirely on how *you* use it.

Interpreting the Label

While it may seem elementary, and you probably know already what the principal words on the label mean, the following simple explanations may be helpful to some beginning gardeners:

An *insecticide* is the over-all name, of course, for the material used primarily to control insects, while *pesticide* covers the entire range of control products.

A *fungicide* is used to prevent and control various types of fungus diseases.

A *herbicide* is a material that is made to control and destroy undesirable plants.

Miticide is a product made particularly for the control and eradication of mites and some related life.

Ovicide is a material aimed specifically at controlling and destroying insect eggs.

Active ingredients are the chemicals which actually have a controlling or destructive effect, while the *inert ingredients* are materials usually incorporated to hold and distribute the active chemicals, but have no actual killing power of their own.

What Form of Pesticides to Use

Whether to use a dust or a spray is primarily a matter of individual choice. Now you can get many effective miracle workers in dust form, in duster tubes, in water-soluble concentrates, in liquid form for use in hand sprayers, with hose attachments, etc.

Perhaps you'd like to try various forms of pesticides and then decide which you like best. In this wonderful art of gardening, *the final choice is your own.*

Top and Bottom Application of Insecticides and Fungicides

Even the most miraculous insecticides and fungicides can't work most effectively, as a general rule, except on those parts of the plant which are covered by the dust or spray.

So, whether you dust or spray, take the extra time and care to cover *top and bottom* of foliage. Think of it as though you're spraying paint on any surface you want to cover and protect —any part of the surface that you miss with the paint has no color or protection whatsoever, no matter how heavily you've coated the rest of the area.

Start Control Efforts Early

Your eagle eye is one of the best protective devices. Check your garden constantly and early for signs of harmful insects and disease.

At the first indication of insect invasion (and in many cases, as suggested in this book, even before signs of damage and infestation are evident), dust or spray. Then, according to label directions, usually repeat the treatment in about a week, especially if any signs of insects remain.

The Miracle of Hormone Weed Killers

While hormones can be controlled today by science to produce miracles of plant growth, you can also get hormone weed killers that will destroy astonishingly! In fact, you can use these miracle destroyers to kill nearly all broad-leafed weeds and undesirable woody plants.

Such weed killers work on a very simple principle. When you apply them, you inject a huge superdose of hormones into the plant. This causes such a rapid and great increase in growth that the plant cells break down and the plant dies a miserable and thorough death, much to the glee of gardeners who justifiably hate weeds.

Killing weeds with the hormone products is not instantaneous. It takes several days to work, but you can be confident that the plant destruction is thorough.

Use the hormone weed killers on your lawn for control of chickweed, dandelions, oxalis, Japanese clovers and many other broad-leafed weeds. Apply as directed on the particular package, and only as directed because while a weed killer may be relatively harmless to some grasses, it can injure others.

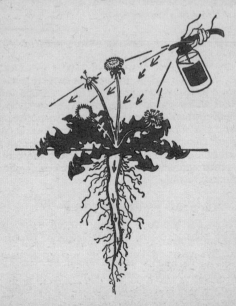

Destroy weeds root deep with new miracle chemicals.

These hormone products are also useful in greater concentration, often brushed on with a paint brush, to kill many really tough weeds, including thistles, docks, poison ivy, wild morning glories and brambles. And, mixed with kerosene, they'll kill tree stumps and prevent regrowth on stumps.

Yes, sensational victories over even the toughest undesirable growth can be yours today, utilizing the extraordinary power of hormone regulators *with intelligent care!*

Fumigating Soil Before Planting

It makes sense to fumigate your soil before planting, wherever it's practical. With some of the new wonder fumigants, you can kill out many undesirable organisms including many weed seedings, certain soil insects, many harmful fungi and nematodes.

Better have all these vicious elements dead instead, of lurking in the soil to attack and destroy your precious new plantings!

These effective new chemicals, usually applied to moist soil before planting, form vapors which clean out the soil quickly, easily and neatly. Simply mix with water and apply either through a sprinkling can or with a mixing proportioner on the hose.

If you wish, you can use special fumigating equipment which puts the chemical down into the soil deeper and faster, but it's not necessary. Apply in your own way, that's most convenient for you, then wet down the earth again after application. This acts to seal the chemical in the soil. In most cases, you don't have to cover the area after application.

Follow the directions on the package you buy, for exact proportioning and how long to leave soil alone between application of fumigant and planting. Your plants, in their clean, healthful soil, and with proper fertilization, of course, will show their appreciation for your soil-cleaning efforts, with lush vigorous growth.

5-Year Miracle against Grubs

Science now gives you the means to conquer one of the worst lawn pests, grubs, and, even more satisfying, to keep them in check for five years or longer with one application of the proper miracle chemicals!

It's important to watch out for damage from grubs through easy telltale clues, *before* your grass dies out. Start fearing grubs if you see starlings and crows popping onto your grass in unusually large numbers. Also, be on the lookout if you see mole runways in the lawn. And, another easy and unpleasant clue that your nose knows best: the presence of skunks visiting your grass. All these invaders may well be going for grubs.

Next step in your sleuthing: examine your grass and seize some sizable tufts here and there on the lawn. If you find that the tuft and surrounding grass rolls back readily like a rug when someone sweeps dust under it, then attack the grub invaders with one of science's new miracle eradicators.

Get some DDT prepared specifically to kill grubs, or chlordane or lead arsenate, and apply according to directions. Within two to eight weeks, these miracle workers will eradicate the grubs. Then you can relax for at least five years, knowing that your grass is happily grubproof.

You can also buy quicker-acting eradicators such as dieldrin, but the others will give you peace of mind grubwise for more years. If you wish, and if the condition seems particularly serious, apply the fast-acting chemicals first, then follow up later with the more permanent killers. In any case, don't let grubs get the best of your grass, since science has given you the weapons to conquer them so you can achieve lawn beauty not possible comparatively few years ago.

Out, Out, Spot Diseases!

Great and thrilling strides have been made in combating and overcoming many fungus diseases which have for centuries caused ugly spotting and destruction of much plant life. Now you have a number of excellent miracle workers to help control and destroy these spoilers.

Captan, an organic fungicide, is an important and effective ingredient in fighting rose black spot, and many spotting diseases on apple and other fruit leaves, as well as brown spotting of some grasses. Look for it on product labels.

Mites hide under leaves.

Cutworms chew away.

Ferbam is another chemical that works wonders in overcoming black spotting, rot, scab and rust of various varieties of flowers and fruits and foliage. Ferbam products sometimes leave their own hardly noticeable coloration on foliage, which some gardeners object to. However, even this fault is far preferable, to my mind, to widespread, unsightly destruction by fungus diseases.

Look for variations of ferbam products, improved even further for specific purposes. *Ziram* is a ferbam derivative containing zinc. *Maneb* includes manganese. You'll note the exact uses specified on the product labels.

Used with care and caution, they're essential and marvelous aids for conquering hitherto stubborn fungus blights!

Killing the Mighty Mite

One of the worst pests infesting the home garden is the mighty mite—now controllable at last through the use of some of science's latest miracle workers. Since most mites are so tiny that they can't be seen with the naked eye, you must be constantly on the lookout for signs of mite invasion.

Since mites feed on the juices in foliage, look for discoloration in the green leaves. Instead of the plant's leaf being a rich, deep, shiny green, an invasion of mites results in gradual mottling and discoloration.

When you see the leaf start to lose its bright green color, with clear evidences of yellow speckling, gradually developing a green-grayish and then brownish "dead" coloring, it's time to grab one of the miracle products and exterminate those mites before the entire foliage and health of the plant is ruined.

Sod worms ruin lawns.

Beetles chew plants.

Reach for Malathion

You can now get a variety of effective mite killers. At this writing, I prefer the products containing *malathion* which you can get in various forms, for application with water.

Apply exactly according to label directions on the product you buy, making sure that you apply to the undersides as well as tops of leaves and foliage. In most cases, you repeat spraying within a week, in order to kill any new mites hatched from eggs that may not have been destroyed by the first spraying.

Mites won't appreciate the new malathion miracle murderers, but your plants will, and so will you as you stop the ugly discoloring of foliage and see your prized plants looking radiantly green and thriving beautifully.

More Power against Insects, with Pyrethrins

Science has developed new *pyrethrin* chemicals which, while not as deadly as some other modern insecticides, are preferred by some gardeners who've used them, because they're comparatively nontoxic to humans and animals.

Even though they're generally less toxic, these modern pyrethrin-type products are amazingly deadly to many garden pests. Check the labels on products available at your dealer, to make sure they'll be helpful to the varieties of plant life in your own garden.

Another plus for you, for more comfortable living in your house as well as garden, these chemicals are miraculously effective in killing houseflies too—quickly, easily and with relative safety in the home.

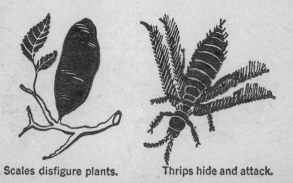

Scales disfigure plants.   Thrips hide and attack.

Giving Plants Bug-killing Power

A new ally in your constant war on insects that feed on your plants is an organic phosphate called "phosdrin." It's one of the miraculous systemic insecticides which go into the plant and kill insects that feed on the plant juices.

Look for phosdrin listed in the ingredients of some of the new insecticides you can buy. Apply easily, exactly as directed on the package. Since the entire plant then becomes a living insect killer, you've accomplished astounding all-over destruction of harmful insects, as never possible otherwise.

In addition, bugs which come in surface contact with a phosdrin insecticide also die. You get these marauders coming —and eating!

With its double-barreled wallop, phosdrin is highly toxic to humans also, but its dangers in this direction dissipate fast. It has been proved that its toxicity vanishes within three days, so that vegetables could be consumed safely after that time. However, it's better to leave the usual interval of seven to ten days between applying a phosdrin insecticide and harvesting.

Study the label for all the varieties of plant life that the particular phosdrin product will benefit. It's a great scientific killer-diller!

Miracle Antibiotics—New Plant Medicines!

Almost every month, experiments with the new antibiotics emphasize their importance in controlling the diseases of plants, just as they're producing miracles in fighting and overcoming diseases in humans.

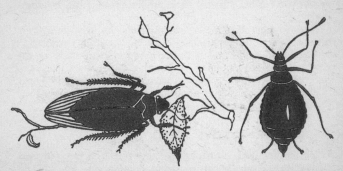

Leafhoppers are destructive.   Attack aphids fast.

Actidione is a miracle drug that you can now get in commercial products which will help you to prevent and control diseases which have previously driven gardeners wild when they ruined precious plants and crops.

Bothered by powdery mildew on beans? Get an actidione product and control it. Also, this same powerful chemical will help you get rid of dollarspot, brown patch and melting out of lawn turf.

Trouble with cherry trees? A spray made of one part per million of this miracle drug will control cherry leaf spot. What's more, in experiments applying the spray at the rate of two parts per million, in midseason, the blight was controlled and no further spraying was needed for the rest of the season.

But, perhaps most important to the average gardener, actidione spray is extremely effective in conquering damping-off. That's a loathsome disease which happens when fungi attack a plant near the ground, often causing the stem to rot and the seedling to fall over and die. It's been difficult to control damping-off because it's usually caused by a number of germs rather than just one.

Therefore a multi-effective drug, a truly miracle drug is required. And that's how powerful actidione goes to work, for this great antibiotic is effective in controlling not just one, but many germs, pathogens, viruses or whatever you wish to call the invaders.

In scientific testing, various soil types were inoculated with a variety of pathogens that cause damping-off. Then a number of drugs were applied to the soil, in different areas, about a day before seeds of tomatoes, peppers and beets were planted in it. Results showed that the miracle antibiotics, actidione, streptomycin and agrimycin—used separately on separate areas—were more effective than any other materials in reducing losses from damping off.

So, for more thrilling, spectacular results in your garden, take action with antibiotics! But—vital warning—apply as directed, and only in quantity according to instructions on the product you buy, because, if you use too powerful a solution, you may kill the plants as well as the harmful pathogens.

However, with proper application, you'll have very happy plants and very dead invaders.

Copper Chases Ivy Spots

When you see dark brown or black spots in front of your eyes on ivy leaves, don't rush to an eye doctor: now you can do something about it to restore the beauty of your ivy fast.

The trouble is caused by harmful bacteria, and you'd better act or the disease can spread and ruin the plants as well as the beauty of foliage. Today the solution is just as simple as this:

First, remove all the badly infected leaves because they won't come back good as new. Second, spray tops and bottoms of leaves remaining, with a good copper fungicide.

Your neighbors may tell you that if you'll just ignore the spots, they'll go away by fall, and sometimes that's true. But if you don't want to take chances, science has put the means to spray away troubles right at your fingertips.

Magic Green Capsules Kill Underground Enemies

Sometimes even though you spray your foliage well with a good insecticide, underground pests remain to feed on the roots of plants, causing them to look sickly, with shriveling leaves and foliage. Now some magical green capsules containing *ethylene dibromide* come to the rescue with quick, clean action.

Many underground pests such as nematodes, garden centipedes, wireworms and sow bugs succumb to the capsules. They're very simple to use. Wearing garden gloves, dig a hole a few inches deep, a few inches from the plant stalk, near the roots. Take care not to injure the roots with the digging tool. Drop in a green capsule, and fill in the hole.

Make sure the earth is moist, as action begins when soil moisture envelops the capsule. Ethylene dibromide, which is a powerful soil "fumigant," is released and kills underground pests that may be attacking the plant's roots.

Far from being a vitamin capsule, these green pellets will nevertheless help guard and promote the health of your plants.

Sensational Results with Systemic Insecticides

Several years ago, an insecticide producer of my acquaintance told me excitedly of "a new development in insect control that will revolutionize garden care and results—the most dramatic advance in the field in decades!"

He had just returned from a visit to Germany where he'd seen remarkable results achieved by scientists there with *systemic insecticides*. He'd watched the men in the laboratories spray the new materials on foliage and roots of plants.

The plants absorbed the insecticides in as short a period as from ten hours to two days. Insects attacking the plants absorbed the insecticides and were killed quickly!

A Death Feast

Thus, the very plants and foliage on which the insects fed were their doom—even when they fed on parts of the plant where there was no direct application of the systemic material.

Now you can get the systemic insecticides in most supply stores; the ingredients are generally listed as *demeton* and *schradon*. Use them as directed on the label, applied on the soil or directly on foliage of roses, chrysanthemums and other popular plants. You'll get remarkable results in thorough control of mites and aphids.

Not Yet Universally Accepted

Although very popular in Germany and other parts of Europe, the systemics haven't achieved as wide acceptance in the United States, particularly on food crops.

Those who favor the systemics enthusiastically point out that while these insecticides stay in plants long enough to destroy aphids and mites, and thus also prevent their breeding, they disappear quickly from the plants and therefore are harmless in food crops.

But government authorities are wisely cautious in checking labels and holding back permission for use on food crops until exhaustive testing is completed. It's absolutely necessary to prove conclusively first that the systemics are definitely safe and nontoxic.

There's little question now that great advances will be made in this class of systemic insecticides, so keep checking for them in stores, and watching the labels for expanded uses. They'll help you get new miracle results in your garden.

Killing Weeds Before They Emerge!

Join me in looking at two experimental plots, side by side— separated only by a small strip of untilled soil—in which cucumbers were planted. We see the two areas looking almost exactly the same.

Some time later, we return to that spot, which hasn't received any further attention. Much to my amazement (and yours, I'm sure), one of the plots has a row of dwarfed cucumber plants, almost choked out by weeds. The other area, right alongside, features rich, healthy, thriving cucumber plants—from the same seed—with only a few spindly weeds in the soil.

Yet . . . neither of these plots was sprayed with any weed killer, nor was any cultivation done, *after the plants appeared above ground*.

The difference was that the weed-free area was sprayed with a *pre-emergence weed killer* after the crops were planted, but before any plants appeared above the soil. You can now get such "pre-emergence weed killers" which are mild in that they won't harm animals or humans, but are death to weeds. I don't know a simpler way to dispose of weeds than before they even emerge above ground!

Observe the Precautions

As with most all weed killers of any type, be sure you restrict use of this "miracle" chemical only to those crops specified on the package, and apply only as directed.

Some of the products point out on the label that you should remove any sizable weeds already on the soil before you apply the pre-emergence weed killer. That's because the product isn't designed to be effective against vigorous, advanced weeds.

But, by all means, don't ignore the benefits for your garden in these pre-emergence weed killers. They can help much valuable growth—many of the vegetables your family enjoys most, also raspberries, strawberries and other berries. I know of excellent results in flower gardens too, with roses, other flowers and bulbs.

And, of course, you can control many weeds that infest your lawn, with these pre-emergence weed killers—within limits covered in more detail elsewhere in this book.

In short, much of your garden growth can emerge more beautifully than possible in years past, if you'll use the pre-emergence weed killers intelligently and at the right time.

The Hydrocarbon Wonder Killers

It has become almost fashionable to discredit DDT because some impossible claims were made for it when it was introduced, and it hasn't proved 100 per cent effective in controlling harmful insects. But DDT, and other advanced chlorinated hydrocarbons, can perform wonders for you in your garden and save much plant life almost miraculously, compared with the destruction gardeners faced only a few years ago.

The fact is that DDT can be a very great help to you in controlling common villains including borers, Japanese beetles, gypsy moths and other garden enemies, as listed on the label of the product you buy.

And the power of DDT is long-lasting—that's why you must be careful not to use it heavily on food crops. However, used very early in the growing season, it will save many crops, and harmful residue will have disappeared by crop picking time.

Don't expect DDT to control pests not listed on the label. It's not effective against some aphids and mites. Also, since Nature has a way of maintaining a balance, species of insects are growing which resist DDT when it's used over a long period of time.

Science Develops New Variations

Each season, science brings forth new products in the class of chlorinated hydrocarbons to control insects and help promote your garden growth. Here are some of the best.

Look for improved products containing *methoxychlor* which performs most of the functions of DDT, as noted in the preceding, but is safer in use—not only for the vegetables treated but also for humans and pets.

Another wonder-worker which is similar to the very effective *chlordane,* is known as *heptachlor*—an excellent ingredient to look for on the product you buy. It's relatively low in price, and is a more concentrated killer, so you use less to get the same results as other popular ingredients. Heptachlor will prove a great aid in combating ants and other pests which thrive in the soil, along with the destructive insects which feed on cucumbers, onions, apples and other growth listed on the label.

Look for these names and others of this class, including *endrin, lindane, dieldrin* and *aldrin.* All these products are powerful insecticides, and must be handled with caution. But used properly, they'll perform miracles in helping you to counteract the insect criminals which stand between you and rich, abundant growth in your garden.

Modern Miracle Against Mildew

With proper day by day care of your plants, whether outdoors or indoors, you can keep them from being afflicted with ugly and destructive mildew. But if unsightly mildew does appear on your plants, now you can do something about it in a hurry.

In fact, that's the key to mildew control, get rid of it fast at the very first sign. Previously, sulfur sprays or dusts were recommended for control of this fungus affliction. But now science has come up with a far better chemical. This modern material appears on product labels under the jaw-breaking name *dinitro capryl phenyl crotonate.*

In spite of the difficult name, the material is easy to handle. Simply spray on foliage according to directions, noting all precautions, and making sure to wet the undersides as well as tops of leaves.

Your mildew troubles will be over in a hurry, thanks to the product containing dinitro capryl phenyl crotonate.

Double-duty New Weed Killer

Two of the most powerful modern miracle killers are now available to you in a combination dust that destroys both crabgrass and many broadleaf weeds. Sodium methyl arsonate and 2,4-D are mixed now to provide a double-barreled wallop.

To apply, dampen down the grass with a light sprinkling, or you can choose an hour when your lawn is moist with dew. Then spread the material with the same spreader you use for seed or dry fertilizer. (Make sure you clean out the spreader *completely* before using again for seeding or fertilizing.)

Just as science reports some astounding results in protecting humans with a combination of two or more miracle medications, garden scientists report that this special twin combination has worked wonders in protecting lawns, in many experiments. It does a thorough job of cleaning out both crabgrass and dandelions, plantain and other ugly broadleaf weeds.

Modern Killer that Kills All

In the places around your home where you want to kill out all growth, such as on driveways and cinder paths, there's been tremendous improvement over the old, dangerous killers which were also a great hazard to pets and humans.

Far safer in use are plant killers and growth inhibitors made with *ammonium sulfamate*. This efficient chemical is nonflammable so that you needn't fear fire hazards if a match is dropped in the area where it has been applied.

Also, there's little danger of spread of fumes damaging desirable plant life nearby. Just take care that you don't apply an ammonium sulfamate product directly on healthy plants that you want to live.

Otherwise it's a powerful chemical ally and a great aid in the places that you want to keep clean, neat, completely free of any ragged growth.

2-Year Destruction with Arsenic!

Improvements have been made with arsenical weed killers which now enable you to destroy and prevent plant growth as long as two years.

You simply apply a good arsenical weed killer with a watering can, as directed. But keep in mind that such a weed killer is actually a *growth killer*. So, use it carefully in such places as driveways, along fences, on paths and in openings on paved areas—where you want no growth at all, and want the effectiveness to last for years, because these harsh and violent killers will kill all plants and make the soil barren for 12 to 24 months.

Also, remember that the arsenical weed killers are strong and poisonous, and must be handled carefully with the respect you give to any poison. Used thus, they'll mean death to the enemy, and will clear up unsightly weed patches where you want no growth at all, for a long, long time.

"One-two Punch" Poison for Poison Ivy

Now, with the aid of miracle chemicals, you can massacre one of the worst weeds that afflicts the human race—loathsome poison ivy!

The wonderful skin-saver is known simply as *amino-triazole* and is readily available to you at stores, in several modern products. Look at the label to identify the chemical, and use according to directions.

Kill Poison Ivy in One or Two Steps

Spray poison ivy leaves and plants thoroughly with *amino-triazole*. Don't worry if the plant doesn't turn up and die immediately. Just as poison ivy thrives vigorously, it dies hard. In a day or two, leaves start to show spotting and damage. Usually it takes a couple of weeks for the plant to die.

Keep watching for any new growth from the seemingly dead plant. Sometimes a second spraying is required about a month later. In practically all cases, the one-two punch with amino-triazole is conclusively fatal.

Be Careful of Other Plants

Because amino-triazole is nonselective—that means it will kill all plants that it hits—take care not to get the spray on any other plant life you want to save.

Use this powerful killer only on days when there's no wind, then you won't have to be concerned about the chemical drifting and possibly harming other plants.

There are some claims that amino-triazole won't harm other plants, even though it's murder to poison ivy. With a division of opinion on this vital point, I'd advise you to play it safe.

Other Effective Chemicals

If poison ivy is growing among valuable plants, you can eradicate it more safely with repeated applications of 2,4-D. A stronger application is a combination of 2,4-D and 2,4,5-T— but this will also harm any other plants it touches.

Another deadly chemical that is harmful to all plants is ammonium sulfamate. Two to three thorough applications, spaced several weeks apart, will usually exterminate poison ivy.

How to Recognize the Pest

If you can count, you should be able to recognize poison ivy fast enough not to touch it. The plants always have three— never two or four or five—leaves, usually dark green and shiny. The foliage might even be called beautiful if it wasn't so poisonous.

Versatile poison ivy's best disguise is the fact that it grows in many different ways. So beware of it everywhere. It climbs trees and fences . . . it may crawl along the ground . . . sometimes it grows in shrub formation. Before you touch any vine, make sure there aren't any poison ivy leaves entwined with the foliage of the harmless beauty. The persistent pest may grow in sun or shade, in swamp or arid spots!

Pulling Out Poison Ivy?

Some hardy individuals still prefer to ignore the wonder chemicals and try to eradicate poison ivy by uprooting it by hand. If you take this dangerous course, better cover yourself completely with rubberized gloves, a completely cloaking shirt, and slacks tucked into your shoe tops.

Then you'd better wash everything you wear in hot water with a strong laundry soap—including your shoes. (Or maybe you'd better rather just destroy them!) Otherwise the plants' poisons will stay on your clothing for weeks.

Don't burn the plants—bury them. Perhaps you're better off just enduring poison ivy and scratching away, if you're so set against using the advances provided by science, for one reason or another.

How Poison Ivy Attacks You

Most infection from poison ivy comes from direct contact with the plant or leaves. Even if you've only stepped in poison ivy, it'll probably infect you when you touch your shoes to take them off.

If your dog has played in poison ivy and you pet him, you may soon start itching! Even smoke from burning poison ivy can carry the infection to you.

But cheer up. These days you finally have the potent killers to attack poison ivy and exterminate it quickly and easily. At the first sign of the "leaflets three"—*spray away!*

Tips on Choosing Sprayers and Dusters

The type and size of the equipment you use to apply the great new insecticides and fungicides depends on the size of your garden and lawn, and on how much you want to pay. In making your selection accordingly, keep these basic points in mind as a guide:

Avoid old-fashioned, one-directional sprayers and dusters, in favor of modern equipment with *adjustable nozzles*. This adjustable feature, in nozzle or tube, helps you to direct the spray or dust to the *underside* of leaves and foliage, as well as to topside. As cautioned elsewhere, both top and bottom application is absolutely essential for proper insect control.

Is It Easy to Clean?

Check the device you buy to make sure it's constructed for *easy cleaning*. It's not only desirable but essential to clean out the equipment after you've finished using a specific chemical each time. Without thorough cleaning, you may get some potent mixtures of chemicals which will be harmful to plant life.

It's best to get equipment made with *noncorrosive* materials. The insecticides you use will stay cleaner in use. And you'll be sure of much longer-lasting satisfaction with the device.

Poisons: Be Grateful and Careful!

Among the modern miracle chemicals, insecticides and fungicides rate near the top for the good they perform. But it's important to keep in mind always that they're poisonous, and therefore rules of safety must be followed. Similarly an automobile is a menace if handled carelessly, but an indispensable aid to better living when you follow common-sense rules of safety.

So, use the insecticides and fungicides provided for you by modern science—but remember always these simple precautions:

- —Handle with care, following directions and heeding precautions on the labels, to the letter.
- —As you handle, mix and apply insecticides and fungicides, avoid inhaling them. Avoid contact with eyes, nose and mouth (when you're working with the chemicals, keep your hands away from your face, for instance).
- —Don't use these chemicals on a windy day, lest you get them on yourself, perhaps inhaling them. Also, you'll avoid having the chemicals blow on nearby foliage where they may do some harm to plants.
- —After working with the chemicals, wash any exposed surfaces of skin with strong soap and water. Change your clothing if you've spilled chemicals on them.
- —If you transfer insecticides or fungicides to other containers, be sure they're clearly labeled. And, of course, store them where children and animals can't get at them.
- —Don't apply insecticides or fungicides immediately before a harvest. Check the label carefully regarding minimum interval between spraying and picking. (The label will state that contents shouldn't be applied "within seven days of harvesting, etc.")
- —Check carefully to note on the labels whether the chemicals shouldn't ever be applied to foliage or fruit that will be eaten.
- —Insecticides and fungicides are not intended for your personal experimentation on plants. So, apply only to those crops recommended on the label. Apply lightly and evenly. Never apply heavier dosages than recommended, lest you cause injury to the plants also.

By using such common sense and reasonable care, the fungicides and insecticides will reward you with all their miracles— without menace or damage.

PREPARING SOIL, PLANTING, MULCHING

Top Priority . . . Testing Your Soil

You haven't grounds for garden or lawn miracles unless you have a fairly good soil to start with. If you find out that your soil is poor, no need to despair. Today there are many ways to improve your soil, described right in these pages, so that you can have a glorious, gratifying lawn and garden—far better than many of those in naturally rich but unattended soils. Gifted men have turned deserts into garden spots, and so can you with your own particular little "desert."

But you can't follow the game without a score card, they say, and you can't garden properly unless you know what your soil is so you can bring it up to par if necessary.

I don't mean that you have to become a research chemist, or trace your soil back to the *Mayflower*. Far from it. As a matter of fact, if the property you're going to garden produced pretty good growth last year, you can start now assured that your soil is good enough to respond with proper normal fertilization.

Nevertheless soil testing is a good idea, and very simple. You can buy a small commercial soil-testing kit, and follow instructions. Or, you can take a soil sample and send it for analysis and report to your state college of agriculture, or state agricultural experiment station, for little or no cost.

Many a time, I've spent an entire day on a farm, taking soil samples from field after field. Farmers who count on the soil to provide their livelihood know the value of soil testing and so give hours and days to collecting soil samples. You can profit by their example.

How to Collect Soil Samples

The primary test is for pH, that is, to determine the soil acidity. All you need for a test is about half a cupful of dirt. Dig a hole about a foot in diameter and about half a foot deep. Stir up this soil, preferably with a wooden stick. Put a cupful or less of the soil in a paper bag or one of those little cardboard containers in which you buy coleslaw or ice cream; don't use a metal container of any kind.

Now mark the package clearly, as to the part of the garden in which the soil was located. In a sizable plot or garden, it's best to take about three samples from different, separated places.

What to Do after Soil Analysis

The test report you get will give the acidity or pH count, and any vital deficiencies in the soil, which you should correct. Best time is just before planting, in early spring, for a real boost to your garden.

If the acidity test shows that your soil has a pH between 6.0 and 6.8, you're all set to grow most flowers and vegetables. I'd advise you to use a good concentrated water-soluble plant food, or dry fertilizer, anyhow—plants benefit most from continual feeding and must be fed abundantly if you want miracle results rather than just ordinary growth.

If your soil tests below pH 6.0, it's too acid or sour, and must be limed. So drive over to your garden supply dealer and get enough lime for your needs, applying according to instructions—which depend on the particular kind of lime you buy. For best results, apply and turn under the lime deeply.

If your soil tests above 6.8, it's too alkaline or sweet. And if your soil has that sweet tooth, it's not good for growth. Again, the best time for correction is early spring. Apply manganese sulfate and borax, in quantity as instructed by your local dealer, for local conditions. If your soil pH is so high as to be "sickening sweet," with pH above 7.6, also use dusting sulfur. You can mix all the materials together, if you wish, in proper proportions, spread the mixture evenly over the soil, then mix it well into the soil, not just on the surface.

Yes, that's all there is to soil testing. And, in general, that's all there is to correcting the average soil unbalance. It's easy, and you get a scientific kick out of dissecting the mysteries of your soil condition yourself. And you only have to repeat the procedure every three to four years, unless you run into widespread troubles—then you'd better retest the soil more often.

By soil testing and correcting, you build a wonderful foundation for seemingly miraculous garden growth—for exceptional beauty that will fill the eyes of yourself, your family and all admiring onlookers.

Special Preparation of Planting Beds for Special Results

If you want to see your garden beds bursting with beautiful, healthy growth, pay particular attention to the vital first step. How you prepare the bed will usually control how well plants grow in it.

Select a spot where the plants will get plenty of sunshine. Then go to work according to the following instructions. Don't pressure yourself too hard and too fast to get the work done in a hurry. Remember that just as Rome wasn't built in a day, neither does your garden bed have to be prepared in a single day. Gardening involves hard work, but above all, gardening must be fun.

So, work a little, relax a little, work a little more. Here's a helpful tip: If you're laboring on a large bed, whether you're spading or cleaning up or weeding, don't look at the whole area and worry about the extent of the job. Just concentrate on preparing or cleaning up that one next square foot of ground. You'll be pleasantly surprised at how much more easily you advance with that viewpoint.

Most important, don't be content with halfway preparation. Do the job right and you'll be extra-happy about your extra-wondrous results. Now dig in:

1. Have your soil tested to see whether it needs heavy applications of lime or other special materials. Most likely you'll find that simply mixing in peat moss, and using a good complete fertilizer, will give the soil most everything it needs.

2. Dig up the planting bed to a depth of 8 to 12 inches with a pitchfork, spade or whatever tools you prefer to use. Break up clumps of earth. Remove large rocks. Realize as you work along that you're loosening and aerating the earth so that seeds and young plants will have an easy time rooting and spreading their roots and growing—unlike planting in a block of cement, as an exaggerated comparison to make a point.

3. This is the time to lime and add peat moss or other materials if soil tests show they're required. In any case, apply a

good complete fertilizer. If you use a dry fertilizer, apply it at the top of the soil after the earth has been thoroughly dug up.

4. Rake the ground to mix in the fertilizer very thoroughly and evenly with the soil. At the same time, remove any debris or growth in the earth. Now you'll have a soft, well-aerated soil, smooth and level.

You're ready to sow seeds or set in seedlings and plants. Now that wasn't so difficult, was it? Stop rubbing your aching back, just exult in the beautiful plants you'll soon have bursting from that lovingly prepared soil!

Important: Plan Ahead When Planting!

There are three points in planting most everything other than vegetables that may seem very elementary, but are worth highlighting here as a caution and a reminder. When you plant, you must keep in mind the *color* that your blooms will be, the height to which they'll grow and the eventual *spread* of the plants.

In respect to spread, don't set in plants too closely, or you'll have a small tangled forest which not only inhibits the growth of all the plants, but also thwarts the sight of their full beauty.

Better have a sparse-looking garden early in the season than a messy mass later. Particularly with the new miracle fertilizers and other helpers, remember at the start to leave room for wide, luxurious growth.

For example, on an anniversary some years ago, close friends gave us a lovely little Japanese red maple tree. We planted it, with more excitement than intelligence, in a spot-lighted corner of our back yard, next to the front of the garage. In three years, the garage door was hitting the spreading branches. We had to move the delicate tree, and it had a severe setback, surviving the transplanting only through loving care. With a little more sense, we'd never have planted the tree so close to the garage in the first place. Don't you make mistakes like that.

You can gauge height in advance by knowing how tall the species will grow, and arranging your plantings accordingly. Unless you plan ahead, you'll be surprised how often you'll have lovely low blooms hidden behind a high-growing border, for example.

As for color, that's almost entirely a matter of personal preference. Most flowers show up best when you mass whites, reds, purples and other shades, rather than mixing them. Certainly contrasting effects, such as borders of bright white alyssum against a mural of dark green foliage, are stunning and desirable. But this is something you'll have to decide for yourself, just as you choose the style and colors with which you like to decorate your rooms.

Don't worry too much about color "mistakes" in your garden, for nature has endowed flowers and foliage with such subtle tones, even in the blazing shades, that somehow most all growing colors relate and live beautifully with each other. The more you garden, the more you'll understand personally the effects that please you most and that you want to achieve.

Your garden is for your personal pleasure, and your own family's, primarily . . . so the only reason you need for planting in your own particular style is, *"I like it that way!"*

The main caution again is *no crowding, please*. Your plants will appreciate that, and show it!

So Sow Seed This Better Way

One of the most exciting steps in gardening is sowing seed. It's creative . . . you're setting the spark of life, in effect. And seeding is fairly simple and swift, even in the most effective way. Granted that the soil has been properly prepared, as described elsewhere in this book, proceed as follows:

1. An important "miracle" step that speeds growth and promotes healthier growth—yet that many gardeners miss— is to soak seeds for a few minutes in a solution made with a complete water-soluble plant food. Prepare the solution as directed on the package—and use it later on the soil.

2. Always begin seeding at the back of the area, then move forward. Instead of packing down the earth with your knees as you work, use a flat board which distributes your weight evenly on the earth.

3. Sow the seed as directed on each package. Fine seed is spread best between your fingers and with your fingertips. When instructions call for seeds to be covered with soil, make sure to sift the covering soil so it's very light and fine over the seeds.

4. Now firm the soil very gently by pressing down with your palms.

5. A very desirable step is to cover the area lightly with straw, to help protect against excessive cold, heat and watering or rain washout.

6. Now, using a fine spray from a nozzle, or a very fine sprinkling can, water in well, using a complete liquid plant food. Keep watering lightly every few days. You'll soon have the thrill of seeing tender sprouts—each a miracle in itself— emerging from the soil.

Special Tips for Planting Seedlings

Give your seedlings extra nutrient as you plant them, and they'll respond with extra growth.

Simply set in the plants so that the potting soil is even with the soil in your well-prepared garden bed. You've selected an area which will get plenty of sunshine (you won't plant while the sun is at its height, of course).

Now soak the mature seedlings gently but plentifully with a complete liquid plant food, one that contains chelated iron and the important trace elements (but don't fertilize *new* seedlings just emerged from the ground). A fine spray will help you avoid "washing out" the tender plants.

For the first few days only, give the young plants some protection from the hottest sun, shading with materials such as shingles or pots.

Water regularly and thoroughly so that the water carries deep down through the root depth, and deeper—always with a gentle spray.

Apply more liquid plant food as directed on the package you buy, and use insect sprays or dusts at any sign of infestation.

Those well-rooted, well-fertilized little seedlings will soon be transformed into vigorous, flourishing plants, delighting you constantly as only your own garden growth can!

Space Out Your Seedlings

This simple tip has proved very helpful to a number of my gardening friends, in growing more beautiful annual flowers, and saving time and work in tending them.

When you plant your annual seeds outdoors, don't trail your hand along continuously, dropping seeds in a row. Instead, spot a pinch of seeds at regular intervals—from half a foot apart to two feet apart, depending on how big the variety normally grows. (Yours, of course, are going to be even bigger and more beautiful, by following the modern miracle methods.)

As the seedlings sprout, the spaces between provide plenty of room for hand weeding, for any necessary cultivating of the soil, for more effective watering and fertilizing. And finally, when you thin out excess seedlings, you can do it far more efficiently, and a great deal faster and easier.

You'll find it a big help next time to space as you seed, and your blooms will be more bountiful as the uninhibited plants feed better and grow faster.

Mulch Ado about Mulching

For the glorious growth you want, there are visible garden miracles in mulch. Doing your garden "mulch good" is one procedure you want to perform after your plants start growing, when they present some sizable growth above the soil. So the right time for mulching is middle or late spring.

Mulching simply means applying good organic matter—peat moss, leaves, lawn clippings, etc.—on the soil, around the base of the plants. You can be sure that you'll have larger, healthier plants and bushes. And once you apply the mulch, you won't have to cultivate the earth there for the balance of the season. If you handle the mulch right, you'll keep most of the bothersome weeds from sprouting there.

And, so important, if you're away from your garden for a few weeks, because of traveling or vacation, mulching will prove to be a garden-saving miracle!

The "Why" of Mulching

When you apply a mulch around your plants and bushes, a number of important benefits result:

1. The mulch is a water-preserving measure . . . it expands the amount of water that the soil will hold . . . it helps the earth take up more water . . . and of course it keeps the water from evaporating so rapidly on the soil. That helps particularly in dry areas, and in cases of drought which seems to be more frequent in most areas in recent years.

2. Mulching helps to insulate the soil against excessive heat. By actual measurement, the temperature of soil under mulch is many degrees cooler than the top of uncovered earth. Especially during hot weather, this coolness of the earth helps roots to grow more sturdily.

The "How" of Mulching

It's hard to beat a good, coarse peat moss as effective mulching material. Just spread it around the soil, particularly around the base of the plants and shrubs, to a depth of about two inches. Make sure that you get thorough coverage, because then you'll get the best results.

If you've built a good compost heap, as instructed elsewhere in this book, apply the compost material in the same way. But you'd better put it on as much as three or four inches deep to make sure you get coverage that will last through the season. The same goes if you use leaves or lawn clippings.

Miracles from mulch? Yes, when you mulch well and fertilize liberally. The resultant rich, luxurious growth will delight you and make you feel justly proud of your healthy, thriving garden.

Garden Magic with Plastic Film

The same polyethylene plastic film that you find on some heads of lettuce and other foods in stores—to keep freshness in— is also producing miracles in the garden.

The film is being used widely in many parts of the country by commercial growers. They report crops doubled and tripled, and ready for market weeks ahead of other produce

Special garden plastic sheeting helps grow better plants.

grown without the protection of blankets of plastic. Now you can buy plastic film in stores for your own garden experimentation.

What might interest you particularly if you're not fond of weeding (and who is?) is the fact that black polyethylene is available which cuts off light from weeds and thus kills them. You save your energies for happier tasks than weeding.

If you're wondering about necessary moisture getting through to the plants, that's solved by many tiny perforations already in the film you buy, which let water and air seep through. At the same time, the film helps hold moisture in the soil so that the earth is more likely to remain moist and loose during drought, while unprotected soil is getting hard, dry, baked unmercifully.

On the other hand, the film helps protect the plants and soil from washouts and swamping during hard, driving rain-storms.

How to use the plastic film? You'll find instructions with your purchase, of course, applying to the particular brand you buy. One method is to spread yard-wide strips of black film over your garden. Over each plant, you cut slits for the grow-ing plants to come through.

Results are truly dramatic with many common garden veg-etables—lettuce, tomatoes, corn, cabbage, beans and such. You can count on over double the ordinary yields. And most likely you'll be chomping juicily on fresh-picked corn several weeks ahead of your neighbors!

Excellent results are also being obtained with seeds (keeping the plastic well slitted so the tiny plants can emerge easily), with strawberries, and with many favorite flowers. They bloom faster, more abundantly, and with practically no weeding.

But, by way of warning, keep this in mind: while you do have miraculously improved growth, and you don't have much weeding, you do have plastic film to meet the eye!

The decision is yours: no superintendent, boss or chairman of the board to tell you otherwise. In your garden, you're the king, queen, emperor. It's all yours to do as you wish, when you wish, how you wish. Isn't gardening wonderful?

Triple Warning Against Weeds!

I've walked with friends in their gardens, and admired the blooms they displayed so proudly, then paused frequently and said, "You'd better get rid of those weeds, here and there and there . . . or you can't ever have a real miracle garden!"

Too often, to my surprise, the response has been, "Oh, weeds aren't so bad. I'd rather spend my gardening time attending to more important things than weeding!" Inquiring further, I found that these gardeners didn't realize that weeds are actually a triple villain.

First, and not least by any measure, is the fact that weeds are unsightly. They should be eliminated just as completely as possible from flower beds as well as lawns, because they tend to spoil the looks of a garden almost as much as heavy dust will ruin the perfection of even the most beautifully decorated room.

Second, weeds act to use up essential nutrients in the soil, thus depriving your valued plants. And they also tend to grow furiously and choke out the plants you're nursing along. Weeds are particularly harmful to young and fragile plants that need the greatest and most complete care and sustenance, in order to survive and grow into the magnificent "miracle" specimens you want.

Third—and this is the point that many gardeners don't realize—weeds often attract harmful insect life and viruses which then infest the valuable adjacent plants. Many a lovely plant and shrub that would be flourishing magnificently has been ruined by infestation that started on surrounding weeds, even though the weeds themselves may not reveal any damage!

So, for the miracle growth you want in the garden, it's almost as important to help prevent spoilage and infestation from weeds as it is to use the new wonder chemicals to promote exceptional growth.

Weed out those weeds steadily and continuously, by hand and with tools, but primarily and most easily and effectively with the many practical weed killers that science has provided for you.

Important Watering Tip

Half a drink is almost as bad as none—that's a tip from an experienced state gardening expert. He says that careful measurement of growth in commercial vegetable gardens has proved this true.

In times of drought, when water has to be conserved carefully, you're better off watering heavily on half your vegetable garden, for example, than giving a skimpy drink to the whole area. *The well-watered half will give you more produce than the entire area inadequately watered!*

Also, when you haven't enough water to go around, give a good deep drink to your newly seeded and young plants, skipping older and stronger plants if necessary. The deeply rooted, established plants have a better chance of surviving drought and then coming back to vigorous strength when you can water them thoroughly or when the rains come. But the striplings will be dead and beyond recall.

It won't be easy for you to leave your older plants or half your garden looking dry and wilted while you water the other half. But, take it from an agriculturist who knows the scientific facts, you'll have a healthier and more productive garden.

Lower Leaves Dying? What to Do

When you find the lower leaves of many flower plants such as mums, asters and zinnias, dying in your garden, it's often due to *bad air circulation*. The solution doesn't require any miracle —just be careful when you plant next season *not to place the plants so closely together!*

Your best action right away is twofold: First, pluck off the lower leaves to help provide better circulation of air, with several inches at least of free air space between the foliage and the ground. Second, water more deeply but not so often, as a moist surface along with dense foliage near the soil tends to kill the lower leaves faster.

In the case of geraniums, when you find the leaves dying from the bottom up, heavy soil moisture is the chief offender.

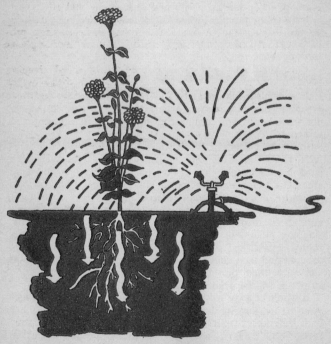

Water deep to promote deep root growth.

Again, when you do water, soak in the water deeply—then, don't water again until the top inch or so of earth is dry.

You'll be delighted to find how these simple tips help keep all the plant foliage green and bright. And next time, give your plants the air—that is, give them plenty of growing room so they can supply their own air conditioning.

New Trick for Hot-weather Transplanting

Now you can get a fine liquid plastic spray which helps keep plants alive and then thrive through transplanting, even during hot weather when the sun beats down at its fiercest.

You can get this helpful product in reusable plastic bottles or in a less costly concentrate. By spraying a film of this liquid plastic on plants, you help lock in the moisture, permitting the plant to "breathe" freely at the same time.

By retaining extra moisture, the plant has a better chance to gain strength, accustom itself to its new environment and establish itself sturdily.

Of course, observe the usual precautions of not planting during bright sunlight hours and giving some shading protection at first. Also, water and fertilize the newly moved plants thoroughly.

Even small trees and shrubs are helped by a light coating of this liquid plastic spray. You'll come through with a higher percentage of vigorous plant survival with this ingenious product.

PROPAGATION

Air Layering—Miracle Brought up to Date

I wasn't there, but I understand that the exciting process of plant propagation known as "air layering" goes way back to ancient days. Now it's having a new revival brought on by the improved polyethylene plastic film available for garden usage.

This is one way of increasing plants without going out and buying them. For anyone in a hurry, or not possessed of the time and patience required, I don't recommend propagation of plants by air layering. But for the scientifically minded, it's a very interesting and personally rewarding pursuit.

How to Go about Air Layering

Now you can buy a complete kit containing all details and instructions for air layering. But, to save a little money and have more do-it-yourself fun, here are relatively simple instructions:

Start during good growing season. On the plant you wish to reproduce, choose a shoot of last year's wood, about the diameter of a pen, or a little larger. (Some propagators claim you can get good results with older wood also.) Select a spot just below a joint or node.

Make a long cut down the middle of the twig, about three to four inches long. Cut carefully and cleanly, and fairly deep, but don't break the twig, and don't cut clear through. (Another method is to cut about an inch strip of bark clear around the branch, down to the bare wood. Both methods are effective.)

Dust the cut surfaces lightly with a good hormone rooting material.

Take a handful of moist sphagnum moss and squeeze it so that you remove all excess water, but leaving the moss still moist.

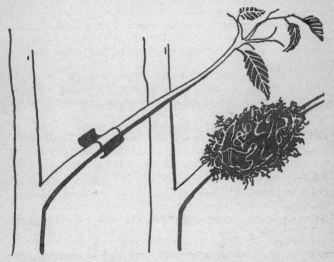

You can multiply favorite species through air layering.

Very carefully and gently so as not to break the twig, pack a little of the moist moss in the cut to keep the cut surfaces from growing together.

Pack the rest of the damp moss around the twig in a lump so that the whole area surrounding the cut is completely covered; use as much moist moss as necessary to do this.

Take a piece of polyethylene plastic film, made for garden use, and wrap it tightly around the moss to keep it firmly in place. You can now get a film that's coated with rooting hormones for added feeding of the new roots, and also contains a fungicide to help prevent growth of harmful bacteria; with such film, be sure the coated surface is inside, of course.

Tie the film carefully at top and bottom. Make sure that the top tie particularly is very tight, so that water that may run down the twig cannot seep in under the wrapping. If water gets in, it will probably cause rot.

If you've followed these simple directions properly, with utmost care, the moistness within the wrap won't escape, and you can leave the layering alone until rooting has taken place.

Don't unwrap the layering until the leaves have fallen and the plant is dormant. At that time, unwrap the film. Lo, there should be a fine rooted layer, ready for planting—a growth miracle come true!

Cut the rooted layer from the plant with delicacy and care. Then pot the growth, handling gently. If you have a greenhouse, that's the best place for the pot. If not, tend it indoors, keeping it moist and in a spot not subject to extreme changes of temperature.

The following spring, set out the pot in a spot protected from harsh winds. Keep the soil moist. By late spring, you should be able to transplant into the garden, and soon have a healthy, thriving plant.

This is the long way around to growing reproductions of your favorite plants, but you'll have the thrill of special parenthood that makes plant propagation a particularly fascinating pursuit. There are other good methods and argumentative adherents, but this is a simple and effective way to introduce yourself to air layering for gratifying results.

Reproducing Indoors Plants by Air-layering

New plastics make more perfect the interesting and rewarding practice of reproducing some of your favorite indoors plants by air-layering. Try it once, and chances are that you'll be embarked on a fascinating new offshoot of your gardening hobby.

At your garden supply store, get some of the new plastic sheets made especially for air-layering reproduction. Then select one or more of your favorite hardy indoors plants, such as a vigorous rubber plant, philodendron or dracaenas. Just follow these few simple steps:

1. Pick a spot on a sturdy stem which permits room to form a moss-and-plastic ball. Carefully make a vertical cut in the stem with a sharp instrument—a little over an inch in length. Insert a little sphagnum moss in the slit, first moistening the moss with a solution of liquid plant food. This slit will be the source of root growth, so you must keep the two inner surfaces apart—a function performed by the little clump of moss.

2. Now wrap this wounded area completely with moistened sphagnum moss, using an amount about half as big as your fist—or enough to enclose the area neatly.

3. Cut the plastic film to size required in order to wrap securely around the moss ball. After wrapping snugly and completely, twist the top and bottom ends of the plastic tightly and tie securely in position with cord.

4. Watch the roots grow during the next few weeks, by looking through the transparent plastic. You'll make exciting discoveries each day as the roots form and gain in size and vigor. When the roots are strong and lengthy, remove the plastic film. Now, using a sharp knife or blade, cut the stem away from the mother plant just below the newly formed roots.

5. Pot the new rooting in good fertile soil and water in with liquid plant food. Set the plant in a shaded, sheltered spot for a few weeks, keeping the soil moist but not drenched.

6. Now set the pot in the permanent position you've selected for it. You'll find special thrills in watching it develop its own beauty and glory near the proud mother plant! Here's another rewarding phase of being *a creative gardener*.

Reproduce indoor plants by air layering with plastic film.

Miracle Growth from Cuttings

One way to feature particularly beautiful plants in your garden is to exchange cuttings with your friends and neighbors. You'll add to your collection of prized specimens that enhance your pleasure from your garden.

When you see some perennials in a friend's garden which are especially exquisite or impressive in size for that variety, ask for a cutting from a stem. By tending the cutting carefully until it takes root, you'll enjoy the same superior blooms in your own garden in succeeding seasons.

Most gardeners are flattered to spread their finest plants around, just as you'll be delighted to do so in exchange. Part of the miracle of gardening is the friendliness that it engenders among people of all classes and callings.

Now—Disease-free Rooting Materials

When you use ordinary sand or soil for rooting cuttings and starting seeds, while you may get excellent results most of the time, you always take a chance that the soil might be diseased and produce contaminated or weakened seedlings. But now, for better and surer disease-free growth, you can get some helpful modern materials:

Natural sphagnum moss is an excellent rooting material that avoids diseases frequently encountered with ordinary soils and even peat moss. Best way to get it is as a finely sifted moss, in packages, all ready for you to use instantly.

Vermiculite, which is a mica material prepared by an "explosion" process, is a clean and very effective product which you can get in different sized granules for different sowing and seeding needs.

New plastic powders and granules are available and are producing some marvelous results in getting rootings and seeds started fast, clean and free of any disease that might be present in the rooting material itself.

Choose from these materials for better, healthier plants than when started in the old-fashioned way. Simply follow directions on the particular package you select.

Hormones for Better Rooting of Cuttings

New hormone preparations now go right to the root of the problem of obtaining faster rooting and better rooting of cuttings. Try them, use them right, and you'll be thrilled to see your tender cuttings sprout stronger, more virile roots in surprisingly fast time.

To prove this modern rooting miracle for yourself, you can root some comparable cuttings side by side—with and without use of one of the good hormone preparations now available for this purpose. You'll see an amazing difference with your own eyes, day after day. Try it—feel like a scientist as well as a gardener!

Some of the good hormone preparations for rooting cuttings contain indolebutyric acid, others list naphthalene acetic acid on the labels. Follow label directions exactly, and don't apply to any cuttings of plants unless recommended on the label of the particular product you buy.

You may get tired of reading the frequent cautions on these pages to "use exactly as directed." But don't fail to follow that advice. Because overdosing with the hormone preparations, for example, may injure or kill the cuttings—and this book aims to help you produce garden "miracles," not massacres.

Use these new hormone wonder-workers correctly, and you'll get truly "miracle results" that you can readily see for yourself, even before you place the cuttings in the soil.

Give Cuttings an Inch

Want miracle results from cuttings that can be rooted in water? Then don't do the usual thing: *don't* put them in a glass nearly full of water!

Instead, only an inch of water in the glass is best. Because this shallow depth provides a higher content of oxygen, so vital for best results.

Keep watching and maintaining that inch of water level until the cuttings have roots strong and large enough for potting in soil. You'll be delighted with the extra vigor of the plants.

Amazing Automatic Plant "Incubator"

Imagine setting some cuttings into the material in a rooting tray, placing them in an incubator, inserting a plug into an electrical outlet, going away from there . . . *and opening the incubator in a few weeks to find the cuttings vigorously rooted and ready to plant!*

That's exactly what happens with an ingenious apparatus developed by a noted horticultural scientist, and now being manufactured for home use. You can place it in your cellar or attic, or wherever temperature stays above a minimum of 50°.

Complete instructions come with this compact, attractive apparatus. It's as easy to install as just pushing a plug into a wall outlet. It's complete with fluorescent lighting to supply vital light and slight extra heat. Controls for proper ventilation and moisture control are built in.

You simply prepare your rooting material in a tray as for any rooting routine, insert the cuttings in the material, water well, place within the machine, close up the apparatus and turn on the electrical current.

When you open up the apparatus at the end of the prescribed time, lift out the tray, and you'll find that the plant roots are fully developed for exceptional planting results.

Here, it seems, is the plant propagation miracle made as easy as can possibly be imagined. Except, of course, that you still have to flip the switch to turn on the current.

Taking the Mystery Out of "Mist" Propagation

For gardeners who enjoy propagation of plants right from cuttings, the "mist" method has long held plenty of fascination. This is a method whereby cuttings are rooted under an almost continuous mist from a special nozzle, or due to a very heavy humid atmosphere. The method has been successful in rooting many soft-wood plants which are difficult and almost impossible to develop at their best otherwise.

The advantage of the mist is that cuttings can even develop roots in full sunlight—healthier, disease-free roots which produce more vigorous plants and more glorious blooms. The mist provides the equivalent of shade, along with the advantages of sunlight, so that the rooting process is also speeded up considerably.

But it's not so easy to maintain a mist from the ordinary watering system outdoors, nor to apply mist in an indoors box enclosure without encouraging root rot and other diseases from excessive dampness.

Science to the Rescue

If mist you must, now you can get an ingenious apparatus which looks like half a huge bubble. You plant the cuttings directly in the soil, preparing the earth for rooting first.

Then you place the large plastic half shell over the cuttings, attach the connection to your water system, and turn on the water. A fine nozzle produces a mist which is turned on and off automatically by an electronic device.

In a short period, the cuttings are rooted vigorously and healthfully, and are soon ready for transplanting wherever you wish in your garden. Lift off the round plastic lid and you find beautiful "plants in the half shell."

Move the plastic-roofed apparatus to another location and go on with a repeat of your mist-ical propagation program!

Multiply Beautiful Coleus Plants

Here's new, quick, multiplying beauty for your house. Enjoy the radiant beauty of plenty of coleus foliage indoors as well as out. Just pinch off or cut out the tips of outdoor coleus plants, leaving a few inches of healthy stem.

Then place the tips in a flower pot containing sand or vermiculite moistened with a mild solution of a good liquid fertilizer. Keep adding water every day or so to keep moist.

The tips will take root and grow beautifully in a surprisingly short time. Renew feeding with the water-soluble plant food every few weeks, moistening but not flooding the soil in the pots.

When outdoors planting season comes around again, you can transfer the strong, colorful, thriving coleus plants to the garden if you wish. Thus you have a practically unending way of multiplying the decorative plants.

You'll also have a renewing source for valuable gifts of exquisite coleus plants, that your friends will appreciate greatly.

Tips on Having "Miracle Seeds"

First rule in buying seeds to enable you to grow the exceptional "miracle plants" you want is not to stint on the cost. While the most costly seeds aren't necessarily the best, it doesn't pay by season's end to have bought certain seeds just because they were cheap. The cost of seeds certainly doesn't amount to much, compared with the time and effort and other things you invest, such as fertilizer money.

Secondly, you'll save yourself a lot of trouble if you buy seeds that are *sterilized*, and guaranteed by a dependable seedhouse that's in business to stay. If the variety of seeds you want is not available already protected, you can quickly sterilize them yourself, as explained elsewhere in this book.

I've had some exceptionally impressive varieties by watching for some *seed specialty* that a good seedhouse offers year after year. The smart seedsman often uses his best offering as a "leader"—so you'll be delighted by your results and come back for his other varieties next year.

So, study the garden catalogs and advertisements each season, and along with your regular supply of seeds of the varieties you love best, order the specialties of each good house. You'll be in for some thrilling and rewarding surprises!

Treat Seed to Counteract Decay and Damping-off

You can treat your seeds before planting, to give plants the best start in life—to counteract the common damage of decay and damping off. A number of modern chemicals are available at stores for this purpose; look for these names on the package listings: thiram, chloranil, captan, or dichlone.

It's very simple and effective to treat a small quantity of seed. Here's how many expert gardeners do it:

(1) Take the packet in which the seed comes, and tear off a top corner.

(2) Dip a small spatula into the chemical dust you've chosen; any small knife blade will do.

(3) Lift out a small quantity of dust with the tip of the blade, and drop it into the seed packet.

(4) Fold down corner of the packet and shake the contents thoroughly for a couple of minutes. Your seed is treated and far better able to resist decay and damping off.

With a large quantity of seed, simply place the seed in a container . . . add a quantity of dust as instructed on the package of fungicide you buy . . . close the container and shake it a few minutes.

You'll have healthier, stronger seeds by taking this modern precaution. And that means healthier flowers, bigger blooms, the extraordinary garden glory you want. Yes, just a few minutes of this special attention to seeds will pay off later in the end result—more magnificent growth than possible without the extra care.

Disinfect Seeds Against Destructive Organisms

When you plant your seeds, you don't want to be planting destructive organisms at the same time! A simple step in time will disinfect the seeds and often save lots of work fighting infestation later—often when it's too late.

You can usually buy pretreated and "certified" seeds in packages, but that's not always possible—or you may have seeds from other sources. In the latter case, here's another simple pretreatment that will prove a crop-saver in many instances.

Semesan is an effective chemical that'll do the trick for most vegetable seeds, and will also help protect the seeds against the damage of damping-off. Use it according to the directions on the package.

By taking this precaution, you can plant the seeds with far less worry about planting infestation at the same time, and with lots more confidence that you'll grow healthy, beautiful and delicious vegetables. You help prevent failures before they happen!

In-between Step for Seedlings

If you've grown seedlings indoors, you'll get much better results in your outdoor garden, and a much higher percentage of plants that survive and thrive, if you don't just move them from indoors to outdoors in one jump.

Best step is to place the seedlings in a cold frame for a while. But if you haven't one, do this: set the seedlings outdoors but not in the ground, for a few hours each day. Then bring them indoors again before evening coolness.

After about four days of this, your seedlings will have become more "hardened," and you can then plant them outdoors with a much better chance for survival, enduring health and a beautiful life in your garden.

Paper-cup Planting Trick

An ingenious gardener showed me a very handy system of starting seedlings in lightweight paper cups. Her seedlings sprouted beautifully, with fine vigorous growth, pushing their roots easily through the light paper once they're planted in the garden soil.

You can quickly see many advantages if you try this homey method. Each cup is easy and pleasant to handle. You simply plant the seedling in your garden in entirety, cup and all. By the end of the season, the cup has deteriorated and practically disappeared, while the plant has thrived and bloomed splendidly.

Be sure to use only the lightweight paper cups, not those made of cardboard-like material. You can even use the cup first to drink from—but water only, please. Skoal!

ANNUALS

_____

How to Grow Annuals for Best Results

Annuals give you a full season of enchanting beauty, then fade
and die away, although some may surprise you by coming
back the next year and for several years. Unlike the perennials, many of which grow in clumps or have tuberous roots
and bulbs, the annual has a single stem or root which lacks
the ability to store up food to tide over through the winter.

But the short-lived annual gives you beauty in a hurry, and
by the basketful. If you sow seeds directly outdoors, you'll
have blooms within six to ten weeks. If you start seeds indoors, then transplant your seedlings outdoors, you'll see their
gay, refreshing colors delighting you in half that time.

The glory of annuals increases as the season moves on—
lasting you from early spring until frost, depending upon the
varieties you grow. The more you pick, the more blooms
you have.

There are more varieties than there are pages in any seed
catalog, so choose according to your personal likes, checking
the descriptions and packets carefully regarding blooming
period and height particularly, before you plant.

Each year, growers are producing new and more exciting
varieties of the favorites—impressive giants and entrancing
miniatures. So treat your garden to some new "miracles" each
year, in addition to the lovely old standbys.

Growing annuals is easy and rewarding. Care in selecting

good quality seeds . . . patience in planting . . . reasonable fertilization, watering and spraying . . . a few hours a week of tending . . . and you'll have beautiful growth and a myriad of colors to delight your sight and glorify your home!

Basic Tips for "Miracle" Growth

Because it's impossible to give tips on all the annuals individually, or for you to absorb, I'll just highlight a few beauties on these pages—but, over all, here are important guides for most thrilling results:

Outdoor and General Growing

1. Prepare soil so it's loose in texture, holds moisture and yet drains off well. Pulverize the earth to a depth of at least eight inches. Make sure no lumps remain. Rake in a complete balanced plant food.

2. Locate for sun at least five hours a day for most varieties. Many will also thrive fairly well with three to four hours of direct sunlight daily and some hours of dappled sunlight. While you can grow many plants in "impossible" shade, you won't get maximum growth, richness and color.

3. Plant seeds according to directions on each packet. Water the soil before planting, preferably with a solution made with a complete water-soluble plant food. Firm the soil over seeds with a flat tool, or back of a spade—but don't pack down the earth too hard!

4. Water thoroughly about once a week to a depth of at least a half inch, if there's little rainfall. Scanty daily waterings are more harmful than helpful. It's better to water seedlings in the early morning and plants in the early evening.

5. Fertilize periodically with a balanced water-soluble plant food such as 15-30-15, complete with trace minerals. This often makes the difference in having "miracle" plants and blooms that are the showpieces of the neighborhood—rather than ordinary results.

6. Control infestation of insects and disease by using the multipurpose or special-purpose modern chemicals about every two weeks, once plants start to bloom.

7. Tend plants regularly by weeding. (But only after plants become established, so you can distinguish the plants from the weeds!) Also, remove blooms as soon as they've faded, to keep them from going to seed and weakening the plants. Thin out when plants are crowded, removing the weaker ones or you'll stunt the growth of all. Those left will give you more than enough blooms, color and foliage in response.

Indoor Beginning

1. Start annuals indoors about four weeks before outdoor planting time. Most all varieties will give you much faster bloom. Use pots or flats.

2. Use vermiculite, an excellent modern planting medium —or ⅔ rich soil and ⅓ coarse sand—or a combination of soil and peat moss (you may have a favorite mixture of your own).

3. Soak planted seeds thoroughly with water the first time, then water lightly and regularly. An application of water-soluble plant food for the first or second watering helps boost growth.

4. Set seedlings out in a cold frame or protected porch area for about a week before planting in the garden, as an extra measure of adjustment to growing conditions.

5. When transplanting seedlings into the garden, water well for a few hours before removing from flats or pots. It helps to leave some soil on the roots as you transplant. Select the low, bushier seedlings with plenty of roots, and discard tall, spindly specimens without much root system. Pinch off a little of the foliage at the top after seedlings are planted.

6. Space seedlings out (same with seeds) so that there's at least a foot of space between rows of smaller varieties, and about two feet between larger types. If sun is hot and strong, give your seedlings some shade protection at first (see tips on other pages); of course this applies to seedlings grown from seeds outdoors too. Go through your garden ruthlessly later and remove weaker plants where conditions are crowded.

Extra Helpful Tips

1. Pinch back your annuals when they're six to eight inches high; that is, gently pinch out the top growth with your fingertips. You'll get healthier, bushier plants that produce as much as twice as many blooms, usually larger and more spectacular.

2. Keep planting annuals of the more hardy types right up to fall for continually renewing fresh bloom and color. Follow same instructions as for spring planting.

3. It helps to mulch annuals in areas where you don't get much summer rain. Use good mulching materials described in this book. You'll cut down on frequency of weeding and watering.

4. *Don't throw away seed packets.* You'll want to refer later to instructions on thinning out plants, and other points.

The choice of annuals with which you'll "paint" glorious colors in your gardens—from abronias to zinnias—is open to you. Joy of selection adds an extra boost to the enjoyment of growing.

Once your garden is blooming richly, don't hesitate to pick plenty of flowers for indoors and for friends—you encourage more and even richer blooms!

If the pages that follow leave out some of your favorite annuals, it's through lack of space only, so forgive me. Now —prepare, plant and pick—good luck!

Grow Alyssum Checkerboard Style

For a dazzling border effect in your garden, hopscotch your plantings of alyssum so that you have a white variety, then a purple plant, then white, then purple, etc.—checkerboard style. This purple-and-white border effect in my garden, edging a large flower bed, made the entire area look lovelier than ever this past season, and won great admiration from friends and neighbors.

Specials Tips: Alyssum is best in low, bushy plants for exciting dense color, so cut back plants frequently, encouraging thick growth and constant display of lovely, gay bloom. A very hardy variety, you can keep planting alyssum all through the season, filling in spaces left bare by removal of some plants that have passed their blooming period.

Super-growing Tip for Geraniums

The greatest growth boost geraniums have ever had comes from the exciting new gibberellic acid available to gardeners. Particularly with tree geraniums which usually take up to two years time for growing a good-sized plant—along with lots of pinching and training to spur extra muscles—you can now boost your plant to full size in less than a year!

Simply apply repeated sprayings of a gibberellic acid product right from the cuttings. Easiest way is with a product available in an aerosol can. Spray with the wondrous gibberellins, feed the plant's increased appetite with a complete water-soluble plant food, and you'll have lusty, luxurious geraniums that'll make visitors' eyes pop.

Better Growth from Cuttings Too

You'll want to multiply your prized geranium plants from cuttings, of course. The gibberellins make it possible for you to multiply short-jointed varieties which have been most difficult up to now.

Treat the plants repeatedly with gibberellic acid, and the internodes will stretch out so you can clip them, and easily make good cuttings. Most amazing of all, when you stop the gibberellic treatment, this variety will go back to its normal size in a few weeks!

Help Cuttings with Hormones

Geraniums are among the best and easiest plants for propagation through cuttings, and the new hormones help you to even happier plants. Here are the simple steps:

1. Clip off the bloom stalks on the selected plant. For rooting, choose hard and woody young stem growth. Cut off the top of the stem, about four inches long, between leaves and a little below where a leaf stem grows.

2. Remove leaves at the lower part of the stem, close to the stem, so you'll be able to insert in the rooting medium cleanly. Let the cuttings dry out on a sheet of paper for about an hour.

3. Now, for help from hormones, dust the lower inch of the stem with a hormone rooting powder—it's a wonderful growth boost.

4. Insert the stem into good sandy soil directly into a pot, or plant in vermiculite for transplanting into soil later, as you choose. Water sensibly and expose plants to a few hours of sun daily at the start.

5. After three to four weeks, the cuttings should be well rooted, and have earned a place in a good, sunny spot indoors or out (during mild season only, of course). You'll have a thriving geranium grove!

More Colors in Modern Geraniums

If you've been prejudiced against geraniums because of their old-fashioned faded red color, you'll enjoy the up-to-date beauties all the more. Now you can grow varieties from white, through shades of pink, into quiet or blazing reds and even exotic purples.

You can enjoy astounding effects in foliage—from bi-color to tri-color leaves, in magnificent red-brown-green and other surprising patterns.

Sizes range from lovely little miniatures to towering tree geraniums, skyrocketing up with the help of gibberellins. In any size, there's new gardening fun when you go-go-go for gorgeous modern geraniums!

Mass Geraniums for Magnificence

A geranium trick that provides a glorious mass of color indoors or on terrace or porch is to combine a number of plants from small pots into one huge pot or planter. You'll find that each plant lends added color radiance to the others, multiplying the effectiveness of each considerably.

Combine four or five plants from small pots, choosing tall plants to provide height rather than a flat, less effective impression.

Main trick in obtaining the most beautiful effect is to turn the tops of the plants toward the outside of the large planter. Space the plants so as to avoid crossing of branches from one plant over another.

After a week or so, when the plants accommodate themselves gracefully to the new group arrangement, you'll be thrilled by the breathtaking display of massed colorful blooms and glorious green foliage.

No Impatience with Impatiens!

Want to have hundreds of perky red faces poking their happy, colorful blooms through lovely, low, bushy, deep green foliage . . . all through your garden . . . from spring until frost? Then you'll want to do as we do—set in plenty of the brightly rewarding impatiens plants as borders or for spots of jewel-like color near shrubs and trees and in front of small garden beds.

This is the single impatiens flower, sometimes known as Touch Me Not, related to the double-flowering balsam. With very little trouble, you'll have healthy plants, blooming profusely and just about continuously, making you smile every time you see them gaily decorating your landscaping. They respond best to full sun but even bloom in areas with only a little sun.

To grow impatiens at their best, set the plants in your garden just as soon as the first cold nights of spring have passed. Dip the roots first for a few minutes in a solution of water-soluble plant food, then plant snugly and water well with the liquid fertilizer.

Soon you'll have lovely low bushy plants, dotted with scarlet blooms up to 1½ inches across, with clean fresh faces to greet you each morning. Impatiens also blooms in carmine, pink or white, if you wish variety.

To paraphrase a familiar saying, I can guarantee that impatiens makes the heart grow fonder . . . of gardening!

Now . . . Giant Marigolds up to 6 Inches Across!

Throw away your old ideas about small, smelly marigolds. Now you can get these garden beauties with and without odor . . . in giant fluffy varieties that grow up to three feet tall . . . with gorgeous blooms from five to six inches across and four inches deep . . . with so many flowers on the sturdy stems that you can hardly see the leaves!

You can get scintillating new medium-sized blooms also, with glorious heads that will remind you of exquisite golden chrysanthemums. You can grow varieties so prolific that simply breaking off stems, setting them in rich moist soil, will produce dozens of new plants in a hurry—that you can give or trade with other enthusiasts.

And you can get elegant little compact pigmy types, with spicy, bi-colored blooms; also, there are lush, thick dwarf doubles.

And try dainty little single French marigolds which grow only six inches high but produce astonishing blooms two inches across! On these little beauties, centers are golden, followed by splashes of maroon on sunny yellow outspread petals.

Special Tips: Plant marigolds for plenty of sun. They grow fast from seeds as well as seedlings, and reproduce prolifically from new cuttings. Apply water-soluble plant food every two weeks for sensational plants and flowers. Allow plenty of room between plants if you want huge, spectacular beauties.

$10,000 Reward!

One of the largest growers has a standing $10,000 reward for anyone who can discover a pure white marigold for him. Some very pale yellow types have come through, but not elusive snowy white. There's a remunerative challenge for you. There's one condition: no fair using bleach!

More Power in Petunias!

You can depend on petunias to give you color almost wherever you want it, because it's the most profuse flowering of any of the bright annuals. Although petunias prefer sun, they'll even thrive in partial shade if helped with extra fertilizer and watering.

The big trick in enjoying petunias at their best is to take advantage of the latest and most beautiful types and varieties. You can get solid and striped singles . . . astonishing giant doubles . . . frilled and flounced petunias . . . in incredibly rich and dainty colors. Trailing types of petunias are wonderful for hanging baskets and garden and window boxes.

A recently developed petunia-type flowers with a deep rose red face on a glowing gold throat, growing almost 1½ feet high. Another has fringed, lacy light blue flowers delicately veined and throated with deep violet—with breathtaking blooms over three inches across.

A new star-patterned petunia adds vivid scarlet and white to this popular species. Another is a deep scarlet beauty that gleams like rich red satin and produces a mass of blooms on each stem.

Before you plant petunias next time, be sure to add some of the modern varieties that are more colorful, richer and more robust than you've ever known these flowering favorites to be before.

Special Tips: To get an early start on petunias, sow indoors from seed, then transplant seedlings outdoors as soon as the soil warms up. You can have a succession of ravishing blooms from midspring to frost!

Petunias are especially decorative planted in solid color or mixed masses. Always plant at least nine inches apart. Take care with the very fine seed to avoid crowding plants badly. It pays to buy top-quality seed to produce more vigorous plants.

Petunias appreciate frequent feeding with a water-soluble plant food, and heavy watering, and they respond amazingly with rapid growth and a burst of bloom!

The Phlox of Life

Gardeners love the hardy phlox because they produce such luxurious flowering and glorious color during the hot summer months. That's when radiant color for your garden from most perennials is scarce (day lilies are an exception). But let's see how you can enjoy extraordinary "miracle phlox" with glowing color that glorifies your garden even in midsummer.

See that the soil is rich, with adequate drainage, and that the plants have plenty of air. Arrange your planting area so that your phlox have more sun than shade.

Note that as the clumps age, the bottom leaves have a tendency to turn brown. Don't waste any time or effort at this point spraying against mites or fungi. It's questionable whether this browning is caused by anything other than the nature of the species. Simply pick off these bottom leaves in a few minutes, and everyone will admire the remaining colorful foliage and gay blooms.

Another important tip: remove phlox blooms when they have passed their colorful, thriving best. If you don't, seeds will form. The seedlings that result will usually crowd out the parent plant and produce harsh-colored flowers.

Select the varieties you like best to start, according to their coloration. You can get phlox in bright reds, variety of rose tints, rich violet blues and others. With proper fertilization, and the tips on care suggested here, your garden will feature glorious "miracle" color in midsummer, when your neighbors may be moaning over the lack of colorful blooms.

Dazzling Showoffs—Shirley Poppies

As I sit typing in our garden, my wife has just interrupted to hand me a lovely pink four-petaled flower, thrilling in its flat wide delicate round shape and enchanting color. She remarked, "Be sure to tell gardeners to try the wonderful Shirley poppies. I don't know any flowers that are easier to grow and give so much delight month after month."

I agree enthusiastically. If you haven't experienced the joy of watching cheerful, colorful Shirley poppies enrich your garden with their glorious colors, by all means plant some. Nothing could be simpler.

Planting in Minutes

Mix the tiny seeds with a little sand or sandy soil preferably. Then broadcast or plant in spots—as a border, as a low growing bed, or wherever you want extra colorful growth among other plants. Most any fertilized soil will do, and full sunlight is preferable.

Growth is fast, and the thin stemmed, delicately foliaged plants are graceful and decorative right from the start. You can choose from vivid scarlets, flaming reds through to pastel pinks and pure whites—or mix the colors for truly stunning effects.

Our Shirley poppies have graced our garden from late May until frost. As I gaze right now at the enchanting coral bloom lying on the table beside me, I wonder who can deny that gardens are filled with breathtaking "miracles"—all ours just for the growing.

Grow Snappier Snapdragons!

An old-fashioned favorite that lost prestige through the years, but is now coming back to soaring popularity—almost as a brand-new species—is today's super snapdragon. You can get varieties now that will grow anywhere from eight inches to well over three feet high!

You can boast of snapdragons in many ravishing colors . . . with foliage gleaming like polished leather . . . with fantastic open-mouthed blooms several inches across, with prettier ruffles than ever before.

Tips for Super Results

For more vigorous and larger blooms, remove some of the early sucker shoots. Don't water late in the day as foliage reacts badly when wet at night. Give plenty of air around plants for healthiest growth and to prevent infestation. Stake tall plants to help encourage their stalwart beauty.

New Fashions in Spider Flowers

Because of their exotic tropical appearance, their bushiness that makes them almost able to double as shrubs, and the lovely new varieties developed . . . the spider flower, more formally known as cleome spinosa, is practically a new garden fashion now.

Strong four-foot stems are densely covered with shiny green leaves that feature up to seven pointed leaflets, for an exquisite foliage effect. Airy, lacy heads of new yellow, pure white, pink, golden or purple-pink flowers wave atop each upright branch. The long, thin stamens, and slender seed pods that climb the heavy stems give the plant its spidery relationship.

Special Tips: Plant as far apart as two feet, to give the magnificent plants plenty of room to develop at their best. Spot about the garden, not too thickly, as massive accents, almost as you'd use a shrub. Stake the plants if they show a tendency to bend over. Count on sturdy spider plants to bloom from two to three months; they flourish very well even during dry periods. They'll serve you beautifully as a background for colorful, low-growing annuals!

Grow Zinnias Big as Grapefruit Halves!

Now you can get and grow astounding varieties of zinnias that produce massive blooms actually as large as grapefruit halves.

Exciting colors are beautiful blends of cream, orange and gold, as well as vivid reds.

Other species available today have long curled petals of glistening scarlet. And you can get striped and mottled giants that produce four-inch-wide flowers on strong three-foot-high plants —in contrasting pinks, reds and purples with white, and red or orange streaked with gold.

You'll probably love the striking beauty of dwarf foot-high zinnias too, and cactus types with graceful loose-petaled heads, in glorious flame, orange and gold colorings. They'll light up your rooms as long-lasting vase flowers too!

Special Tips: Zinnias grow well from seeds, if planted as soon as the soil is thoroughly warm. You might also give them an early start indoors, and you'll have bright blooms in your garden in a hurry. The more space you give to the giant varieties, the bigger they'll grow—so don't fence them in!

PERENNIALS

Beauty in the Shade

If you love perennial blooms, you'll avoid failures by resigning yourself to the fact that most of these lovely plants just won't thrive in full shade. No amount of fertilizer or care can really compensate for the lack of some sun.

That's one of the sad facts of gardening life. Once you realize that, you can go on to success in having some delightful blooms in the shade with practically no sun, by careful selection and tending.

Just given a little sun during the day, but shaded the rest of the day, you can get excellent growth and decorative color from these beautiful perennials:

> *Day lilies* . . . choose from varieties available that will bloom right from early summer through to fall.
>
> *Primroses* . . . you'll enjoy their delicate beauty primarily in the spring.
>
> *Bleeding heart* . . . they'll enhance your garden with their enchanting foliage and colorful blooms in mid-spring.
>
> *Myrtle* . . . will give your garden beauty in partially shaded areas from late spring into fall.

More Success in the Shade

Even with just a little sun, you can grow balloon flowers, monkshood, bugbane and a few other varieties with real success.

The secret is to treat shaded plants particularly well—choose sturdy plants to start with, cultivate and fertilize the ground deeply before planting, water adequately but don't swamp the plants, and give extra feeding every few weeks with a good liquid fertilizer.

You'll accomplish what some gardeners think is hardly possible—a beautiful succession of bright, colorful blooms in shade, with only a little sun.

Color in Deep Shade

With the extra care detailed above, a few hardy perennials will even thrive for you without sun.

Try your luck with vigorous varieties of lily of the valley, myrtle and bugle. Coddle them with constant care and you'll have gay blooms and graceful foliage that seem to bring sunshine into the shade.

Annuals in the Shade

Four popular varieties among the lively plants that last just for a year or so, but bring you color in shaded areas, are some species of tuberous begonias, cornflowers, nasturtiums and pansies.

I've had good fortune with lovely impatiens (one of my favorites) in deeply shaded spots, but here again, extra loving care is needed, as with perennials that are deprived of sun.

For rich, green foliage, many varieties of ferns will give you rewarding results in the shade.

Keep trying, and surprisingly, you'll come up with your own impossible "miracles" of growth in shaded areas—with plants blooming that "can't bloom" in the shade. But don't count on it!

How to Grow Exhibition-type Chrysanthemums

No gardener can or should keep mum about the magnificent mums he can grow easily in his garden. For profusion of bloom, richness of color and beauty of foliage—September through November—mums are truly garden marvels. You can grow them by the armload—or single exquisite mammoth blooms—depending on the varieties you plant and the kind of care you give them.

In general, chrysanthemums require little more than plenty of sunshine (although many varieties will even do fairly well in partial shade), good complete fertilization, and plenty of moisture.

A special tip, to grow very special exhibition blooms, is to fertilize several times during growing season with a complete water-soluble plant food containing *plenty of chelated iron*. Mums appreciate particularly this modern nutritional "seasoning."

Tips on Planting

Spring is an excellent time to plant chrysanthemums, but you can also put them in right up to July and still get lovely fall flowering.

Plant in a rich soil, for full sun, working in plenty of modern peat moss, and adding a complete fertilizer. Apply more fertilizer about once a month, liquid or dry. Go heavy on the water, making sure to water deep—none of the scanty surface swishing or you won't help produce the deep vigorous roots that mean high robust plants and extraordinary blooms.

Space out plants with plenty of room between, particularly if you're going to grow exhibition-size blooms. Crowding cuts down the height of the plants and width of the blooms.

Pinch to Produce Exhibition-size Flowers

If you want floral showpieces, you'll have to keep after the grooming of your plants. Pinch back your plants early, about mid-July, and remove all but three to five branches.

If you're set on huge beauties, limit the plant to one branch. Allow only one bud per branch! Fertilize as previously directed, water plentifully, and you should grow some really showy masterpieces!

For Masses of Mums

In addition to growing some overpowering beauties, you'll certainly want armfuls of mums for indoors, as well as for outdoor glory in fall months. For this purpose, pinch out the tip end of each plant when you set it in the earth. As side branches develop, remove the tips also, until you have enough leaves per branch so that two sets remain.

Maintain this system of pinching out until the end of July,

and you'll have vigorous compact plants that'll give you loads of blooms.

It's also a help to cultivate around the soil regularly, to keep the earth well aerated and discourage weeds. After the plants are eight inches or more tall, it's also desirable to apply a light mulch for current and later winter protection.

Spray Bi-weekly for Protection

Start a regular spraying program with a good general insecticide-fungicide about ten days after planting. Repeat the application about every two weeks. As always cautioned with an insecticide, be sure to hit the undersides as well as topsides of leaves.

Multitudinous Varieties for You

You can grow all kinds and colors of mums, from tiny button mums to huge beauties . . . those with cactus-type petals and changeable colors . . . sunburst giants such as you see in florists' . . . disease-resistant new loose-petaled varieties . . . cushion mums that produce many bushels of blossoms in blazing jewel tones . . . and many, many more. New varieties are being propagated each year, so keep up with them if you want the latest.

Follow the simple suggestions here, and you'll enjoy bursting beauty in mums each fall, multiplying their magnificent displays year after year.

More Beauty with Bleeding Heart

Your garden is missing one of the finest gems of the flower world if you don't grow bleeding heart at its best. This exquisite plant, with its graceful foliage and delicate sprays of deep pink heart-shaped blooms, brightens your home for over a month in spring and gladdens your brimming heart.

For bleeding heart at its most glorious, plant in rich soil that is well fertilized and conditioned for looseness to hold plenty of moisture. Dig deep and plant the roots straight down as possible, keeping the crown just below the top of the soil. Water in well with a good liquid fertilizer. Be sure the plants have plenty of sun.

You'll want to multiply healthy thriving plants to glorify more spots in your garden, and to give to grateful friends. It's easy and fun. In early summer, as soon as the foliage is starting to fade, lift out old clumps and cut the heavy roots into pieces three to four inches long. In a shaded area, cover the pieces with about an inch of rich soil. Water often but don't flood the place.

By fall you'll notice that foliage is springing up. In the spring you'll have lovely young plants, ready to spread their radiance wherever you wish to plant them.

Another simple way to multiply bleeding heart is simply to divide a large clump, after blooms have faded, into a few good-sized divisions. Then plant in rich soil and tend well, fertilizing and watering plentifully.

Each year, tended as described here, bleeding heart will reappear more glamorously than ever, with more and lovelier blooms. Particularly as a background for majestic tulips in spring, the effect in your garden will be breathtakingly beautiful!

Asters That Rate "Ahhhs!"

Few flowers are more attractively gay than asters at their best. Like so many plants, there are many varieties of asters, each loaded with a frightening technical name. Don't let that faze you—just select at the start *perennial* asters, not the annuals which some experts claim aren't asters at all. The perennials are bigger, lusher, lovelier, and the best choice for aspiring gardeners.

These daisylike beauties respond best to lots of sun, with average moisture. They resent swampy soil and show it by signs of rot. So keep asters well watered but not "drowned," for radiant beauty.

Plant in spring and enjoy happy gorgeous blooms in fall. Divide the clumps and replant each spring; take three strong shoots from the outside of a healthy clump, for each division. Throw away the center of the old clump, after a vote of thanks for its pretty performance the preceding fall.

Shasta Daisies

I've been partial to these giant, hearty, optimistic flowers ever since I saw some radiant beauties growing on a windswept cliff overlooking a wide expanse of blue sea, while visiting some friends. They gave us some healthy divisions which we planted and enjoy even today, years later. Treated right, they'll grace your garden for years with their white and gold natural beauty.

To grow Shasta daisies that will be the envy of visiting friends, start with healthy plants. Set them in early spring, preferably in soil that is well fertilized and aerated for good drainage. Fertilize generously: I've always used a good liquid fertilizer and obtained excellent response.

It's very important to divide the clumps at least every second year, or you'll find the plants stifling and fading on you. In that case, blame yourself, not the plants. It's very simple to lift out a clump, pull it apart gently in several husky divisions and replant. (Throw away the woody center portion.)

If bugs or beetles attack your Shasta daisies, apply a good dust or spray containing wonder-working methoxychlor and rotenone. But usually, healthy plants won't cause you any trouble.

So it's up to you. Unless you divide regularly, your Shastas will love you not. But with the little care outlined here, you'll love the special beauty of vigorous Shasta daisies in your garden.

Choice Columbine Spreads Good Cheer

"The bells are ringing," and they're ringing gaily in your garden when you grow columbine at their loveliest. These bell-like, trumpetlike flowers range in color tones from creamy white to deep reds, yellows, purples and even two-toned varieties. They bloom gloriously in late spring and early summer.

It's simple and it's fun to grow columbine from seed, and enjoy them in their fullest glory, by following just a few tips. Plant the seeds in a fertile bed and keep them shaded and well watered, feeding early with a good liquid fertilizer. The seedlings will sprout within two to three weeks, and can then be transplanted most anywhere so long as they get plenty of sun.

You'll note that columbine plants have very definite crowns, a clear marker for you so that you plant with the crown right at the surface of the soil.

This is important for greatest production of blooms in your garden. As soon as a flower fades, pinch it off, and another lovely bloom will replace it fast, adding to the color glory of your surroundings.

Just one major warning: Leaf miners love to attack your delicate appearing columbine and will ruin the foliage unless you act quickly and keep on the watch. At the first sign of infestation—you'll see ugly white tunnels on the leaves—use one of the new miracle sprays containing *lindane*. Nip off the leaves first, then spray weekly—bottoms as well as tops of leaves—until every sign of miners disappears.

Let some of the blooms go to seed instead of nipping off blooms, then use the plentiful seeds and start the whole wonderful regrowing process to produce more seedlings the following spring. You'll have a dazzling display of especially beautiful and enchanting flowers.

Spicier, Perkier, Prettier Pinks!

One of the loveliest, brightest little flowers for garden or buttonhole is the perky pink. These gay beauties grow easily and abundantly, requiring very little care—just a lot of sunshine and plenty of moisture.

Here's your vital guide to having plenty of the spicily fragrant carnationlike blooms—from assorted seeds that blossom into a delicate palette of pinks, salmons, reds in many shades, and white. Only fertilize lightly—yes, strangely enough, the caution is *don't overfertilize*. Too much nitrogen particularly will mean that the foliage will be thick and heavy, but the flowers will be few and stunted. But apply less fertilizer than to the rest of your plants, and you'll have plenty of pretty pinks smiling happily above the green foliage.

Another tip. Cut off the blooms just as soon as they fade, and pinks will renew themselves through the summer, getting their second wind in the fall when their dainty tints are especially welcome and refreshing.

I recommend planting clumps of single pinks from seed, and double pinks from plants, for an enchanting aura of spicy fragrance which will fascinate your guests as you lead them about your garden.

Aspire to Higher Spires of Delphinium

Now you can get giant delphinium which grow up to five feet tall, with exotic spikes of double florets in delicate pastels to rich deep hues. Planted and tended correctly, you'll get two long-lasting showings—in late spring and in summer. For a rare garden thrill, seek out this new giant variety. You can also enjoy medium and midget delphinium, from plants or seed.

It's important when placing plants in the soil to make sure you don't bury the crowns, but keep them just above the soil. Fertilize when planting, and several times during the season. Delphinium are particularly responsive to a good water-soluble plant food.

As an extra growth boost, mix some superphosphate well into the soil when preparing for planting. You'll find that between the superphosphate when planting, and the liquid fertilizing shortly after, you'll have the most majestic delphinium in your neighborhood.

A few more tips: Cut back flowers rapidly as they fade, to make way for quick new blooms. As the foliage wilts, cut way back and new growth will appear surprisingly fast. If you find foliage growing black, apply a good anti-mite spray, and usually you'll overcome infestation quickly.

If seed and plants aren't very hardy, crown rot may attack and ruin the plants almost overnight, so they topple over, or separate from the roots at the least pull. If this happens, dig up the plants, roots and all, and throw them away. Disinfect the ground with an application of bichloride of mercury before planting anything else.

But don't worry about disaster which probably won't occur. You're sure to be delighted with delphinium if you get top quality plants or seeds, and tend carefully as suggested here.

ROSES

Variety Is the Spice of Rose Life!

When the noted author Gertrude Stein wrote the famous line,
"Rose is a rose is a rose is a rose," she was all wrong in respect
to the multitudes of varieties from which you can choose to
have the rose garden of your dreams.

There are old-fashioned roses and exciting modern varieties,
new each year . . . hybrid teas and hybrid perpetuals . . .
grandifloras, floribundas and polyanthas . . . climbing roses,
miniature roses and rose trees . . . and hundreds upon hundreds of differently named roses, of all sizes, shapes and colors.

I won't even begin to advise which varieties will please you
most, other than to suggest that you choose from the catalogs
and offerings of reputable nurseries and dealers. Don't be at-
tracted by low-priced "bargains" except from reputable firms,
for you usually get no more than you pay for.

Very low prices, out of line with the rest of the offerings in
the field, usually mean that you'll get very young plants, inferior or mass-produced plants, and often plants that aren't
hardy enough for your area.

Keep in mind when you buy roses that you invest just as
much time, work and soil preparation and fertilizer money
in a poor, cheap plant as in a top-quality plant that will survive
and delight you for years and years.

Above all, choose the varieties of roses that suit your personal taste. If you love these blooms particularly, you'll prob-

ably get much extra pleasure by joining the excellent American Rose Society, and benefiting from their publications and activities.

The true "miracle" of roses is the uplifting thrill their beauty will bring you day after day, the feeling as stated by the poetess Christine Rossetti almost a hundred years ago ". . . a rose, the joy of all the earth!"

Planting Roses for Best Results

Build a home for the precious rose bush just as carefully as you prepare a home for yourself. For you want the radiant blooms to be with you and enrich your garden and your life for a long time. Here's a simple method, with a few special steps, that will assure you better results:

1. Soak the roots in a solution of liquid plant food while you dig the hole in a spot that will get plenty of sun. Save the solution for use later in the planting. Modern radioactive tests prove that the roots will soak up a good deal of nutrient in just a few minutes from a good liquid plant food.

2. Dig a hole large enough so it's wider than the natural widest spread of the rose-bush roots, and deep enough so that the graft on the main stem will sit exactly at ground level. That extra-wide digging is important so you won't cramp the roots and inhibit fast, easy growth right at the start.

3. Set in the bush so it stands straight up. A good method is to build a mound of soil first in the hole and spread the roots over it. Then slowly cover the roots with rich fertile soil or topsoil, well mixed with peat moss. Drift the soil gently between the roots, firming the earth lightly with your fingertips or with a blunt stick, handled carefully. Continue adding soil to fill about two thirds of the hole, firming as you fill, packing down with your flat palm as you fill higher than halfway.

4. Pour in a gallon of complete liquid plant food (you can use the presoaking solution), then another gallon of water, pouring slowly, giving the water a chance to sink in, rather than washing the soil about.

5. Now fill the hole to ground level with the soil. Firm the earth, but don't stamp it down.

6. Prune back the tops of all new rose bushes to little more than a foot from the ground.

7. Now mound up more soil about six inches high around the new bush, regardless of whether you're planting in spring or fall. When the plant is thoroughly established, you can level out the soil again for cleaner appearance.

8. Water well every few days until the bush is sturdily established.

With this extra care in planting, your rose bush will produce its maximum beauty for you.

Exciting Development— Sub-zero Everblooming Roses

After a lifetime of experiments and thousands of field trials, the famous rosarian, Dr. Walter D. Brownell, has developed a sub-zero rose that blooms without any special protection— even after winters as cold as 35° below zero!

These dramatic rose bushes are so vigorous and hardy that they not only survive the severest winters but are also far more resistant to the ravages of summer drought. Also, they fight off common black spot and many other rose troubles, so that they require much less spraying than other varieties.

Perhaps most exciting of all, these sub-zero roses are said by the reputable growers to be practically "lifetime" bushes. The claim is that they'll increase in size and beauty year after year—and results to date bear this out!

So, even though sub-zero roses seem costly at first, they'll prove economical as they thrive and give you exhilarating beauty in abundance—often over a hundred huge and ravishing blooms on a single four-year-old bush—flourishing year after year, without the cost and work of replacement.

Many Glorious Types and Varieties

You can now get these magnificent sub-zero roses in many of your favorite exquisite varieties, in practically every color and shape . . . tea roses . . . pillar roses that climb and frame your porch, fence, garage or the side of your house, and even the beautiful and astonishing tree roses which are like a new race of roses in themselves.

Eye-level Tree Roses

This is truly a sensational development in gardening, combining roses that laugh at the cold, live through sub-zero temperatures, and, in addition, bloom beautifully at eye level!

The double-grafted, heavy, straight trunks are about three feet tall when planted. And the planting is similar to other roses, requiring rich, fertile soil and full sunshine.

As day follows day, a great rounded head develops atop the trunk. Gradually, large buds appear along with rich, dark green foliage. Finally, the buds burst into large, exquisite blooms, radiating rare and overpowering beauty and fragrance.

Sub-zero rose trees are fairly costly to start with, but they last a long time and provide a queenly conversation piece even when planted as single specimens. You can choose from deep, velvety, fully double varieties that bloom abundantly week after week, producing breathtaking roses up to five inches across.

Also, now you can get delightful white roses with creamy yellow centers . . . two-toned pink blooms . . . large, yellow, deeply fragrant blossoms.

Here's rose enchantment for you, never available before this modern age—and literally on a higher level!

Enjoy magnificent new bush and climbing roses.

Entrancing tree roses are garden highlights.

Astonishing 4-in-1 Rose Tree

You'll have the entire neighborhood staring admiringly in your garden when the sub-zero 4-in-1 rose tree is in full bloom. This astounding new garden wonder flourishes four different varieties and colors of magnificent roses, all on the same high rose tree!

Horticulturists have produced this amazing new development by budding four different varieties of hardy roses on a single three-foot trunk. Thus, the crown not only exhibits four different colors and varieties, but also, the foliage is many times thicker, richer and more luxuriant.

Blooms keep repeating on the 4-in-1 rose tree from spring through fall, improving year after year with even less than average rose care. All through the season, this one costly tree will be radiant with these four varieties and colors: bluish-pink, blazing velvety red, deep buttercup yellow, and a glamorous two-tone rose combining tints of orange-red and pink.

Enthusiastic friends will hardly believe their eyes, but the proof is in the seeing, and the fun is in owning and growing your own 4-in-1 rose garden wonder.

Ever-new thrills like this one await you as one of the band of privileged people who enrich their lives with gardening.

Astounding Everblooming "Living Fences"

"Definitely the outstanding shrub for use in fence-rows and hedges." That's what the U. S. Department of Agriculture has to say about the amazing "living fences" of everblooming multiflora and other special varieties of roses.

If you want a dense, supertough fence of meshed and inter-twined rose bushes, for a large property or lot or farmland, this

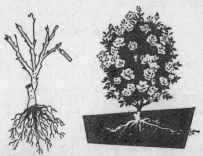

Plants with long, unwithered roots produce better bushes.

may be exactly the thing for you. They're so sturdy that even a charging bull can't break through a full-grown, vigorous hedge!

But don't expect the "living fence" to begin to compare in beauty with fine varieties of roses, or to be as decorative around your home as the most popular roses—they're not for that purpose at all.

And the blooms on these rose hedges don't compare at all with choice roses—they're rather lovely in themselves, as all flowers are, but they measure less than two inches in diameter usually, and aren't "exhibition roses" in any sense.

Blossoms . . . Foliage . . . Berries

So much for the negatives; strictly on the positive side, everblooming rose fences have much to recommend them. They reveal dense clusters of roses in spring, a mass of many dozens of roses on every plant. Their foliage is bright green through the summer. And they exhibit colorful scarlet berries in the winter.

Requiring just a little fertilization each year, and at least some sunlight, the bushes shoot up to about six feet in height. Then, umbrellalike, the branches arch down gracefully. The thick, thorny branches intertwine and form a mesh that's as strong in its way as a steel net! It's fast-growing—often an inch a day.

From the safety factor, it's a fact that neither animal nor man can normally plunge through a strong, established living rose fence. The plants resist drought by reaching far underground with their deep roots for moisture. They're much cheaper than wire fencing, and far more decorative. But, remember, if you want roses for sheer beauty, these plants shouldn't be your choice. For utility on large property, you can hardly do better.

Easy to Establish

For a "living fence" or continuous flowering effect, get your plants from a reputable nursery or dealer, preferably 2-year number-1 quality if you want blooms and growth fast. Many colors are available now—white, pink, dark red and variegated blooms. Plant about 1½ feet apart in rows, in fairly fertile soil, then stand back and watch the muscular growth develop daily, weekly, monthly.

Your best bet is to try a few everblooming rose hedge plants where you'd like to establish a "living fence." Then see how you like them in a season or two before spreading out. You

MIRACLE QUICK-TIPS
FOR BETTER GARDENING OUTDOORS & INDOORS

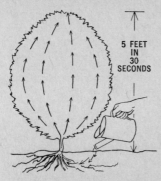

5 FEET IN 30 SECONDS

Boost growth fast with instant-action water-soluble plant food. In university tests using tracers, nutrients reached top of 5-foot rose bush in 30 seconds.

Grow stronger dahlias and get more blooms. Set in four stakes and black plastic roof over plants to shade during hot months. Remove as weather cools.

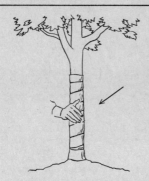

Protect young trees from gnawing animals which chew bark and ruin trunks. Wrap with ordinary household foil around lower tree trunk. Tie with strong cord.

CONCRETE

Save yellowing evergreens. Chemical lime from concrete house foundation leached into soil. Feed chelated iron in water-soluble plant food "for acid-loving plants."

Repair lawn bare spots speedily. Cut cross-lines in soil at least an inch deep with hoe or other sharp tool. Then sow seed and keep soil damp daily.

Paint flower pot quickly and all over without smearing hands. Paint inside top of pot. Then set pot upside down on old tin can. Remove after paint dries.

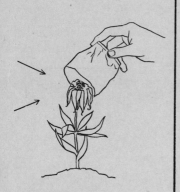

Save precious seeds on plants before they fall off. After flower has died, tie plastic bag over it. Dried-out seeds fall into bag instead of on ground.

Protect house plants. Keep soil chemicals from harming foliage. Wrap aluminum foil around rims; change monthly. Use foil "dishes" under pots.

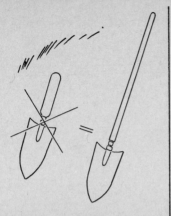

Make a better tool out of an old trowel. Remove handle, replace with old broom handle. Use "new" long-handled trowel to dig without bending.

Get more roses. When cutting blooms, cut stem above the topmost five-leaflet branch. If you cut below, new shoot may not produce roses.

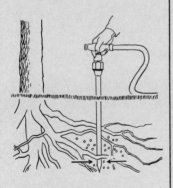

Water trees deeply with a root-feeder device which attaches to hose. Push hollow spike right down to tree roots. Water flows through, soaks roots.

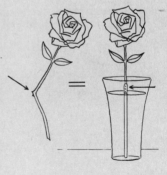

Fix broken flower stem if too short for vase. Push stem into ordinary drinking straw until it is right length. Use sticky tape to hold firm.

Keep plants from spreading.
Cut top and bottom from tin
can. Sink can into soil all
around plant to keep roots
from spreading too close to
other plants.

Seed with a salt cellar. For
faster planting of tiny seeds
like petunias, mix seeds with
fine sand. Sprinkle on soil with
salt cellar for easy control.

Grow an ivy tent. Place three
long chopsticks or other sticks
in pot, tie at top. Train ivy to
climb up, down and around the
sticks.

Shelter young seedlings from
hot sun when first planted.
Place wooden slats into ground
on south side of plants. Remove after about a week.

Prevent plant breakage from hose rounding corner of a garden bed. Hammer heavy wooden pegs into corners of beds to keep hose under control.

Make tool handles glow so no one stumbles over them in dark if left out. Paint handles with luminous paint, all over or strips. Prevents accidents.

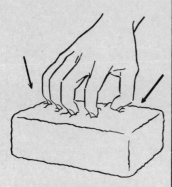

Keep fingernails clean when gardening without gloves. Push fingernails deep into soft soap beforehand. Later wash out soap and nails are clean.

Start seedlings indoors in small space. Place little pots or peatpots in an old muffin tin. Easy to carry to sunny windowsills, then to outdoors.

Protect young plants from cold in early spring. Make a little "hothouse" by pulling plastic bag over four stakes placed as a frame support.

Keep names readable on plant markers. Write name on top with crayon or felt marker, cover with transparent sticky tape. Name won't wash off.

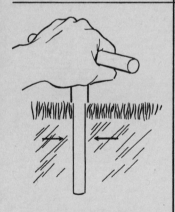

Check lawn moisture with a "soil probe" tool. Push hollow tube into ground, twist, bring up soil. Shows depth of moisture, other soil conditions.

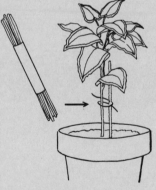

Use pipe cleaners as supports for weak little indoor plants. Push pipe cleaner into soil, tie plant stem to it. Soft covering won't rub the stem.

Make garden work easier by carrying small tools on belt. Cut slits in an old small purse, push belt through. Holds clippers, plant sticks, seeds, etc.

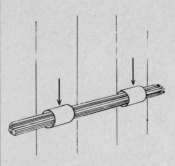

Keep stakes handy. Remove tops and bottoms of two tin cans. Paint attractively. Nail to wall about 18 inches apart. Push stakes through.

Save your shoes. Cut pieces of old hose, slit. Fit over top of spade as cushion for shoe pushing down. Also use piece as pail handle grip.

Start tomatoes faster. Beam extra warmth from sun on young, strong tomato plants. Place wooden slats or shirt boards as reflectors on north side of plants.

Support tall plants by tying to stakes with soft, strong nylon strips. Cut up old, discarded nylon stockings into strips to size needed.

To speed planting, make a garden measuring stick of your long rake handle. Paint line every six inches, place handle on ground, set in plants.

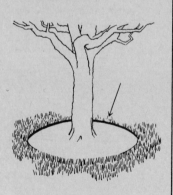

Keep grass away from a tree or shrub for better growth. Sink a hoop in ground around the tree trunk. Looks neater, keeps grass from creeping up.

Save your knees when working in the garden. Stuff an old hot water bottle with insulation material or other padding. Soft, protective, durable.

may be one of the enthusiasts who will also love these sensational plants for beds, borders or for specimen planting and decoration here and there about your property.

Protection Program to Produce "Miracle" Roses

For the many hours and days and weeks and even months of enchantment you get from exquisite roses, you must trade from five to fifteen minutes or more a week in the average rose garden to protect these beauties from spoilage by harmful insects and disease. Otherwise, you'll never have the perfection of blooms and foliage which roses offer in such thrilling abundance—in exchange for only a little care.

Years back, before the development of many of the wonder-working chemicals available to you today, keeping invaders of the rose garden under control took hours of hard labor. But now science has simplified such control so that only a few minutes of spraying or dusting each week will usually keep your roses healthy and thriving gloriously.

The key words of rose protection are *"each week!"* Otherwise, while you can kill off many insects or diseases after they appear, they will have already marred some foliage and blooms. Spraying (which many find more effective than dusting) is even more effective if done twice a week, but usually a thorough weekly spraying is all that your roses require from you to fight off infestation.

You'll find more about wonderful "miracle" chemicals elsewhere in this book, but the following brief guide will serve you in protecting your roses *weekly:*

BLACKSPOT. This is a common affliction of rose bushes. Black spots appear on the edges of leaves. The spots spread, leaves turn yellow, die and fall away. At the first sign of this, *act in a hurry*. Spray thoroughly with a *captan* solution and repeat in a couple of days.

For prevention, spray your plants even before the leaves have unfolded, then at least once a week throughout the season. Ask for a product containing a "sticker" solution, or buy such materials separately to mix with the captan solution; the marvelous "sticker" material forms a film which helps hold the spray on the foliage for days, preventing washoff by rain!

Don't overlook this easy step toward controlling dreaded blackspot which was practically impossible to overcome not too many years ago. Use this same captan spraying to combat *rust* (orange spots instead of black) which attacks rose plants in some areas of the country.

APHIDS. These little greenish or brownish pests are bound to collect on the tips of shoots particularly unless you guard against them. They suck out vital juices from new, soft growth and cause weak, marred blooms and shoots if you don't destroy them. Spray with a DDT solution of nicotine sulphate, and do it regularly, because these tiny invaders return to the battlefield again and again. Science has given you the means to lick them, but you must be just as persistent as they are.

RED SPIDER MITES. So tiny that they're almost invisible, these vicious pests attack the undersides of rose leaves, suck out juices and turn the leaves yellow and brown, with a burned, withered look. Instead of blaming drought, turn up the leaves and you'll find traces of white cobwebs. Fortunately, powerful chemicals are now available that work wonders in mite control. Spray a solution of malathion, dimite or aramite (look at the insecticide package label) and apply regularly as directed on the package. *Be sure the solution covers the undersides of the leaves when you spray!*

POWDERY MILDEW. You'll recognize this common rose affliction when you see ugly whitish "powdering" on foliage and new shoots. Usually caused by high humidity—such conditions as cool nights following very hot, moist days—the fungus is easy to control by applying a *karathane* product as directed on the package. But be sure you act at the first sign of mildew or your rose bushes can be stunted and injured. (As with other insecticides, don't apply in the full heat of day.)

BEETLES. Formerly a horrible scourge of rose bushes, you can now control beetles easily with good sprays and dusts containing *methoxychlor*. Apply thoroughly and regularly. Don't rely on old-fashioned beetle traps which seem to act as magnets in attracting more of the armored invaders. Dusting the area with chlordane is also effective, but so far as your rose bushes go, the methoxychlor application gives you quick and concentrated on-the-spot control.

ABOUT ALL-PURPOSE SPRAYS . . . there are good "all-purpose" sprays which will perform a quite effective all-around job in helping to keep your rose bushes healthy and thriving. Naturally, they won't be as efficient in combating specific ills as a specific-purpose product, but will save you time and work. Many gardeners successfully use all-purpose sprays, and then also apply the specific chemicals when special conditions show up that need special attack.

Be sure that any all-purpose product you use is up to date, taking full advantage of modern wonder chemicals. Look on the labels for one or more of these marvelous aids: malathion, captan, methoxychlor and even (but not *only*) good old DDT.

To shoot for the ultimate in perfection—exquisite "miracle" roses—never forget to use that spray gun early and often!

Tips on Pruning Roses for Protection

To enjoy roses at their best, some judicious pruning will add to the health, vigor and grace of the bushes themselves, and to the size and beauty of blooms. Here are some general pointers, and more detailed tips which will help you to have an enchanting rose garden that you can really eye with pride:

Make sure that your tools are sharp and clean, lest you mutilate and injure the plants, along with straining your own temper.

If you're unsure, it's always better to cut off too little than too much. You can always trim off a little more, but as with a haircut you can't patch on again what you've cut off, once you've cut it off!

Do your pruning about 30 days before growth generally starts in your area in the spring.

In most cases, clean out twigs and tangled top growth. Clear off all dead wood, of course. Work so as to keep the center of the bush fairly open. Get rid of any side growth you don't want, by cutting off even with the cane surface. To promote growth in the direction you wish, cut the twig or cane off just above an eye which points in the right direction.

Don't chop a bush back close to the ground if you want plenty of large blooms. In most cases, don't cut off canes much thicker than your little finger. And, to repeat, at any point where you're a little afraid that you'll be cutting back too much—*don't!* A good rule is that if you spare the clippers, you won't spoil the bush.

Here are a few more detailed instructions for general types of roses:

GENERAL ROSE BUSHES. Keep the four or so main canes growing fairly high; don't cut back much more than twigs and top growth. Remove other old or crossing canes down almost to the base. With sensitive tea roses, trim only very lightly or leave untouched except to remove dead wood or tangled twigs.

CLIMBING ROSES. Trim lightly in general, but cut out all dead, unwanted and old wood. Aim primarily to promote neat, graceful appearance. Most gardeners act to maintain a lush, rich look which is neither skimpy nor thick and tangled in effect.

With good sense in pruning, working with a gentle hand and artistic eye, you'll help nature to endow your rose garden with the utmost in gracious beauty. But to chop a healthy bush too far back is the unkindest cut of all.

Merry Merry Christmas Roses to You!

They're not really roses, but the lovely little flowers known as Christmas roses will delight you with their pretty white blooms even at Christmastime in tough winter weather.

These small plants stand only about eight inches tall. Their deeply cut leaves are palmlike in shape, and stay evergreen all year. The plants start producing buds in the fall which flower into dainty white blossoms, radiant against the rich green foliage.

Christmas roses have amazing built-in protection. While in bloom, if a cold snap hits them, the buds will close up and you may think they've been irreparably injured. But when a comparatively warm spell comes on, and the sun shines, the buds open and the gay white flowers wink at you once more.

Best planting time for Christmas roses is in spring. Choose a semishaded location where the plants will be protected from hot summer sun. But make sure they're able to get sunshine during the winter or they won't thrive for the exceptional results you want with everything you grow.

It's smart to plant Christmas roses close to, and even under, evergreens . . . under trees . . . in shaded areas near walls. They'll give you refreshing green color and blooms on wintry days when you particularly welcome the thrill of flowers around your home.

But, a warning again: Just because they're called "Christmas roses," don't expect these plants to be anything like your beloved rose bushes. Just enjoy their own particular kind of beauty as a low-growing winter gardening wonder.

BULBS, CORMS, TUBERS

For Best Results from Spring-flowering Bulbs

For enchanting fresh color in early spring, you must have flowering bulbs glorifying your property. Plan for a variety and succession of blooms and colors, suited to your personal taste. Count on snowdrops and winter aconite to start your season, followed by other beauties such as crocus, hyacinths, daffodils, and above all, those superior new varieties of tulips available now!

Here are basic tips for handling and enjoyment of spring-flowering bulbs at their best:

Scatter bulbs throughout your property . . . as early flowering borders . . . in small batches . . . in large, colorful masses in a flower bed (but not where they'll leave empty gaps after blooming) . . . as gleaming jewels in front of shrubs and evergreens.

Remember, if you start with poor bulbs, you'll wind up with inferior blooms, no matter how much care you give them. Get your bulbs from reputable suppliers only . . . beware of bargain offers that seem too cheap to be true (they're probably not true, delivering poor-grade, tiny bulbs).

Check every bulb before planting; if there are any signs of rot, or if they're soft or pulpy to the touch, instead of solid and firm, get replacements or refund.

Fertilize the soil and plants well, as recommended on these pages for flower gardens in general. Soil should be well aerated and with good drainage, not boggy. For most vigorous health, plant for full sunlight. Don't plant too close to tree roots, for the bulbs will lack moisture and nutrients from the soil in competition with the roots, and you won't get the wondrous growth and beauty you want.

Helpful general planting guide: Small bulbs should be planted so the *tops* are about two to three inches below the level of the soil . . . up to six inches deep from bulb top to soil level for large bulbs. If in doubt, figure on about twice to three times as much soil above the top of the bulb as the bulb's diameter . . . and spaced out about four to five times the diameter.

Plant crocuses, daffodils, winter aconites and other "early" bulbs in mid-September to first weeks in October. Then plant most tulips, Dutch iris and other bulbs from mid-October to mid-November. If you want to put in all your spring-flowering bulbs at once, mid-October is the safest time.

For bigger, more beautiful blooms in successive years, remove seed pods as soon as the bulbs have finished blooming. If you let pods ripen, they may well steal strength from new bulbs, and you won't have the large, vigorous blooms you want.

Break off decaying blooms before the petals drop, because decaying blooms invite and encourage disease. *But don't remove the leaves in a hurry!* Wait until the leaves turn yellow, then cut them off about level with the earth.

For most rewarding results the following year, dig up the bulbs carefully after the leaves have yellowed thoroughly. Remove the tops and clean off the soil. Set the bulbs out, not touching one another, in a shaded, airy place. Later, when dried, store the bulbs in shallow boxes in a dry, cool place. Then plant in the fall, most any time before the ground freezes.

You'll have increasing beauty from your bulbs next year! But after three years, bulbs have produced about their maximum in size and beauty, and you'll probably wish to replace them. By then, they'll have paid their way many times over in the enjoyment they will have given you.

Tiptoe Through Exciting New Tulips!

Step from one thrilling new variety of tulip to another in your dramatic and colorful spring garden. Treat yourself to these and other exciting varieties, according to your personal taste:

Lily-flowered tulips will attract admiration with their long, slender, ladyfinger petals. Long, stiff stems in the newly developed varieties feature fantastic colors . . . mahogany-red velvety blooms with gleaming yellow edging . . . reddish-browns

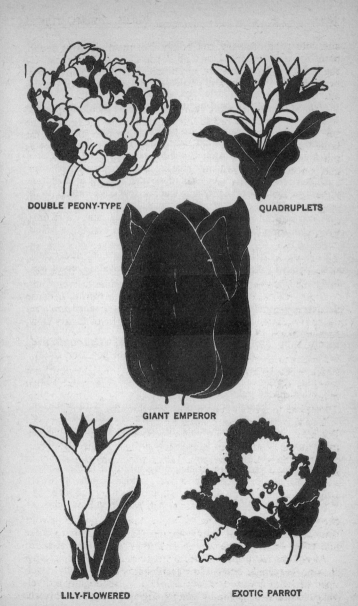

DOUBLE PEONY-TYPE

QUADRUPLETS

GIANT EMPEROR

LILY-FLOWERED

EXOTIC PARROT

Tulips are lovelier than ever.

and other unique, decorative shades . . . all yours for the planting.

Double-peony flowering tulips produce feathery-edged peony-like double blooms, rich and heavy. You can grow clear yellow flowers with scarlet-red striping, and other thrilling combinations. Many blooms of this species are delightfully fragrant too.

Vigorous Darwin varieties are now better than ever, growing to almost three feet in height, with large blooms that last and last, glorifying your garden for a long happy time. You can choose from almost as many shades as on an artist's palette!

Robust red emperor can be had now in species that bloom as early as the first of April, and even a few days before, with good luck. You'll enjoy flaming scarlet flowers as big as large coffee cups. And now you can also thrill to a new white emperor, featuring lovely pure white petals with a striking black center.

Keep up with the new species in your garden, and you'll greet spring in an aura of ever new "miracles" of color enchantment.

Quadruplet/Quintuplet Tulips!

Imagine seeing right in your own garden an exciting tall graceful tulip, growing two feet high or more, with four to five gorgeous blooms on one stem! Now you can get such multi-bloom tulips, each one a bouquet in itself when you place it in a vase on your table. There's a magnificent floral centerpiece to impress guests indoors!

With just ordinary fertilization, and with an extra watering with a good liquid plant food as an extra growth boost, these multibloom tulips will thrive beautifully. They'll produce extra clumps each year for you to separate and then multiply their stunning effect in your garden.

As the plants grow, they branch out about nine inches above the ground, and produce four to five glorious blooms in May. A variety of enchanting colors is available: satiny red, creamy white, red with yellow streaking, and sunny yellow with a contrasting red border.

Try some of this exciting new variety of tulips. What a joyous way to have quadruplets or possibly even quintuplets!

Ten-inch-wide Titanic Tulips!

You'll want your spring garden to feature at least a few of the exciting giant tulips which are now available from quality suppliers. These new species grow up to two feet tall, and measure as much as ten inches wide in bloom. They're thrilling showpieces for your garden. Some even have unique green-and-brown striped leaves.

The colors of these mammoth tulips are so radiant as to seem almost fluorescent in effect. They'll glow in your garden in blazing red, white, violet, pink and even in a rare sunny golden shade.

A good idea is to start with a few mammoth bulbs, as they're fairly costly, and add some each year, planting where you want bright splashes of spectacular color. Spray a few with a gibberellin product—and feed with extra water-soluble plant food —and you may well produce some phenomenal blooms such as no one in your area has ever seen before!

"Parrots" Bespeak Special Beauty

For flamboyant tropical beauty in your garden, bursting forth in late May, be sure to plant some of the modern, highly developed parrot tulips.

This exotic strain has been improved year by year so that now you can enjoy lush blooms with large petals fringed like multitinted feathers. These spectacular tulips actually resemble the plumage of flamboyant tropical birds, right in your garden, flaming in the spring sunshine.

Because of their exciting fringed blooms and spectacular colors, parrot tulips are particularly decorative as vase flowers too. You can grow many rich colors: rose pink with green markings and splashes . . . deep orange with a glistening yellow base.

Don't be without a few black parrots, exceptional glossy ebony fringed blooms, very large when grown at their best.

Plant and care for parrot tulips as instructed for other varieties, and they'll speak up for themselves each spring with their dazzling beauty!

Exotic Peacock Tulips

Just as a peacock proudly spreads its colorful tail feathers wide, this exciting variety of tulip opens its cups in widespread arcs which reveal their inner beauty with unusual effectiveness.

The interiors of modern peacock tulips display many variations of brilliant contrasting colors. An added feature is their unique, distinctly striped purple and brownish foliage.

Plant peacock tulips in front of taller flowers and shrubs, as they only grow from eight to eighteen inches tall. A long-lasting species, they'll strut and show their colorful feathers continuously in spring, all through the duration of other early- to late-flowering tulips.

"Drown" Your Tulips for Dramatic Blooms

It's difficult to emphasize too strongly how important water is to having exceptional tulips. Of course, good strong bulbs and healthful, fertile soil are vital too. But extra-heavy water-ing can work miracles!

So, as soon as buds appear, and as they open into bloom, water heavily. You'll be thrilled at your exhibit of the largest tulips around. Here's the secret: the heavy watering gorges the plant cells and forces the stem and flower to stretch to their fullest possible size!

In addition, the blubs grow larger and your radiant blooms will live longer. Yes, tulips love to drink and will reward you beautifully for drenching them.

Enjoy Crocuses by the Dozen

For fresh, lovely colors, plant the "heralds of spring" in batches of a dozen of each shade. Get the new larger varieties which will give you bigger splashes of white with blue stripes . . . golden yellow . . . deep purple . . . pure white.

So easy to grow, simply plant crocus bulbs about three inches deep and three inches apart. They require practically no care and will return for years, but for specially radiant response give them a growth boost with a complete modern water-soluble plant food.

With this little extra stimulant, as these lovely blooms pop above the ground with their fresh beauty, they'll herald a season of exceptional garden glory for you.

Go Daffy Over New Daffodils!

To get the greatest pleasure out of delightful daffodils (nar-cissi) that trumpet the beauty of spring with their colorful crimped nozzles and spreading petals, plant a great variety of sizes and shapes. Instead of just the lovely but commonplace yellow daffodil, you can now plant a thrilling range of new specimens, from three-inch-high midgets to giants eighteen inches long and half a foot wide!

For delirious daffodil beauty, far out of the ordinary, fol-low these few simple tips. In spite of what you may have heard, daffodils do respond to plenty of sunshine—within limitations. For the ideal, plant so they're a half day in sun, a half day shaded, and you'll get vigorous blooms that last longer.

Also, remember that daffodils always turn toward the sun, so plan accordingly when you plant, so the bed will enable them to face in the direction you want. Plant four inches deep in good, loose, fertile soil. Divide every two years.

Feed spring and fall with a complete balanced fertilizer, liquid or dry, and your daffodils will thrive beautifully and bloom twenty years or more.

The good news about modern daffodils is that you can now get a showpiece beauty that's almost perfect pink! It's a startling contrast to white trumpets especially, in your garden. And now you can plant bi-colored beauties with white or yellow petals and red trumpets . . . frilled orange centers with a gleaming white backdrop . . . double clustered centers against oyster white petals . . . tiny gems . . . or huge trumpets so robust you can almost hear them!

Thank modern selection and breeding for these new beauties that you can add to your old-fashioned favorites. Set them glowing for you among tulips, under trees, against evergreens, wherever you want fresh, cheery color in the spring.

How to Have Superfragrant Hyacinths

Mammoth species of hyacinths have now been developed which excel in color, beauty, size and fragrance! They'll produce large spikes of thickly clustered bell-like blossoms that flourish their glamorous colors and spread their exhilarating fragrance for weeks in your garden!

Be sure you get top-size Holland bulbs, plant in October, in rich, loose, well-drained soil, in places where they'll get half a day of sun. Cover with at least four inches of soil. Fertilize with a complete, balanced water-soluble plant food, for most magnificent response.

It's not necessary to dig up hyacinths, for they'll come back in their full glory regularly for six to seven years usually if you fertilize them well and give them a little care. Remove the flowers when they have faded each season but don't remove leaves until they've yellowed thoroughly.

Get a variety of colors, or concentrate on your favorite, for you can now choose from bright porcelain blue, pure white, rosy pink, lively yellows, carmine red, deep lavender, and other rich or subtle shades. The scent and sight of these gay blooms on their graceful spikes tell you doubly that "spring is here!"

Now . . . Gladiolus Magnificent Beyond Belief!

Modern growers have outdone themselves in producing new gladiolus so magnificent that you can hardly believe your eyes. But you will—when you see them flourishing in your own garden, with proper selection and care.

The new *double and dragon* gladiolus repesent a tremendous advance in this spectacular species. Varieties are being developed which are practically double-double—with as many as twelve petals on every flower—as double as a full-petaled rose! Imagine one flower after another like this, clustered on the stalk so thickly that you think they're too crowded to even open.

These double dragons have, on the reverse of the petals, small spurs, like horns, which produce an exotic nubby look that adds exquisite form and texture to the already beautiful florets. New varieties are available to you in gleaming alabaster white, deep orchid, and glistening yellow with a dramatic splash of red. New garden thrills for you indeed!

Amazing Skyscraper Varieties

Imagine gigantic gladiolus blooming in your own garden actually man-high in size—five to six feet tall. This floral miracle is possible now when you plant the giant queens that have been developed for you.

These garden wonders have flowering heads up to a yard long—as many as two dozen flowers on a single stem, each blooming the size of a saucer, up to eight inches wide, plants growing up to three inches in a single day. Plant and tend them properly, and they're all yours.

Dainty Miniature Beauties

Like large or small diamonds, you can have both huge and small jewels of gladiolus in your garden. You can grow an exquisite small variety with florets about three inches wide . . . about twenty buds opening ten at a time . . . on graceful flowerheads about two feet long . . . on a vigorously erect plant three to four feet high.

Colors are beautiful—including a remarkably attractive clear rose-red, with charming heavy ruffles. If you wish, you may display a graduated stand, from miniature to medium size to giant skyscraper varieties—a variegated wall of flowering glory!

Planting Glads for Best Results

Space your glads at least six inches or more apart, depending on the size of the variety you're planting. Work the soil well and deeply. Set each corm in with the pointed end up. Cover the corms with at least four inches of medium to heavy soil, or six to eight inches if you have light, sandy soil.

It's important to plant gladiolus this deep because the high stalks need plenty of underground support. Plant for full sun. Water plentifully.

Apply liquid plant food or dry fertilizer upon planting, and several times during season, especially after the plants have finished blooming. Fertilization then helps develop the new corm forming on top of the old one that has produced the blooms.

After plants are established, cultivate the soil lightly to remove weeds. An extra, helpful modern measure is the application then of a pre-emergence weed killer.

Time your plantings so that you set in new corms in the spring at two week intervals. They'll bloom seventy to ninety days later, in a succession of glorious flowers over a long period.

From the time plants are about six inches high, it pays to spray with DDT at least every two weeks.

For outdoors beauty, remove flower spikes after they've passed their full blooming; cut with a sharp knife low on the stem, so that the graceful foliage will be unmarred. For indoors decoration, wait until all the flowers are open, then cut early in the morning, for longer-lasting pleasure in the vase.

Proper Care of Corms

About two months after your blooms have faded, and before severe frost, dig up the corms for preservation over the winter. Handle these delicate "hearts" very carefully.

Cut off the old stems with a sharp knife, close to the corms. Remove the old, withered corms out from under the new ones, and discard. It's wise to sort out the corms by sizing, marking them clearly for color.

Place the corms in paper or plastic bags, sprinkling well with a 5 per cent DDT dust for protection against insects—leaving the dust right in the bag. Then put the bags away in a dry place where the temperature doesn't go much below 70°. When the soil warms up, start replanting.

Special Tips for Gladiolus

Just about everything you need to know about gladiolus is covered in the preceding. But here are some extra helpful hints which you can apply if you have the time and interest:

You can double the number of favorite glads you grow, by halving the larger corms. Remove the papery husk so you can see the buds on the corm. Then slice the corm in half, leaving a bud on each half. Sprinkle with sulfur dust for protection and to promote hardiness. Plant each half as though it were a full corm.

Boost ordinary corms into giant growth by cutting out all the side buds and leaving just the one single top bud. All the vigor will pile into that bud, producing a much bigger plant and blooms. Scoop out the side buds by slipping the knife under in a shallow cut.

For extra-fast and extra-large growth, soak the corms for a few hours in water-soluble plant food before planting. Try it with a few corms and compare the growth with others left untreated.

To help keep moisture in soil, and keep down weeds, some modern gardeners lay strips of aluminum foil between rows of gladiolus. They report greater ease in tending the plants, reducing both watering and weeding. Other experts apply a sawdust mulch immediately after planting.

Try the new varieties, plant and tend them properly, and when you see the extraordinary flowering beauty in your garden from exceptional gladiolus—you'll be glad you did!

How to Grow Irresistible Iris

Here's a beautiful bloom that comes in so many dazzling colors that you can think in terms of choosing a whole palette of scintillating shades. Then consider the gorgeous floral heads as paint brushes, to create an enchanting mural of living beauty about your home.

Irresistible iris has exceptional appeal in color, variety of shapes—and the great "plus" of dependability and easy growing. You can enjoy all kinds of iris, from dwarf plants hardly bigger than your outstretched hand, to supergiant new varieties rising almost high as a pretty young woman, and with exquisitely formed heads up to half a foot wide!

Fall is the best time to put in iris, but you can also plant in midsummer, since some varieties bloom not only in spring, but also provide a double feature by bursting into flower in late summer. Choose carefully the variety you want—for height, shape and color.

Best way to judge the color you'd like best, since the shadings are so variegated, is to actually see a specimen in bloom, if that's possible. If not, take a chance—every iris color is so lovely that it's bound to please you to some degree anyhow.

Suggestions for growing the most spectacular iris are fairly simple—the *extra* care will make the difference between ordinary or showplace blooms. Here are your tips on iris:

How to Plant for Best Results

Prepare the earth to a depth of about a foot, using good loose soil, and mixing in modern, improved peat moss and plant food. Dig the hole wide enough so you won't crowd the roots. Fill in the soil practically to the top, then lay in the rhizome and spread out the roots a little lower in the earth. Now cover the rhizome so it's just below the surface, not more than an inch down, with the fan facing high and to the front.

Depending on the space you have, and the arrangement you plan for your garden, place the plantings anywhere from eight inches to two feet apart for most varieties—leaving room for growth. Water in well, but don't drown the new plantings. Firm the soil sensibly over the rhizome.

Iris is very hardy and will grow with little extra care. The species responds well to periodic boosters with a complete water-soluble plant food, but doesn't need as much fertilization as most other plants. For best results, plant for full sunshine.

General Care of Iris

When new shoots appear in the spring, clean off the old foliage carefully to help the plant grow vigorously and help prevent disease. Press down with your fingers to make sure that the plant is firmly in the ground, as sometimes wintering tends to heave up the rhizome.

Fertilize well, preferably with a complete water-soluble plant food, for a faster, vigorous boost, or circle the plant with dry plant food if you prefer.

Heavy watering when the plants are bursting into bloom will make the flowers bigger and more flourishing, filling them out in effect. Remove faded flowers to keep them from going to seed, and for your garden's clean good looks.

The tall varieties may need staking. If so, insert stakes carefully into the ground, in order not to injure the roots.

A Measure of Protection

While the iris is very hardy, it's subject to attack by borers. A very quick and easy protection is to apply DDT or rotenone soon after growth begins. Repeat application about once a week until the plants bloom, and harmful borers won't develop.

Why take a chance on ruining your glamorous plants, when modern protection is so easy?

Separate for Magnificent Blooms

For spectacular plants and flowers, you'd better separate iris clumps every three or four years. You'll enjoy more of your beauties, too. It's quite easy, and scientific fun.

Dig up clumps in the fall preferably, with gentle care. Cut back the foliage to form fans about eight inches high. When the clumps are up, clean off soil with a hose; don't let the rhizomes or roots go dry at any point. If rhizomes are large, separate into single or double fans (three or four fans if small). Cut separations with a sharp knife or razor tool, leaving a portion of rhizome and roots on each fan.

Throw away the original rhizome, and any that seem weak or defective in any way. Replant as instructed for regular planting. You've multiplied your iris treasures, and you'll have increasingly beautiful specimens!

Guide to Varieties

There are too many varieties of iris to list with any helpful clarity for you. There are dwarfs that bloom in April, then Siberian and bearded iris flower in May and June, Japanese iris bloom in July, and some varieties repeat in late summer and early fall.

Buy from a reliable grower. Seek out some of the new species which are extra-resistant to the rigors of hot sun, drought or too heavy rain and cold winds.

Your best guide is to choose the shapes, colors and sizes that you personally like best, depending also on where you'll plant the iris—such as dwarf varieties for a rock garden—tall miracle species for a spectacular garden background.

Probably your widest choice is in the popular bearded iris varieties, and there are multitudes of them to enjoy, including new versions for you to discover, such as the exciting deep pinks that many growers rave about.

The Happy Horned Iris

A fairly new and distinctive variety is the showy horned iris —a tall bearded species in which the beards project straight out like horns. You'll probably want at least a few of these exotic beauties about your home.

The Joyous Japanese Iris

If you want special admiration from visitors, the Japanese iris is unique enough to win rapturous praise. The blooms are large, the colors are striking and sensational, but mostly, the shape is distinctive—with flattened-out petals that seem to drift in the atmosphere like fantastic, light, artistically tinted discs.

The blooms grow from four inches across to magnificent specimens almost a foot wide! If you want to produce such mammoth showpieces, give them extra care and fertilization, lots of sun, and especially *loads of water* before and during the blooming time.

Another tip to help you have extraordinary plants and blooms, is to apply a booster once or twice a season with an excellent water-soluble plant food made especially for acid-loving plants. Japanese iris seem to love this feeding, and spread their astounding single or double blooms to prove it.

You'll be glad you planted at least a few specimens of this unique variety. The blooms stretch from three to six weeks, from early May along toward late July. The flowering stems are straight and formal, reaching three to four feet tall, and surrounded by delicate foliage that is grasslike in structure. Plant, protect and divide like other iris.

No matter what other flowers you have in your garden, you'll find that as you walk around on your "admiration stroll" each early evening, you'll get more than the average eyeful of pleasure from the irresistible iris, in all its exquisite varieties.

Pointers for Peony Perfection

Scratch a peony enthusiast and then run—lest you be overwhelmed by the flood of praise about his favorite plant! And you can't much blame him, because this magnificent variety provides a rare combination of big, spectacular flowers, delightful fragrance, glorious range of colors, exquisite foliage through the growing season, fairly easy care, and many many years of life.

Well cared for peonies are thriving beautifully ten to fifteen or more years after being planted. You should certainly have some peonies in your garden, and also one or more specimens of the breathtaking modern tree peonies.

Follow these tips and you too will probably go raving glad over your gorgeous blooms:

1. Planting. This is the vital step where many people fail by improper handling, and blame anything but their own mistake. *Never plant peonies any deeper than one to two inches below the surface.* Don't plant any clumps with less than three eyes or they'll take too long to grow into sizable, blooming plants. Face the eyes upwards, and with no more than two inches of soil above the eyes, or they may not bloom at all.

2. Where to plant. Because you want big, lusty, showpiece specimens, plant where peonies will get plenty of sun, with no chance of eventually being shaded by trees. Also, peonies require plenty of soil nutrients, so don't plant where tree roots or other large growth will interfere. Plant about four feet apart, preferably in fall when results are usually far more satisfactory than from planting in the spring. At least for the first winter, mulch lightly with straw, then remove the mulch in the spring.

3. Preparing the soil. Dig a hole large enough so you won't crowd the root when planting. Mix leafmold and a complete 5-10-5 fertilizer with loose soil. Don't use any fresh manure, which injures peonies. Prepare the soil to a depth of eighteen inches, since peony roots like to go down deep. Fill with the prepared soil almost to the top, since the top of the eye should only be an inch or two from the soil surface. As an extra precaution, before planting, firm the bottom of the hole with a flat tool or with your foot, to make sure the eyes don't go down below the two inches.

4. Protect against fungus blight. Although peonies are a very hardy plant, they're often afflicted by fungus blight, the most common one called botrytis. This causes buds to turn black, wither, and fail to bloom. Take modern scientific measures against this. As soon as your plants are a few inches high, spray with captan, Bordeaux mixture or ferbam. Apply at ten-day intervals, until your beautiful peonies burst into bloom.

If ants invade your plants, dust a light ring of chlordane under the spreading foliage, on the earth. Repeat as often as may be necessary (unless the ant invasion doesn't occur at all). The ants don't actually harm the blossoms, but they're undesirable tenants from the viewpoint of clean good looks.

5. Proper fertilization and watering. In addition to fertilizing when planting, your peonies will respond well to good fertilization soon after new shoots are 10 inches high—particularly feeding with a complete water-soluble plant food. Repeat the nutrition boost after the blooms have faded, to give extra vigor to the plants. And water *deeply* whenever plants show signs of wilting during dry spells.

6. *For spectacular blooms.* If you want prize-winning types of specimen blooms, remove side buds from stems, channeling growing power into the big terminal buds. However, if you're interested primarily in a glorious showing for your own pleasure, don't trim off any buds. Let the plant dazzle you and your friends with many showy blooms!

Remove blooms after they've faded, so they don't go to seed. When you cut flowers for indoor beauty, leave at least two bottom leaves on the stem remaining on the plant. Cut flowers judiciously so as not to denude the plant. They'll last longer indoors if you place the flowers in a basin of water alongside the plant immediately upon cutting.

Stake your peonies if necessary, if the heavy blooms and foliage cause the lush plants to bend over. Use rings and ties that won't cut into stems. Handle gently, of course.

7. *Choosing best varieties.* Get your peonies from reputable suppliers, because they're going to adorn your home for many years. That's why they're worth the extra care suggested in planting, too—they're a long-term investment in tremendous pleasure. You can now get marvelous single and double types in white and lovely shades of pink and red.

Follow these basic tips and you'll enjoy enthralling peony perfection!

Exceptional Thrill . . . Tree Peonies!

One of the most exciting of all garden treasures is the tree peony at its best, an enchanting ornamental bush. It will light up your landscaping with its sensational color glory. And it's an easy bush to grow.

Take care in planting the root so that the graft union is two to four inches below the surface of the soil—no more. Otherwise prepare the soil, fertilize and spray like regular peonies.

However, never cut back any of the woody branches on your tree peonies. Remove the faded flowers. Each year your bushes will grow larger and more spectacular, reaching a maximum height of about four feet tall, then spreading richly and gracefully.

Starting with fine roots, and tending properly, you'll have marvelous big blooms, measuring up to eight inches across, showing their lovely reds, whites, pink or maroon against deep green foliage. Extraordinary new varieties are now available, imported from Asia.

Here's enchanting beauty almost beyond belief—and it's all yours for year after year, as an alert gardener!

Now—Miniature to Mammoth Dahlias for You

While you want to have the fun of growing mammoth dahlias with blooms that measure up to a foot in diameter, you can also enrich your garden with smaller sizes of this colorful favorite. And they'll glorify your home indoors as well, for good dahlias last for many days and even for weeks when cut. Here are a few beauties to look for:

Perky Pompom Dahlias

Plant masses of these dainty pompom, button-size dahlias for armfuls of blooms—each about 1½ inches in size. Mix bright pinks, reds, lavenders, ambers and white. Just fertilize well and water heavily, and they'll keep blooming week after week for you.

Medium Cut-flower Dahlias

Especially if you love dahlias indoors, as well as big splashes of color in your garden, put in plenty of the medium tubers that produce excellent cut flowers. Each plant will give you *hundreds* of blooms each season, for the more you cut, the more they bloom!

Cut these strong dahlias in the cool of the day, when flowers are at full maturity; set immediately into fresh, luke-warm water, and they'll last as long as two weeks, radiating their bright beauty for you.

Exotic Cactus Dahlias

This lovely variety was developed for exceptional "oohs" and "ahhhs," it would seem, because they evoke surprised admiration in your garden or in a vase. Petals are thin and grace-ful, spreading out in a five to six inch airy circle.

They're among the brightest and best of dahlias—now in sunkist orange, deep pink, flaming red, delicate peach and a pastel yellow that's almost chartreuse. They're something new to many people and thus a rich centerpiece becomes a con-versation piece!

No wonder these cactus dahlias are "dahlings" of many gardeners. Pardon, please.

Grow Dahlias Big as Dinner Plates!

Dahlias are the delight of many gardeners because they can be the showpieces of the garden when grown properly—featuring incredible blooms actually as big as dinner plates, up to 12 inches in diameter! You can grow prize-winning beauties of deep orange-red with white tips, gleaming cyclamen-pinks, glowing yellows, rich lavenders, blazing reds.

If you want huge "miracle" blooms that will have your neighbors gasping and gaping with admiration, follow these steps:

1. Start with top-size, firm, plump, healthy tubers, of course. Don't accept little types, or any that may be shriveled or with any sign of rot, if you want giant blooms. Certainly there are many exquisite smaller varieties, but right now you're aiming for mammoth masterpieces.

2. Check that soil with a test, if it hasn't been done recently. Dahlias prefer a slightly acid soil (to be technical, about 6.5 pH). Application of a little limestone will often help here. Pick a spot with rich, loose, well drained soil, with plenty of sunshine. Fertilize the soil with a 5-10-10 dry plant food, or good liquid plant food upon planting.

3. Plant tuber or plants in late May or first of June. Mix a few handfuls of modern activated peat moss with the planting soil. Water thoroughly right after planting, and frequently thereafter in dry season. Dahlias thrive better with plenty of soaking.

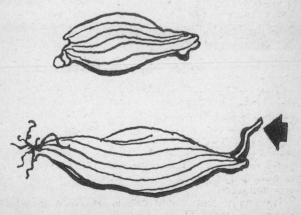

TOP, wrong—Dahlia tuber cut off without any stem.
BELOW, correct—portion of stem left on (at arrow).

4. For huge size, pinching and disbudding are very important. After the growth has developed about three pairs of leaves, pinch out the centers of the plants. Your plants will branch better and grow more sturdily.

5. Start your preventive spraying program when your plants are thriving, and repeat weekly, using a 6 per cent chlordane dust or DDT. You'll be sure of more perfect blooms.

6. Fertilize plentifully, with a good water-soluble plant food, or repeat with the 5-10-10 dry fertilizer—a couple of handfuls ringing the plant about a foot away from the stalk. About mid-July, a mulch of peat moss or straw between the plants will help greatly, as you water heavily every few days.

7. Apply more fertilizer every two weeks, liquid or dry, right on top of the mulch. Support the vigorously sprouting plant with a stake, tying loosely with soft material—never hard or tight. You can practically see the plant's "muscles" developing!

8. Now for vital disbudding. Don't remove the single big terminal buds, but take off all the small side buds and sprouts, leaving only one bud per cane—much as it hurts you to toss away the other tender buds.

Keep watering plentifully, and take a look each day as the flower spreads into astounding, breathtaking bloom—yes, big as a dinner plate, and more beautiful than any dinner plate you ever saw.

You'd better take snapshots of these magnificent showpieces, or no one will believe you when you tell about them around the fireplace next winter!

How to Store Dahlia Tubers for Multiplied Beauty

Those dazzling dahlias you enjoy in summer can multiply their beauty in your garden many times over, but only if you treat them right. Each plant will give you a number of extra tubers, and they'll be showpieces too, if you care for them the best way. It's a process that's interesting, pleasant and productive:

1. Like many people, dahlia tubers hate the cold, so you'd better get them up and out before the ground freezes. But don't just dig them out, put them on a shelf and then replant. First, after the first frost, cut off each plant about a foot above the ground, and get rid of the foliage. Wait another week, which gives the tubers time to ripen well.

2. It's time for exercise. Dig up the tubers with a strong pitchfork—but with extreme care. Since tubers grow out, sort of like spokes from a wheel hub, start digging almost a foot

away from the stalk, all around, then get the fork under and lift out the clump. Handle gently. Turn the clump over and let dry for a few hours, then shake off the soil.

3. Soon after they're out of the ground and free of soil, take a sharp knife or long-handled razor blade, and cut each tuber off the main stem, *leaving a small portion of stem on each tuber*. The stem is essential in forming the new bud.

4. Separate the tubers by variety, marking them with tags or crayon, or according to your own system. Store each type in a different box or tray, as an identification aid, if you wish. Spread out the tubers so they don't touch each other, and in a place where they'll be kept warm for three weeks, in temperatures as high as 80° to 85° for best results. Sprinkle with water lightly every few days and turn them over gently each time.

5. Your prized tubers are now ready for their warm winter nap. Wrap each tuber in paper, even newspaper will do—or in new plastic material—and place in shallow trays, with plenty of room for each. Or, set them loosely in a deep carton, but separate each layer with a mixture of two-thirds dry peat moss and one-third fine sand. Cover the trays or cartons, and store in a dry place where the temperature stays about 50°, more or less.

7. When spring comes, plant all the tubers you have room for, and give or exchange the others with other gardeners. You'll be glad that you took such care, because the beautiful plants and blooms will multiply the gardening enjoyment of your friends and yourself many times over.

New Disease-resistant Lilies

Often flattered as "the Queens of the Garden," lilies have declined in popularity somewhat through the years because of their susceptibility to disease. But they're starting to boom again as science has conquered that failing to a great degree in two ways:

Now, when you buy lily bulbs, seek out the new varieties, which are listed as *disease-free* or, more logically, disease-resistant (because there can hardly be a plant so perfect and hardy that some disease can't attack and injure it!). These better varieties are astonishingly vigorous, and flourish beautifully, rarely marred by disease of foliage or flower.

Secondly, with the new sprays and dusts perfected to counteract infestation by disease and insects, you can usually protect your plants and drive away invaders at the very first indication of attack.

Special Growing Tip

We've had particular success in our garden with lilies by feeding them frequently with a 15-30-15 water-soluble plant food, producing such vigorous, healthy plants that they showed no evidence of disease.

It's of specific interest to note our results as compared with other gardeners who didn't use the miracle liquid plant food. We shared a batch of bulbs with two friends when they arrived from an acquaintance in the State of Washington.

In the two other gardens, the lilies grew three to four feet tall, decorative but not spectacular. In our garden, the same bulbs produced magnificent plants that shot up over six feet tall (we have a snapshot of the plants towering above my wife, to prove it) and produced eighteen gigantic, magnificent blooms from one bulb—miracle results indeed!

Such results can be yours too—just by selecting special disease-resistant species, and giving them a little special care.

Stop Lily Root Rot!

When your magnificent lilies start to wither and wilt, showing the effects of root rot, use a wonder chemical to overcome the disease quickly and safely. Remarkable results are reported by state agricultural scientists after extensive tests.

The miraculous ingredient to get is *oxy-quinoline sulfate*. Be sure to get the chemical in a pure quality state, which will produce a bright yellow solution, not murky or cloudy or off color.

Usual mixture to overcome the common "rhizoctonia" root rot is ⅓ teaspoonful to each gallon of water. Apply so that the roots are drenched thoroughly.

In a short time, even badly infected plants throw off the rot, grow vigorous new roots and produce beautiful foliage and blooms.

A Light Tip on Tuberous Begonias

Tuberous begonia blossoms are beauties, but they can cause you heartache in drab blooms, or none at all, unless you're careful to *avoid heavy shade!*

You may think you're giving the plants enough sunlight, but if hedges or high plantings nearby, or the wall of a garage or other building cut off enough light to cut down length of day as much as an hour you'll not get the miracle results that are the gardener's delight.

The *double* caution to keep in mind is that tuberous begonias are sensitive to both the *strength* and *length* of light.

For best results, pick a place where these gorgeous but temperamental plants have full sun until about 9 A.M., then light, filtered shade until 4 or 5 P.M., then full sun until sunset. You may be branded as a begonia clock watcher, but you'll be praised as a master gardener when you show off the magnificent blooms well into August.

Quick Moisture Miracle for Tuberous Begonias

Here's a quick, neat and simple trick to help you get remarkable results with tuberous begonias. It's based on the fact that these exotic beauties like plenty of moisture *in the air* . . . they're constantly hungry for humidity, unlike you and me.

In addition to making sure there's plenty of moisture in the soil, give them a light *overhead* sprinkling every few days, and wet down the grass or paths *near* the begonias. This "moisture in the air" often promotes marvelous extra growth!

Sparkling Velvety Red Sensation— Sprekelia

A specially colorful floral gem you'll enjoy is the Sprekelia, grown from a bulb, indoors or out, producing glorious velvety scarlet blooms every spring. The relatively unique Sprekelia will win lots of compliments for its unusually rich color and delicacy of bloom.

Important tip is to plant the bulb so that the neck is *not* covered, but projects above the soil an inch or two. Feed with a good water-soluble fertilizer. See that it gets some sun daily, Exquisite Sprekelia requires little other care, except for watering that will keep the soil reasonably moist but not soggy.

Outdoors, plant Sprekelia bulbs in front of the flower bed, as the flowers are short stemmed and will reveal their exotic beauty best out there. Except in very warm areas, dig up the bulbs in fall and store them over the winter like gladiolus bulbs.

Indoors, choose a container a little larger than the bulb. Place a layer of up to an inch of sand or gravel at the bottom. Set in the bulb and add a porous soil, remembering to leave the neck exposed.

Another beautiful specimen for your garden of floral masterpieces!

A Surprise Miracle!

You and your family will get an amusing thrill out of Lycoris (also known as the hardy pink Amaryllis) in your garden. This beautiful comedian is sometimes called the "surprise lily" or "magic lily." Here's how to help Lycoris put on his act best:

Plant bulbs in late August or early September, or you can even get good results by waiting to plant until early spring. Use a rich soil, keeping the bulb tops about four inches deep. Fertilize and water well, then await delightful results.

Your plants will produce foliage of ribbonlike leaves which disappears by summer. But then—surprise!—in late summer, colorful rosy-lilac blossoms of this "mystery lily" pop out *without a sign of foliage.* Each stalk is topped with up to a dozen florets. The stalks grow as much as seven inches a day, and the beautiful blooms last about a week, either in your garden, or as lovely cut flowers.

The sight of the bursting blooms beaming atop the high

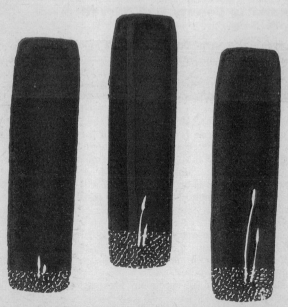

See the amusing "surprise lily" spring up high.

bare stalks, sometimes as high as 25 inches, causes much amused comment, and will fulfill its place in the garden as an unusual conversation piece.

"Hole-in-one" Bulb Planter

If you're a golfer, you'll get your greatest thrill from a "hole-in-one" drive—from golf club to hole in one shot. As a gardener, you can get a lot of help from an ingenious little gadget that's a "hole-in-one" bulb planter.

This tool looks like a metal cup with a handle on top of it. Here's how it works. Just push the "cup" into the soil where you want to plant a bulb. Twist the tool a little, then pull up.

You'll find a clear flat-bottomed hole, just right for setting in a bulb. You can control how deeply you go down by how far you push the planting tool. Use it for other plantings too that have a limited root area.

Push-pull-plant . . . it's as easy as that with this simple little wonder-worker. Like the good old safety pin, the least complicated inventions are frequently the most useful.

From first sight to tall full bloom in 8 days.

Quick Tips on Storing Bulbs and Tubers

Identify with grease pencil. If you find that tying labels on bulbs and tubers is tedious work, just grab a black or dark red grease pencil and print the color right on the tuber or bulb . . . if it offers a large enough surface.

Use household plastic bags . . . just as you store foods in the freezer or refrigerator. Put the bulbs in an ordinary household plastic bag, tie the top with the same wire or plastic strips you usually use. The plastic holds moisture in, and you can look through to see how your bulbs are holding up. If they're growing any mold from too much moisture, punch holes in the bag to let in more air.

"Season" with DDT. To help protect gladiolus bulbs from common insects, sprinkle on DDT powder when storing—like you'd season with salt. With bulbs that are stored moist, sprinkle on a fungicide powder first, as extra protection.

Use a good storing product rather than shredded paper or such. A fairly coarse sand, or vermiculite, or sphagnum moss, for example, are excellent and not costly—and they hold moisture much better.

VEGETABLES

How to Grow "Miracle" Vegetables

You've never really tasted a wondrous salad bowl until you've munched on greens grown in your own garden! There's no flavor as fresh and luscious and satisfying as the delicious taste of vegetables you've picked a few minutes before cooking. Never such thrills of pride as when guests rave about the zesty sweetness of delectable vegetables you've grown yourself.

But vegetable gardening involves work and care. If you're not willing to apply yourself week after week, with little let-up, you'd better buy your vegetables at the nearest store or roadside stand. If you're ready to work for the super enjoyment of home-grown greens, here are some general tips that will help you produce vegetables at their best:

Fertilize and prepare the soil in the same way as suggested for flower gardens in this book. Make sure your soil is rich and freely aerated.

Check the drainage by testing with a soaking of water in one spot, to make sure the liquid is absorbed quickly and doesn't puddle, because most vegetables won't produce in volume in soils that stay overwet.

Fertilize *heavily* with a good dry fertilizer for vegetables, applying half when digging up the earth, and the other half on top. Or, you'll get even greater size and production with repeated application of a modern water-soluble plant food, complete with potent trace minerals.

Guard against insects and disease with the "miracle" dusts and sprays described elsewhere in these pages, heeding the warnings not to dust for a period before harvesting. A general methoxychlor-malathion-captan dust is practically a "must" to help produce unflawed vegetables.

Buy top-quality seeds that are pretreated against rot and damping-off (look for the marking on the package). Choose varieties that thrive best in *your* area.

Start planting early, as soon as the danger of cold weather is past. As your crops finish, replant with the same or different varieties, according to season, and you'll keep your table heaped with successive harvestings of delicious vegetables right up until cold weather returns.

Store the late vegetables in your freezer for taste treats all winter.

To grow vegetable giants, have some special fun spraying a *gibberellin* product on a few plants of different varieties —but not on lettuce, which tends to shoot up like celery under the influence of this amazing stimulant. Try it on some corn, for example, even if you have to pick the robust ears off a mammoth plant from a stepladder!

There's a deep thrill of accomplishment in seeing the results of your labor grow, and then harvesting choice vegetables for the enthusiastic enjoyment of your family, and yourself. Start with a small vegetable patch the first season, then decide for yourself whether to spread out or not.

If you pile too much work on yourself, parts of your vegetable garden will necessarily be neglected and fall behind. But begin sensibly and small, and you'll find that you have wonderful vegetables, instead of the vegetables having you!

6 Steps to Miracle Tomatoes

Mmm, when you bite into a juicy tomato plucked fresh from your own plants, or lay out the moist, gleaming, rich-red slices on a dish for your appreciative family and guests, you'll feel more than rewarded for applying a little extra care and know-how to growing exceptional tomatoes. These steps will lead to gratifying results:

1. Begin by selecting strong, sturdy young plants of varieties that are specially suited to your area. Wrap a small paper cylinder around the stem a little above and below the point where it emerges from the ground; this bars cutworms. Set the plants deep, this helps extra roots to develop along the

stem below the ground. After you fill in the soil, apply two measuring cups full of liquid plant food. This will provide a quick start for the hungry young plant.

2. As the plant begins to grow, set a five- or six-foot stake in the ground gently alongside each plant. It's best to tie the plant loosely to the stake as it grows. This is important: as small, leafy side shoots appear, pinch them off, thus training each plant to one strong stem. But be careful not to remove blossom spurs.

3. About three weeks after planting, apply liquid plant food again to foliage and soil. This will help maintain and promote vigorous growth.

4. After the feeding, cultivate to loosen the soil around the plant, and carefully remove all weeds in this area particularly.

5. Then spread a mulch (grass clippings are good) on the soil around the plants and between them. The function here is to hold moisture in the soil for the plants; it also helps to prevent blossom-end rot. Spray the plants thoroughly with a good fungicide to help prevent blight and leafspot.

6. As a vital extra boost, spray the first blossom clusters on each plant with a fruit-set hormone, directing the mist right down into the open blossom. This will keep the blossoms from dropping in the event that the weather suddenly turns cold, so it actually saves the first fruit in many cases.

In a short time, you'll be picking luscious, firm, super-satisfying "miracle" tomatoes, often weeks before your neighbors. Try new hybrid high-producing varieties, improved strains extra-high in vitamin C, also cherry, pear and plum types.

Please pass the salt!

Fruit-setting Hormones Multiply Tomato Yields

Here's what I've seen happen in controlled tests of tomatoes. One plant bearing four tomatoes. Another plant next to it, of the same variety, grown in the same kind of soil—*but where the tomato flowers were treated with a fruit-setting hormone* —bearing 28 tomatoes by actual count, bigger and tastier tomatoes!

Miracles indeed. While results aren't always as extraordinary as these, you can increase your yields of tomatoes double and triple the usual with proper usage of some of the new "miracle" fruit-setting hormone products.

Easy to Use

Easiest way to use these wonder-workers is in liquid form, diluted with water, or, even more convenient and speedy, you can now buy aerosol cans which are more costly but even easier to handle.

Follow the instructions on the product you buy. Be sure you direct the spray right into the face of the tomato flower, and not on the back of it. Don't spray on too much or you may get some faulty fruit—but with reasonable care, you'll be thrilled with your improved results.

Beat the Regular Season

You'll miss out on many benefits if you don't use this fruit-setting hormone miracle on your tomatoes. With proper application when the flowers appear on the plants, you'll find that you pick ripe, red, juicy tomatoes—all rosy and ready for eating—weeks ahead of the usual time!

And the tomatoes will be not only far more abundant, but also bigger and of better quality—apparent in the meaty, luscious slices or chunks in your salad bowl.

Conduct Your Own Experiments

As a garden "scientist," to have more fun out of experimenting and proving that garden miracles really do happen, I suggest that you leave one tomato plant untreated, and see the difference in tomato production and quality for yourself. You'll be convinced that using a fruit-setting hormone spray is worth many times more than the cost and the extra effort.

Please remember, however, that the hormone spray is not a substitute for healthy plants, good soil and proper fertilization. All these elements work *together* for the exceptional results you want.

I happen to be writing these lines on a typewriter set atop a table in my back yard. Alongside the machine is a small bowl with several just-picked garden tomatoes gleaming invitingly in the sun. After the last paragraph, I reached over for one of the shiny red tomatoes and bit into the juicy meat. As I "feel" the energizing and delicious vitamins racing through my system, I give thanks again to nature and science for these "miracles" of health and pleasure from our garden.

New Disease-resistant Tomato

When you plant tomatoes, get some of the marvelous new *Manalucie* variety. In many nursery tests, this vigorous newcomer survived disease where many other common varieties succumbed.

While the Manalucie won't conquer all disease, it will thrive under very tough infestation conditions. And, if you spray with a good modern fungicide—as you should—you'll enjoy more firm, delicious tomatoes from your plants than with many of the weaker varieties—with amazingly little loss.

Let Us Have the Best Lettuce

One of the most rewarding and enjoyable vegetables is luscious lettuce that will fill your salad bowl with fresh flavor and health month after month. Since lettuce loses flavor rapidly after it's picked, it's a particularly gratifying crop because you can pop out into the garden, pick it, wash it, and be eating it in minutes after deliverance green and juicy from the soil.

For top enjoyment, select and plant the types that suit your personal taste best—tight-headed, loose-leaf, or others that make your taste buds tingle. Plant in fertile soil with plenty of sun.

Of prime importance, *water plentifully*. You just can't grow top-quality lettuce without lots of moisture! Dust weekly with a general complete methoxychlor-malathion-captan dust (but not within ten days of picking).

If you want specially huge, rich green heads, apply a complete liquid plant food every few weeks.

To assure the delicious tender leaves you want, don't let plants go to seed, but replant successively every three to four weeks, starting several weeks before usual date of last frost, until a little over a month before usual first winter frost.

You'll bowl guests over with your own just-picked salad bowls of lettuce at its very best.

A Bonus Miracle . . . Second Crop of Lettuce

There's no salad like the salad made from crisp, delicious lettuce fresh out of your garden. So, by the time September comes around, you're saddened that your garden lettuce is all gone. But, instead of sighing, sow and you shall reap!

Yes, even in early or mid-August, you can plant more

lettuce and get a good crop before frost. Some people claim that this fall garden lettuce is even better than the spring and summer growth. That's because the lettuce gets a good start during warm August days, and then as the days and nights cool in September, the leaves develop more crisply.

So, here's your tip: plant a new crop of lettuce in early or mid-September, after your earlier crops are gone. Fertilize again; another application of concentrated water-soluble plant food is very effective. *Make sure to water well,* as plenty of moisture is a must in order to grow healthy, quality heads of lettuce.

If you see any sign of yellowing, water heavily, and also apply a good complete commercial garden dust. (But don't use the dust up to two weeks before the lettuce is to be picked and eaten and, even then, wash the lettuce thoroughly; do that always for cleanliness and protection.)

Mmm, can't you just hear the crisp crackle of your fall lettuce salad between your teeth, and taste the miracle of fresh, juicy flavor? There are few gastronomic joys to beat that!

Roquette—A Minor Salad Miracle

Dining in a very fine restaurant in New Jersey, I raved to the waiter about the delicious salad bowl, distinguished by the unique tantalizing flavor of the greens. When I asked him for the secret, he fetched the proud chef from the kitchen.

The chef, in turn, led me to a small garden behind the restaurant. There he plucked a few leaves from a growing plant and handed them to me, ordering "Taste!" He watched me chew enthusiastically as I savored their piquant mustard-y flavor. In a heavy European accent, he managed to spell out the name of the plant: "r-o-q-u-e-t-t-e."

A Discovery for You

A few leaves of roquette, mixed in a salad with crisp, fresh lettuce, lend it a special tangy flavor that you can't ever get with lettuce alone. If you and your guests have gourmet tastes, roquette grown in your garden will augment your reputation as a cook and prove a real conversation piece.

However, if anyone doesn't like odd and unusual tastes, better serve the roquette in a side dish, for each to add to his own salad after nibbling on a piece of leaf.

A Little Extra Care in Growing

While roquette seeds aren't common, some seedhouses can supply you. Since the plant doesn't like intense summer heat, you'll get best results if you start the seeds indoors. Figure about six weeks from seed-planting to setting the small plants outdoors—about as early in spring as the ground permits.

Plants grow from 1½ feet to almost three feet high. The leaves are fairly long and deeply scalloped, so they're decorative as well as tasty in a salad. *Pick the leaves when they're young and tender,* as older leaves tend to develop too strong a flavor and odor.

Roquette is also sometimes called "rocket" or "rocket salad." It's related to the mustard family, and is quite popular in Europe and Asia. Eventually it produces yellowish white flowers and beaked pods. People used to eat the seeds as a delicacy, but now the leaves are the most popular.

Gourmet poets have written about the plant as far back as 1597, to my knowledge. Roquette will add to your gardening a little extra fun and flavor, and something "a little different."

Spinach Sensation!

If you're one of those who wouldn't like spinach even if it didn't taste like spinach, turn the page right now. But if you love spinach, you're in for a special treat by growing one of the improved disease-resistant varieties in your own garden.

When buying or ordering seeds, make sure of two things: that the variety is definitely disease resistant, such as *Virginia Savoy,* which produces beautiful rich green tender leaves and is relatively trouble-free, and that the seeds are marked pretreated against seed rot and damping off.

Plant early, about four weeks before the usual date of last spring frost. Then plant some other crop after harvest, since spinach won't do well in summer heat. Come back with another planting about a month and a half before the usual date of first winter frost.

A gourmet taste tip: try some young, tender, freshly picked and cold-washed spinach leaves in your salad bowl for sparkling, appetizing color and zesty "different" flavor.

Grow Radishes That Win Raves

The big improvement in radishes is that you can grow varieties now with short green tops but big round red beauties under-

ground—*that retain their crisp, solid meat* . . . no hollow-
ing out or pithiness . . . even when they reach the size of
a silver dollar! And these radish giants keep their rich red
color, no fading to a dull pinkish shade, even at their largest
size.

Get 6 Crops of Radishes!

Because these luscious, tart-sweet radishes mature in about
three weeks, you can get as many as six crops before frost, by
planting just about as soon as you can cultivate the earth in
early spring.

In good fertile soil, sow seeds about an inch deep and in
rows a foot apart. Thin out later—giant types at about three
inches apart for strong seedlings—smaller varieties about an
inch apart. Keep watering thoroughly, and refertilize as you
replant.

Radishes are a particularly good crop to start kids gardening. That was the first planting I ever made. I was thrilled with
the "miracle" of growth in the soil, even though I'd pull up a
dozen tops to find a single "swelling" big enough to chew on.
But my first grew-it-myself round red radish brought a happy
excitement I'll never forget!

So don't forget the great new radishes, even if only for planting as a border, or a come-on for the future generation of
gardeners.

Smoo-o-ooth Carrots You'll Care More About

They taste so extra good, and they're so good for you, the
new smooth-skinned, deep orange, tender carrots you can
grow in your own garden. You can pull up plenty of beauties
—each slick and tempting and bursting with vitamins—if you
apply just a little special care.

Soil Preparation Is the Key

For perfection in carrots, you must first cultivate the soil so
it's very fine, practically pulverized, and down deep, not just
the top crust. Mix in plenty of peat moss or other organic
matter and fertilizer, to help keep the soil loose and airy.

Plant the top new varieties just as soon as danger of frost
is over. Mix the tiny seeds with sand for sowing thinly enough,
then plant about one-half inch deep, in rows 1½ feet apart.
This is extremely important. When seedlings have de-

veloped, keep the strongest, and thin out the others ruthlessly so tops are about three inches apart. Water well and you'll have straight, smooth, uniform carrots that you can serve with pride and eat with rich enjoyment.

You can make several replantings and harvest fresh carrots right up to frost. Fertilize again with each planting. Merry munching to you!

Garden Bonus—Fresh Bermuda Onions

Imagine having a barbecue in your back yard, and just a minute before the hamburgers are done, you pick a plump onion right out of your garden a few feet away. You clean it off, cut a thick, luscious, gleaming slice dripping with juice, and place it on a sizzling burger. That's *living!*

Now you can grow better-than-ever Bermuda onions. First, it's vital to select stock no more than ¾ inches in diameter —these smaller specimens are far better than bigger sets.

Special Soil Preparation

For the "miracle" onions you want, ordinary soil isn't good enough. Mix in plenty of modern peat moss, add a little lime for sweetening, and plenty of compost or other organic matter that's most convenient.

Plant choice white Bermudas about an inch apart. Hill them up as they grow. Or, if you prefer, plant top-grade seeds in early spring. Seeds won't give you pickin' onions as fast, takes several weeks or a month longer, but you'll have even better flavored onions.

When you serve fresh-picked onions to others, you'll probably gain more friends with the superior flavor than you lose through onion breath.

Peppers—More Appealing Than Ever

Grow 'em sweet, hot, red or green—peppers are gaining in popularity as our taste goes for more Italian types of foods, more salads, more unique flavorings with meals. Garden-fresh peppers especially have a juiciness and zesty flavor that really perks up the taste buds.

You'll probably enjoy growing fresh peppers as a change from ordinary vegetables. Choose improved sweetmeat types for eating raw in salads, and for stuffings, or red-hot species for spicy sauces and side dishes.

Tips on Growing Best Peppers

Get sturdy, heavy plants about five or six inches tall. Set out in May. Plant about two feet apart in rich loam, in a spot that gets loads of full sun. Combine plenty of peat moss or other organic matter in the soil. Fertilize when planting and when buds appear.

Keep your pepper garden watered heavily. Shade young plants with shingles or tents for the first few days in the earth. Peppers are quite pest-free and seldom need spraying.

When those beautiful glossy peppers mature, pick sweet peppers while still green, but let hot types turn red before plucking. Pick every peck of precious pretty peppers (say that ten times fast) well before frost.

Modern peppers are sure to please your palpitating palate!

Zimply Crazy About Zucchini?

There's a recent miracle plant you should try in your garden, developed by the University of Connecticut. It's named Black Beauty, and it has many beautiful advantages for you.

Black Beauty bears a week earlier than most other varieties of zucchini, and it keeps on bearing. Each plant has a single upright stem which keeps on blooming. As each new bloom fades, the new fruit forms very fast and is ready to eat in a few days! The more you pick, the more this amazing plant produces.

Try picking Black Beauty at various stages of growth, and discover which best suits your taste. You can eat the fruit small, or let it reach large cucumber size. You'll find the meat rich, creamy and of specially luscious flavor, truly beautiful eating in every way.

Pause for Refreshment

A witty gardener remarked recently, "Considering the current prices for topsoil, they'll have to change the simile 'cheap as dirt'!"

Grow Mouth-watering Midget Watermelons

Whether you live in the northern parts of the country or elsewhere, now you can grow delightful new species of midget watermelons in your garden. These little wonders are delicious, juicy and low-calorie! And they take up little room in the garden or the refrigerator. Try growing some for a new gardening thrill.

Plant in most any good, well-drained soil, in full sun, following directions on the seed packet you buy. Be sure to water well.

You can tell that the melon is ripe when the tendril nearest the stalk shrivels and turns brown. (That's much more dependable than the old test of hitting the melon with the finger and listening for a hollow sound.)

These little miracle watermelons grow to only about seven to ten inches long, and five to eight inches in diameter. Most popular varieties are New Hampshire Midget, Rhode Island Red and Takii Gem, a Japanese variety. You'll love their tender sweet, fresh flavor and juicy crispness when you bite into a bright red, inviting slice. Happy eating to you!

Now You Can Stop "Sprouting"!

No more worries about your precious potatoes, onions and other root crops sprouting "horns" when you store them away for future use.

There's a simple solution today. Buy a "sprout inhibitor," and apply to your root crops before you put them in storage. Follow the easy directions and you'll be delighted to find that you eliminate a great deal of the usual waste. You'll discard very few potatoes and such because they're spoiled or ruined by sprouting.

Of course, don't treat any of your root crops that you may intend to use for seed, because they'll not produce at all for that purpose. But for eating . . . yum!

Beautiful, Edible Garden Borders!

Here's a practical gardening idea that's in good taste in more ways than one. Plant a garden border that combines beautiful flowers and delicious vegetables.

I've seen just such arrangements in lovely borders hiding the drab side of a home garage, for example. At the back of one narrow garden strip, glorious red gladiolus, yellow mums and huge white daisies displayed their rich, happy colors.

In front of the flowers, I watched the lady of the house pick luscious greens for the evening salad bowl from a decorative border of glowing robust lettuce.

High-growing flowers in back, low-growing vegetables in front—(Why not try such a border as part of your garden?) —looks good enough to eat, and is!

Special Gardening Thrill— Window-sill Vegetables!

If you're an apartment dweller, or if you live in an area of long, harsh winters, you can still enjoy the miracle of fresh-picked vegetables all year round in a limited amount—grown in your own soil and by your own efforts! Simply set up a number of large flower pots along south windows, where they'll get plenty of sun, and start planting.

Of course, I don't recommend or even suggest that you grow large species of corn or cabbages. But it's perfectly practicable to have your own home-grown endive, species of small lettuce, chives, tiny onions, radishes, parsley and such.

Simply use good small plants preferably, or even seeds (but that takes longer), a good, loamy soil, keep the earth and plants well fertilized—a complete water-soluble plant food is easy to apply and spectacularly effective. Watch out for harmful insects and fungus growth, and control them with the same wonder chemicals you use in your garden, just being very careful about the quantities you apply.

I have a friend who delights in serving her especially delicious endive salad at winter parties. When her new guests remark that the endive tastes "garden fresh," she loves to answer calmly, "Of course, I picked it from my garden an hour ago!" Then she exhibits her prized potted vegetable garden.

You can do the same and add extra thrills and length to your gardening year.

BERRIES

Bigger and Better "Hormoned" Berries

The wonderful fruit-setting hormones work miracles too in helping you to grow bigger and tastier strawberries, raspberries and blackberries than you ever grew before!

Gardeners report with astonishment that they've grown blackberries twice as big as the season before—and strawberries and raspberries that dwarf previous specimens—simply by spraying with the special berry fruit-setting hormones now available in stores.

Actually very little work is involved. Make your spraying solution according to directions on the package you buy. About two weeks after the berry plants have started blooming, most of the flowers should be open and tiny whitish berries start appearing. At that point, spray on the hormone solution. Spray again about five days later.

Then get ready to enjoy at picking time the biggest and most delicious berries you've ever tasted!

Treat Your Family to Plum-size Strawberries

The first time I saw the improved empire variety of strawberries, I picked one of the giant berries and looked it over in amazement. Without thinking, I said, "Wow, these strawberries are as big at plums!" So I take credit for nicknaming these beauties "plum-size strawberries." But the growers get all the credit for developing them so that gardeners like you and me can enjoy them all year round.

No, these plum-size marvels don't grow all year round in the garden, but they react exceptionally well to freezing. So, if you own a deep-freeze unit, be sure to pack plenty of plum-size strawberries away when you fresh-pick them from your garden. Then you and your family and guests can delight in this rare treat even during a blizzard in deep winter—if you live in blizzard areas. You'll love them wherever you live.

Strong and Drought-resistant

The big, sturdy empire plants are exceptionally good growers even during hot, dry spells. With just average fertilizing and watering, they'll survive when weaker varieties may fail. They're also lovely in foliage and in bloom, with large white and yellow blossoms.

Good plants are powerful producers. I've checked records showing an average production of six pints a year per plant, in carefully conducted tests year after year. And, in spite of their giant dimensions, these plum-size beauties are firm, juicy, bright red and extra delicious when you pluck them right from your own plants.

Grow them yourself and you'll find that these plump, plum-size specimens are sure to win "oohs" and "ahhs" when you serve them at any dinner party!

Enjoy 3-Season Strawberries

Now, from one planting, you can pick strawberries from your garden in spring, summer and fall—with choice plants of the superfection variety. Field tests by a state experimental station showed that superfection produced as much as three times more berries per square foot as other older varieties tested. And home gardeners report similar exciting results!

Choose Choice Plants

It doesn't pay to stint on superfection plants, because poor specimens will produce meager results. Be sure you get top-grade plants with heavy fibrous roots containing many hair-like long feeders. Plant in good soil in an area that gets full sunlight, fertilizing regularly.

Put in your guaranteed disease-free plants in early spring, and you'll pick abundant crops of luscious strawberries in June, during the summer and into fall, often up to freezing weather.

Not only will you proudly present your family with fresh-picked berries season after season, but you'll hear them rave about these big beauties. With proper care, they'll grow as big as an inch in diameter. The flesh is firm, juicy and so sweet that you can usually keep the cover on your sugar bowl.

Superfection strawberries are versatile too. Their double-appeal to the eye and the palate makes them superperfect for those big, tempting, "company" strawberry shortcakes, not to mention strawberries and cream for breakfast and desserts.

They're excellent for jam too, and they last exceptionally well in the freezer. Yes, you can brag at the office about your own fresh strawberries in January—something that used to be reserved just for kings. (Aren't you glad you're a gardener?)

Smart Idea—Superfection Borders

Try a flock of vigorous superfection plants as an unusual and delicious border for your flower garden, also along walks. You might even scatter some plants in your rock garden, since they're so decorative as well as satisfying to your stomach.

First the plants develop rich, green foliage, then bright white and yellow blossoms pop out among the green leaves, and finally, sparkling red berries make their appearance—but not for long, because you pick them eagerly as they ripen.

As a border, set healthy top grade superfection plants about a foot apart. As they thrive and burst into foliage and blossom, friends will tell you that they look as good as they taste.

New Pyramid Garden Is "the Berries!"

An amazing new "aluminum garden" now enables you to grow a lot of strawberries or raspberries in limited space. This pyramid garden is a round "tray" six feet in diameter, of strong, rustproof corrugated aluminum, with four terraces, each a few inches higher than the other, rising in a pyramid shape.

You can plant between fifty and one hundred strawberry plants, for example, utilizing all the terraces. A special nozzle at the top sprays the entire pyramid area when you attach a hose and turn on the water.

Accessories you can get with this unique contraption include a plastic cover of the new porous material which converts the pyramid into a miniature greenhouse for very early planting. A special net can also be secured which fits over the entire pyramid construction and protects berries from invasion by birds.

Concentrated in so small an area, and going round and round, the pyramid garden is easily tended and offers particular advantages to city and penthouse gardeners. When in full bloom with bright foliage and glowing red berries, the entire effect has been likened to a huge "strawberry shortcake" (although personally, I prefer whipped cream instead of green leaves).

The manufacturer states proudly that the pyramid garden will keep the average family supplied with enough berries for an entire season. One thing sure, it will keep the gardener going around in circles.

Many strawberries in a small area in a pyramid garden.

Mulch Weed Control for Strawberries

Most scientists agree today that a combination of chemical weed control and fall mulching with straw will perform miracles in keeping strawberry patches producing healthy luscious fruit year after year.

The trouble with most straw mulches is that they contain the seeds of many weeds. Thus, once the mulch is placed on the strawberry patch, the seeds germinate, many weeds grow and smother out the strawberry plants!

Fumigate the Mulch

But here again science has come up with a modern chemical miracle in the form of a fumigant which destroys all the weed seeds in the straw before you apply the mulch. You simply get the product and apply as directed, placing both the fumigant and the straw in a sealed bag for a day, then applying the weed-seed-free straw mulch to the strawberry beds.

An enterprising gardener has found that a plastic garment bag is very good for the purpose. He places straw and fumigant in the bag, zips it closed, then empties it a day later. He cleans out the bag and says he finds many other uses for it around the garden after turning the bag insde out and cleaning it thoroughly.

You'll be delighted at the way such a mulch suppresses weeds and promotes the growth of more abundant, juicy strawberries.

Winter-hardy Blackberries—a Taste Bonus

Developed for you by the New York State Experiment Station in northern New York, the giant Bailey blackberry is now available in hardy, vigorous bushes that have survived temperatures as low as 22° below zero!

The berries themselves are well over an inch in length, juicy, delicious and proverbially sweet as sugar. You can get them from a good supplier with a guarantee that they'll be 100 per cent fruitful, so that you know you'll enjoy crops of these luscious and attractive favorites for many seasons.

Tending Tips

You're best off getting two-year plants that have proved their survival of tough winter weather, and will produce crops fast. Be sure the bushes come with strong canes so that they can hold a heavy crop without breaking down.

Plant in ordinary fertile soil, with at least four feet between bushes. Keep well watered and fertilized, but avoid fertilizers very high in nitrogen content. For sturdiest growth, cut back two-year-old canes after fruit crops have been picked and fruiting is over completely. Watch carefully and spray at any signs of infestation by insects or disease.

With reasonable care, these hardy bushes will bring you exceptional eating delight year after year.

Pick Raspberries 3 Seasons

Now you can enjoy your own fresh-picked, delicious raspberries in late June, more in the summer, and another crop in early September, continuing to bear up to November. Just plant the improved "Sweet September" everbearing variety.

When you get vigorous two-year plants and set in the soil in fall, you'll pick basket after basket of sweet, firm, flavorful berries the following spring.

Tips on Planting and Care

Be sure you get healthy plants that have strong, well-developed roots with many long fibrous feeders. Plant in fertile, well-drained soil, about three feet apart, either in rows about six feet apart, or in groups of a few plants together as ornamental features about your property.

Set in holes plenty wide and deep so as not to crowd roots. Firm the soil gently. Wet down liberally with a starter solution of complete water-soluble plant food.

Frequent spraying may be necessary to guard your plants against insects and disease, so be on guard against any sign of infestation, and act promptly.

As winter approaches each year, after fruiting, cut out any dead canes right down near the soil. Prune out any weak and fragile growth also, to help encourage development of sturdy wood that bears fruit.

When new leaves and shoots appear in early spring, cut back any dead tops, down to live, healthy wood.

With very little work you'll get a lot of benefit and add greatly to your family's pleasure when you dish out sparkling servings of red ripe luscious raspberries week after week, season after season, with these three-season delights.

Now . . . Double-inch Decorative Blueberries

You can now enjoy the ornamental beauty of gorgeous flowering blueberry bushes growing five to six feet tall, loaded with plump giant-size blueberries that measure as much as two inches around by tape measure! You can prove this yourself to wide-eyed neighbors—using an honest tape measure.

These are beautiful ornamental shrubs as well as producers of delicious berries. The foliage is almost evergreen, with glossy blue-green leaves. As the cool weather comes on, the leaves gradually change color until they're a brilliant red as winter sets in.

During July and August, healthy bushes produce large clusters of juicy giant blueberries. You'll enjoy them for desserts, in cereals, for luscious preserves.

Planting for Best Results

For vigorous growth, plant three-year-old bushes about four feet apart in well-aerated, richly fertilized acid soils. You must plant two or more different varieties for pollination. Mix in plenty of peat moss or other conditioner with the soil. Plant for full sun.

Feed liberally and often with water-soluble plant food made for acid-loving plants specifically . . . for lusty growth and fruit production (special dry fertilizer for acid-loving plants is also very good but not nearly as fast-acting). This acidifying action is of extreme importance for desirable growth!

If you plant these new, improved blueberry bushes in spring, you'll be munching the luscious berries the same summer. Prune old, dead, unproductive wood each spring. The shrubs will beautify your property as ornamentals in most any spot.

Like Sawdust on Your Blueberries?

Most people like cream on their blueberries, but new miracles of growth have been reported by using sawdust—yes, common sawdust—around blueberry bushes.

One prominent experiment station did this. A mass of sawdust was sieved with water (known as the "leaching" process). The solution obtained was then applied to the soil around the plants of some blueberries in a patch.

The bushes thus treated with the sawdust solution *doubled in growth,* compared with adjacent untreated bushes. And far greater yields of delicious blueberries resulted.

Exactly why the sawdust solution works so effectively hasn't been defined precisely. But obviously the wood residue contains elements of great benefit to blueberries particularly.

Yes, Nature often plans miracles with the most commonplace materials, and man seeks them out. Why not stop in at your local lumber yard, get some sawdust, strain it through water, apply the solution to your blueberry bushes, and see what exciting results you get.

Please pass the sawdust—I mean the cream!

SHRUBS, TREES, VINES

Choose from a New World of Scintillating Shrubs

Whether you choose types of shrubs centuries old or brand-new varieties, today you can find improved specimens of practically every species.

Out of the hundreds upon hundreds of types for your choice, here are just a few stars to help you get started in your initial selection or additions to your landscaping:

SILKY DOGWOOD: This is a supremely decorative shrub which gives you a variety of beautiful colors in flowering and in changing foliage, all in one dramatic bush. In late spring, this fine species is covered with a net of tiny lacy white flowers, which turn into glistening little blue berries. Comes fall, the foliage turns a rich red, which disappears as wintry weather comes; then goes into the next act of its performance, revealing attractive bright-red bark.

A great advantage of this excellent shrub is that it's quite trouble-free. It thrives best in soil kept quite moist, but is so hardy that it survives dry periods well. All in all, silky dogwood is an exceptionally worthy ornamental shrub.

WHITE FORSYTHIA: Perfected white and the popular yellow forsythias are decorative and dependable shrubs. Both are covered with a profusion of bright blooms that light up your grounds early in spring when color is needed most.

Compact bushes grow to eight feet in height and usually thrive beautifully with ordinary care. The bright white or yellow radiance of forsythia is always a happy harbinger of spring and the rich seasons ahead.

PINK SAUCER MAGNOLIA: This glowing shade and other varieties of this highly romantic shrub give you magnificent color in the air at tulip blooming time. It's true spring magic to watch the fat buds unfolding the exquisite saucerlike blooms six inches and more across.

Later, the glossy leatherlike leaves are very decorative to enrich your indoors, and for large floral arrangements. Magnolia is an excellent lawn planting because it branches so openly, enhancing rather than obscuring the landscape.

OREGON HOLLY-GRAPE: Here's a growing favorite as an outstanding beauty which provides a more ornamental variation from the ordinary yew. It usually stays low and bushy, no more than three feet high, with sparkling, prickly dark-green leaves and delightful blue-toned berries.

Orange holly-grape is decorative through the winter, with its richly beautiful leathery foliage. It thrives at its best when planted for north or east exposure.

FRINGETREE: You'll find this a really fantastic beauty, so showy that you'll want to feature it in a spot where it can flaunt its beauty alone!

It grows tall and gracefully, adorned with an exquisite lacework of fleecy white fringelike flowers in late spring. The leaves too are beautifully long and graceful.

This specimen is so unusual, hardy and yet delicate, that it will win much admiration from your neighbors—and from you!

VARIEGATED DOGWOOD: Almost too dramatic to be true, this shrub is a decorative delight in spots with light shade where you're seeking special color accent. The gracious branches are covered fully with rich green leaves marked heavily with creamy-white stroking. You may be able to find other colors of leaf patterns too that you'll like even more.

The variegated dogwood is very hardy, thriving best in moist soil. This species grows slowly, but makes up for it by its strikingly impressive foliage.

GIANT BLUE HYDRANGEA: This improved version of an old favorite is now available in exciting bushes that produce huge, dense, plump flower heads as large as a foot across! The effect of the immense balls of ravishing blue against the wide green leaves is an enriching sight.

Plant in partial shade and apply a protective mulch for wintering. For the rich true blue, acidify the soil with frequent applications of fertilizer prepared especially for acid-loving plants.

THREE-COLOR ROSE OF SHARON: This amazing triumph actually has three different colors grafted on a single bush! From midsummer until early fall, this unique bush features large double blooms in lovely white, rich red and deep purple—all flourishing at the same time. This triple display of color makes this specimen an exciting showpiece.

The newly developed species is very hardy, and requires only normal care and fertilization. It's a graceful, loose-branched beauty which will spotlight the area where you plant it.

These specimens are just a minor sampling of the wonderful variety awaiting you in the world of constantly improving shrubs. Study the many offerings carefully and then choose the types of foliage, coloring and bloom that will fit in best with all your plantings and that will delight you most.

How to Plant Shrubs and Evergreens for Best Results

A neighbor stood beside me and chuckled disdainfully as I carefully planted a new shrub, checking measurements, going slowly step by step.

"All that care you take is a lot of foolishness," he said. "I put in my shrubs in a third the time, just plopped them into a hole in the ground, and they're growing great!"

I looked down the street at the adequate but uninspiring growth in front of his house. I answered pleasantly, "Good-enough isn't good enough for me. I want 'miracle results' right away, and lasting through the years. The only way I know to get the results I want is to apply that 'little extra' to every planting."

I recommend this same step-by-step method in planting shrubs and evergreens. You'll find it very much worthwhile in resultant bounteous beauty and personal enjoyment.

1. Choose a good quality, healthy shrub or evergreen, and, for best results, get it with the original ball of earth around the roots, well wrapped in burlap.

2. Dig a hole with fairly straight sides, about six to twelve inches larger in diameter than the soil ball, and about an inch deeper.

3. Slide the ball carefully into the hole, and set it in gently, so you don't jar or break the roots. Leave the burlap on. After you've filled in part of the soil, cut away the burlap at the top, but don't remove the burlap as it'll eventually rot away, and meanwhile it holds and protects the roots and root soil.

4. Start filling around the ball with good rich soil and top-soil, well mixed with peat moss. When the hole is half filled, make sure the plant is set straight. Firm the soil lightly.

5. Water slowly with a hose after you've removed the nozzle, for a few minutes. Then add a gallon or two (depending on size of the hole) of a complete liquid plant food, such as a 15-30-15. Let the liquid all soak in well.

6. Now fill in the rest of the soil as before, until level with the ground. As you firm the soil, build it into a slight basin shape around the plant. Don't cover with grass sod.

7. Water again with the nozzleless hose, and add another gallon or two of liquid plant food. Let the liquid soak in.

8. Cover the basin area with several inches of a good mulch, such as peat moss, grass clipping, ground corncobs, whatever is most convenient for you.

9. Prune the top back a little, removing any broken or criss-crossing branches.

10. You're finished, except to water every two or three days for the first few weeks if rainfall isn't adequate. Make sure that the waterings are deep and thorough.

Best planting time is early fall, so that the plant is well established before winter really takes hold. Your new shrub or evergreen should thrive beautifully, with extra special growth for your extra effort.

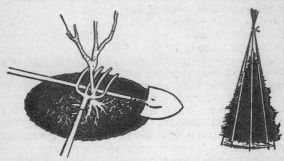

Set bush at right depth.   Stake tepee protects shrubs.

Plant Bare-root Shrubs and Trees with Extra Care

For growing shrubs and trees that have the surest chance for survival and fast, vigorous growth, your best bet is to choose "B and B." That refers to a shrub which has ball and burlap—

the complete root ball of soil in which the shrub grew, just as it was dug from the earth and all carefully wrapped in burlap.

However, for best results with bare-root shrubs and trees, if that's what you have, here's how to go about it. If you do this job right, the bare-rooted citizens can give you marvelous results and many years of pleasures.

1. Dig the hole plentifully wide, so that the roots can spread out normally, with several inches to spare beyond the root tips. Dig deeply enough to set in the shrub or tree at exactly the same depth that it grew originally.

2. Sift a rich, fertile soil to a very fine texture. Cover the roots gently and then fill the hole halfway, fixing the shrub straight. Firm the soil but don't pack it down too tight.

3. Water in about a gallon of complete liquid plant food. When this soaks in, fill the hole to the brim with water running slowly from the hose, after removing the nozzle.

4. After all the water soaks in, fill the balance of the hole with the soil. Then water liberally again with the hose, after applying another gallon of liquid plant food.

5. Now cut out any very thin and weak-looking shoots entirely from the shrub or tree. Prune away about one fourth of the length of branches on the rest of the shrub or tree. That will encourage sturdy branching.

Water thoroughly at least every few days, and you should have a fine, responsive shrub or tree.

Pruning for Perfection in Shrubs

You can help produce "miracles" in the increasing beauty and perfection of shrubs and bushes by proper pruning. *But,* you can also ruin many plants if you hack away without knowledge and care.

Each spring, I wince as I imagine shrubs shrinking in fear as the demon gardener approaches them eagerly and recklessly, gleaming clippers in hand—to hack, hack, hack. That's a peculiarly irresistible kind of spring fever you must throw off before you damage many of your precious plantings.

A good rule is to prune wisely but not too well. Heed the following general guides and apply your own good judgment and restraint, as well as artistic taste, as you prune for perfection.

WHY Pruning?

1. Improve the health of the plant by removing dead, withered or diseased branches, along with tangled growth that interferes with proper advancement.

2. Cut down excessive growth to keep the shrub within desired ornamental size; in other words, enjoy most beautifully shaped plants.

3. Help a too tall or spindly bush to grow into a lower, denser, more graceful shape.

4. Increase production of flowers and fruit.

Basic Tips

1. Always use sharp, clean tools for neatness and most rapid healing.

2. In practically all cases, cuts should be made at a slant, rather than vertical or horizontal. Wherever possible, slant so that the lower side is exposed rather than the upper surface, as the cut will heal more rapidly.

3. Where there's a choice in removing stems, cut out those with fewest leaves and buds, as leaves are vital assets to the plant's nutrition.

4. With most plants, prune in very early spring, before vigorous new growth has really started. *But don't prune spring-flowering shrubs until right after flowers have faded.* Otherwise you'll cut down the number of future blooms. Also, by pruning right after flowering, you direct the vigor in the bush to new growth rather than to making new seeds.

5. Don't go in for wholesale slaughter by chopping down the shrub to within a foot or so of the ground. Instead, cut out about one third of the weakest and oldest canes, and cut them right down to the soil—to avoid unsightly, decaying, disease-inviting stubs.

6. Soon after extensive pruning, when new shoots develop, thin out the shoots to avoid tangled growth and to shape the plant the way you want it to grow.

7. When one branch grows closely over another, it's usually wise to remove the top branch lest it shade and weigh down the lower. Here again, use your judgment as to general shape of the branches and the plant. Cut close to the joining, at a slant.

8. When a very narrow crotch develops, there's danger of a split appearing. It's usually best to cut off one branch, preferably the thinner and weaker.

9. Always remove any dead, withered, diseased or tangled branches and twigs, all through season. Be careful in cutting out dead wood not to cut into healthy, live growth.

10. Always cut all the way back, snug to the other limb, in order not to leave a stub (of course, don't overdo it and cut *into* the surviving limb).

11. In light pruning, make your slanted cut right above a strong bud. However, if you're cutting down to two directly opposite buds, make a horizontal cut.

12. Keep in mind that if the bush is about the height and shape you like, thinning may be all that's needed. Also remove spindly growth and suckers at the base of the plant.

13. Avoid a top-heavy "umbrella shape"—a long trunk with foliage bunches at the top. This comes from cutting all canes back evenly a foot or two above the ground, or from trimming off all side branches in one area. Cut here and there like a good barber, not in square or rigid formations.

14. When branches intertwine and interfere with one another, remove the weaker, older stems. Also, when possible, take out a few central canes that crowd the bush—keeping in mind, as always, the graceful shaping of the bush.

Cut off withered tips.

Cut off top branch
too close to another.

On too-close crotch
cut off one branch.

Special Health and Beauty Boost

After pruning, it's a marvelous pickup for your plant when you apply a little extra plant food—dry, or preferably a liquid feeding for a quick boost, since the liquid is absorbed in minutes by the stems and foliage. The extra nutrients help the shrub produce vigorous new growth for a beautiful flourishing appearance all through the following seasons.

Of course, pruning alone won't overcome troubles from crowding of plants, poor location, inadequate roots and such ills. But it's a fine aid in its own right, as part of good gardening routines—so prune right and you'll beautify your plantings bountifully!

Now There's Gold in Them Thar Lilacs!

Imagine glorious golden lilacs, with their heavenly lilting fragrance added to exquisite new color, growing right in your garden!

Actually the new lilacs are a creamy yellow rather than deep gold, but they're definitely yellow in color, not just a tint. The color deepens as the plants age.

With wonderful horticultural developments, you can grow lilacs also in bright white, pale lavender, rich purple . . . in single or heavy double clusters . . . shrubs that grow about eight feet high (or lower, if you keep pruning) and trees that reach up to twenty-five feet in height.

Also, you can now get varieties that have mildew-resistant dark green leaves—magnificent foliage that turns a glorious deep wine-purple shade in the fall.

As for tantalizing scent, you can sniff the gamut from light to rich spicy perfume—and even unpleasantly odorous species which you want to avoid in acquiring lilac shrubs.

Tending Tips

Always plant lilacs for full sun, otherwise you'll never get full satisfaction in growth or bloom.

Lilacs do well in most any well-drained soil that's fairly fertile, but thrive better in rich alkaline earth. Light annual liming is recommended, with complete fertilizing at least twice a year.

Some varieties tend to show mildew on leaves, and are susceptible to scale insects. At the first sign of infestation, spray with the new wonder chemicals.

Cut off dead flowers as soon as they've finished blooming. to prevent seed formation which robs the plant of vigor. When you cut off dead flowers, be sure not to injure the closest of leafy branches, as these produce blooms the next year. Remove all suckers.

Plant like other shrubs or trees, provide this simple care, and you'll enjoy armfuls of these supremely alluring blooms, early or late in season, depending on the variety you plant. Despite the brief period of bloom, few flowers are so gratifying and "loverly" as your lilacs.

Ravishing Colors in Rhododendrons

You'll love showing these majestic beauties blooming on your property in May and June—now in glorious gleaming white, dainty pale purple, delightful deep pink, and favorite fiery red!

The huge many-flowered blooms contrast dramatically with the large, bold, deep-green leaves. And the evergreen foliage all year round makes the best rhododendrons just about indispensable among your foundation plantings.

Important Tips

To grow rhododendrons at their best, prepare a good loamy acid soil, rich in organic matter, to a depth of about fifteen inches. Mix plenty of modern peat moss or compost into the earth. Acidify the soil with special water-soluble or dry fertilizer made specifically for acid-loving plants.

Plant for semishade. If close to the house, make sure to remove all mortar or building debris in the area, as lime in any form may kill your valuable plants.

Keep a good moisture-retaining mulch around your rhododendrons, using peat moss, pine needles, wood chips or other material that will remain in place even in windy spots. Mulch to a depth of about three inches.

For a profusion of blooms the first season, be sure to get three- to four-year-old top-quality plants.

Hardy Imported Azaleas Win Top Admiration

You'll enjoy blazing new color in varieties of Holland hardy azaleas now being imported in a beautiful range of glowing shades. You can choose from soft pinks, apricot-yellows, salmon-orange, raging reds, and other bright and subtle tones.

Plant sturdy, top-quality, three-year-old specimens in early spring, and you'll be thrilled by magnificently colored blossoms in full bloom before the end of the first season. These hardy varieties have survived temperatures below zero, and will come back in blazing glory for you year after year.

Planting and Tending Properly

Instead of creating an acid soil, provide a rich organic environment by mixing plenty of peat moss or leafmold in the planting hole. Plant for full sun or partial shade.

Fertilize regularly; for best results, use a complete water-soluble plant food made especially for acid-loving plants. Be careful not to cultivate deeply, as azalea roots grow close to the top of the soil.

Remove faded flowers immediately to prevent them from going to seed. You conserve the plant's vigor for new branching and production of a mass of blooms next year!

Miracle Prevention of Azalea Petal Blight

If you have azaleas, and live in an area where these exquisite and exciting blooms are popular, you've probably been horrified by the sudden destruction sometimes caused by the disease called azalea petal blight. In just a few hours, the gloriously colored blossoms suddenly go brown. But now there's marvelous new prevention for this overwhelming disease.

Get one of the modern weed killers based primarily on *calcium cyanamid*. This wonder-worker acts doubly to release nitrogen plant food into the soil.

A month *before* your prized azaleas usually bloom, spread the chemical on the soil under the plants, as directed on the product you use (usual application for this purpose is about a pound per hundred square feet of soil).

Thus, you kill the spores that can spread azalea petal blight over an entire neighborhood overnight. This beforehand treatment will help insure the jewel-like radiance of your valuable azaleas, and your deep pleasure in seeing their vivid colors light up your home.

Miracles for Acid-loving Plants

Have you ever stepped out of your house one morning and been horrified to see your prized and costly evergreens turning yellow while you turned pale? Now science makes it possible for you to remedy that "yellow anemia" in a hurry in practically all cases—by acting in time. The miracle worker is concentrated water-soluble plant foot made especially for acid-loving plants, quick and easy to use.

I've seen yellowing evergreens, laurel and rhododendron bushes turn rich green soon after applying this special plant food. I've watched laurel that seemed dormant burst into bud and then produce lovely blooms. I've been delighted to find my small dogwood trees enriched with lovely flowering branches when other gardeners said I'd have to wait several more years. And all thanks to quick and easy watering with the specially compounded plant food.

Here's the reason. Yellowing of broadleaf evergreens and acid-loving plants is usually caused by one of two things. Either the soil isn't acid enough, or the plants aren't getting needed iron in a form they can use efficiently for healthy green growth. So they become ill with "yellow anemia" or "chlorosis."

This condition is so common because broadleaf evergreens are so often planted close to the house. The concrete foundation, with its natural lime content, affects the soil nearby so it's not acid enough for best growth of evergreens. You must correct this or your plants suffer the consequences.

Prescription: More Iron

Just as your doctor prescribes iron if you have a deficiency, you can provide iron for your evergreens with the special water-soluble plant food "for acid-loving plants." You can rescue and give a new lease on vigorous life to firs, spruce, yews, hemlock, berry bushes, azaleas, dogwood, rhododendrons—in fact all acid-loving plants, shrubs and trees.

The miracle plant food supplies chelated iron—that's a new form of iron which plants absorb easily (more about wondrous chelated iron elsewhere in this book). And since the iron in the food is readily absorbed through both roots and foliage, improvement is usually astonishingly swift.

In addition, the water-soluble plant food supplies other nutrients, which work with the iron to help the plants improve and flourish. Prompt and proper application, according to instructions on the package, can save your evergreens and beautify your landscaping.

Dry Fertilizers Also

There are also excellent dry fertilizers for acid-loving plants which you sprinkle on the earth from the trunk to past the spread of the branches in the spring, and again after flowering season. But I prefer the water-soluble plant food, applied with a sprinkling can or hose applicator, for amazingly fast action—especially important when you see that telltale yellow appear. One application and happily you'll "wonder where the yellow went!"

And you'll thank modern science again as you save precious broadleaf evergreens and acid-loving plants worth hundreds of dollars, with just a few dollars' expenditure and a few moments of pleasant, productive effort.

More Fun with These Fungi!

One good way to assure being a "miracle gardener" instead of a dud is to avoid troubles that happen commonly otherwise. Many people complain about bad luck in trying to grow some acid-soil plants from seed away from the accustomed native ground. With such varieties as azaleas, pines, rhododendrons and trailing arbutus, *lack of fungi* is frequently the trouble.

The fact is that certain fungi which live on the roots of such plants don't cause disease but, quite the opposite, seem essential to the plants' growth. Scientists happen to disagree at times about just what these fungi do, but they admit that without the fungi, the plants don't thrive.

So here's your vital tip. Buy some plants and insist on a large ball of earth surrounding the roots. This earth will contain plenty of the necessary fungi which, in turn, will spread throughout the rest of the bed. Then your new plantings will have the *friendly fungi* they need for a solid, vigorous start.

Shot-in-the-roots for Young Shrubs

Here's a natural "miracle" booster for valuable young shrubs, especially those planted right next to grassy areas. Attach a *water lance* to your hose. The way to use this inexpensive gadget is to push it carefully down into the ground, several inches beneath the surface, right next to the shrub.

When you turn on the water, the lance pipe by-passes the grass which is competing for a drink, and carries the fluid right down to the shrub's root level in a hurry. With such a periodic custom-tailored deep soaking, your shrubs will respond with faster and healthier growth.

This is an easy and important way to help grow exceptionally beautiful and hardy shrubs.

Keeping Evergreens Ever Green

There's very little that gardeners prize more than a proud, virile, rich-green evergreen. To have "miracle" beauty decorating your home, you want to take action in a hurry, if you see one of your beautiful evergreens starting to turn to dull, grayish green. Now you can do something about it!

More and more troubles with evergreens are caused by tiny redspider mites which attack other garden plants too. If not controlled and annihilated, these pests will suck the green glory from your evergreens too.

The first sign is that the brilliant green turns dull and grayish, then brownish. Examine the needles closely and you'll usually detect tiny webs woven among them. You can frequently see the needles mottled and losing color—particularly when you step far back from the evergreen and note that it's losing color, compared with nearby growth. Another signal is that needles start dropping off.

Too Tiny to Detect

Unfortunately you can't usually even see the redspiders on the foliage because they're so tiny. Actually they're not even spiders, but mites only about 1/60th of an inch long. They attack the evergreen needles in a mass, sucking out the juices, so that the gleaming chlorophyll green gradually disappears.

Here's a simple test to track down the presence of the vicious mites. Hold a white sheet of paper or cardboard under a branch. Hit the branch sharply with a pencil or stick. If tiny specks appear on the white paper and start moving about, the evergreen has been invaded by redspider mites. Rub them with the point of the twig and they'll become brownish smears on the white surface.

Science to the Rescue

If you haven't a good *malathion* product on your pesticide shelf, better get it right away. You must destroy these vicious invaders early or they'll ruin the valuable evergreen amazingly fast. Spray on the wonder chemical in the solution directed on the package you buy.

Repeat the spraying as often as instructed. Be sure you direct the spray also at the *underside* of the needles, wetting them thoroughly, because that's where the mites usually prefer to pierce the needles and feed on the plant juices.

Your lush, magnificent evergreen will reward you by coming back to thriving, colorful beauty if you act in time.

A Miracle with Holly Berries!

The amazing fruit-setting hormones now work one of the most astounding "miracles" in helping to produce holly berries. Many gardeners complain that they find they have female holly trees which don't produce berries because there's no male tree near enough. Even that can be remedied now!

If you have this problem, ask your garden supply man for the proper fruit-setting hormone product. Mix the solution as directed on the package. When the holly flowers are fully open in the spring, spray right into the face of the flowers with the hormone solution.

Your female holly trees will oblige and surprise you by forming berries as lovely as you could wish for.

Modern Chemicals Make Junipers Popular

An impressive example of how the advances of science improve our enjoyment of plant life is shown by the popular comeback of junipers.

These extraordinary and beautiful evergreens had lost their appeal over the years because they were constantly attacked by and infested with scale and spider mites. But now that science has produced powerful "miracle" chemicals which control and kill these pests, you can go ahead and enhance the beauty of your home with the joys of junipers.

Simply spray thoroughly with a solution of *aramite* or *malathion*, as a preventive measure each year, and your junipers will flourish, free of scale and spider mites. If the pests do appear, a few sprayings will clean them out.

Many Decorative Varieties

There's an exciting choice of colors for you to choose from in junipers: rich black-greens, cool steely blues, gorgeous gray-greens and even gleaming golden hues.

You can get tall growing plants, medium types that ball out beautifully, and low-growing spreading forms.

Don't overlook how these graceful juniper evergreens can adorn your landscaping with their glorious, colorful, year round needle foliage. For now, with another bow to science, your health worries are over in respect to owning choice specimens of this spectacular species.

Simple Protection for Young Evergreens

After planting young evergreens carefully, it's heart-breaking to see them damaged frequently before they can take hold. Children running by the tender shrubs and hitting them, dogs hurtling past, even careless adults brushing against the growth can injure them.

You'll be kinder to young evergreens and to yourself if you simply do this. Take a few tall sticks or bamboo stakes and protect the new shrubs by forming a protective "fence." Just three or four stakes, tied at the top, either in a tent shape or square, will usually do the trick. They keep the new plant firmer and shielded against damage.

And when cold and severe weather sets in, use those same stakes as a frame for a burlap covering.

That little extra care will pay off for you in stronger, lovelier evergreens, and will sometimes save you the cost of complete replacements!

Death to Dogwood Borers!

To keep lilacs, dogwoods and other woody shrubs thriving healthfully at their beautiful best, clean out any borers. You'll have more vigorous shrubs that will produce more and more radiant blooms.

Look for the holes in trunks and branches that are your clue to borers within. Fill a simple oiling can with a solution of effective *carbon bisulfide*. Squirt the solution into the holes. Then close up the holes by plugging with slightly moist mud.

The excellent chemical compound works fast. In a short time, the destructive pests will be bored to death. Your rescued shrubs will respond with extra growth and more glorious flowering.

Hormones Keep Cut Evergreens Weeks Longer

One of the loveliest of nature's decorations indoors is a collection of graceful branching evergreens. Now, using one of science's wonder products, you can make the cut evergreens hold their green, rich beauty and brightness weeks longer than usual.

Simply spray the cut foliage with one of the fruit-setting hormones which are now available in stores, and recommended on the label for varieties of flowering evergreen trees, particularly holly. While it may not be worth getting the product just for your cut evergreens, this is a great "plus" you can enjoy if you already have the product around for use in your garden.

Choosing Trees for Home Improvement

There's no question that trees enrich your home and property. But when you set in new trees, make sure you choose a species that doesn't grow higher than twenty-five feet at maturity. The towering giants belong in parks or the forests primeval, but not around today's homes. The smaller trees will give you shade and beauty.

Gigantic trees are undesirable from many points of view. The huge roots eat up a lion's share of soil nutrients, spread amazingly, and inhibit the growth of adjacent or nearby grass and plantings. And when it comes to spraying and pruning, costs are much higher than for low-growing, more graceful and more accessible foliage.

As for the death of a giant tree, if it should become infested by insects or disease, you'll be stunned when you get estimates for removal. You can prevent such high costs beforehand by limiting your choice to trees of moderate height.

Of course, if you have some gigantic trees, you'll live with them and love them, as we do at our home!

More Delicious Delight in Dwarf Fruit Trees

An exciting and relatively new delight is provided now for you, the modern gardener, in enjoying the large, wholesome and delicious fruits that can be grown right around your property on dwarf fruit trees.

These little "miracle" trees don't grow any higher than eight to ten feet, yet produce loads of sizable and perfect fruit when planted and tended properly. They're desirable from every viewpoint because they're triply wonderful in providing lovely flowers, graceful green foliage, and the best of hand-grown, hand-picked eating.

Another great boon is that these low-growing trees are easy to spray with insecticides, even with a hand spray or dust gun. And one thing you have to recognize if you're going to grow fruit, you must spray with the wonder-working insecticides regularly, or you won't have either edible fruit or decorative trees!

Marvelous Varieties Available Today

Each season, nurseries and growers are developing the dwarf fruit trees better for you. Whereas you once could get only apple and pear trees in dwarf size, now you can also get dwarf plums, cherries and peaches for your family's delight.

With apples and pears specifically, and with some varieties of other fruits, you must plant two or more varieties for cross-pollination in order to bear fruit. Check the nursery or catalog, in respect to the varieties you buy.

Remember, the fruit itself will not be dwarfed, but will grow to full size, of rich color and perfect shape—with proper planting and regular attention.

You can get fine varieties in apples of red and yellow delicious, Cox's orange, McIntosh and others. Choose from Bartlett, Clapp's, covert and other fine types of pear, and so on with other fruits. Make the choice that matches your family's flavor buds.

How to Plant Properly

1. Choose an area with full sunshine. Fruits need plenty of the sun's healthful rays to develop vigorous specimens bursting with nature's vitamins and sparkling juices.

Set in your trees where they'll be decorative as well as productive, as close as ten to twelve feet apart.

2. Dig the hole extra wide so there are several inches of free space beyond the ends of the roots when you set in the tree and fill in with soil. Homespun philosophers caution "Don't expect a four-dollar tree to grow in a four-bit hole!" Roots won't develop as fast or thrive as vigorously if you make them stub their toes against compacted earth.

Set the tree in to a depth that brings the root stock point of union (which you can see clearly) about four inches *above* the soil surface. If you plant with the point of union below the soil, your dwarf may grow into a giant!

3. Fill in with fertile soil combining rich earth with modern activated peat moss. Mix in a good 5-10-5 dry fertilizer, or for even swifter response, apply an excellent 15-30-15 liquid fertilizer complete with chelated iron and valuable trace elements.

4. Soak water in deeply, then—as an extra help—spread a light mulch of straw, grass clippings, leaves or other mulch convenient for you. Keep watering the tree deeply during dry periods, not just surface watering, or the life-giving moisture won't get down deep to the roots where needed.

Help support the tree with a stake if it seems at all shaky, although this isn't always necessary with a dwarf tree.

5. *Dust or spray regularly* against insects and disease, in proportions recommended by the product you buy. Best all-around protector is a combination of marvelous malathion-methoxychlor-captan, which is readily available these days.

Modern dwarf trees just naturally go with the trend to modern low houses, and with efficient do-it-yourself care. Nothing else gives you so joyous and decorative a combination of the three "f's": foliage, flowers and fruit!

You'll enjoy the beauty of good dwarf fruit trees right from the start. And, depending on the age of the trees you buy, you'll be picking delectable fruit of your own—the first crop paying in full for your whole investment—in just a few short years.

Distinctive Dwarf Columnar Fruit Trees

Here's an exciting idea in flowering fruit trees that's come over here from the magnificent old-time estates in Europe—trees that grow only ten feet high, in graceful narrow columns, yet produce full-size delicious apples or pears!

Since these trees were developed in cold northern areas, they're hardy and will thrive most anywhere in this country with proper fertilization and care. In spring, they're covered with beautiful fragrant blossoms. Then, into summer, the blossoms are transformed into exquisite little fruits which grow and ripen into big luscious apples or sweet, juicy, colorful pears.

Easy to Plant

Plant these columnar beauties as instructed on these pages for other dwarf fruit trees, in full sun. But since they're so narrow and vertical, you can plant them as close as two to three feet apart.

These trees require usual fertilization and regular spraying. In addition, prune them lightly. During the early summer, simply prune back the new lateral shoots, so that you keep the side branches trimmed to about eight inches in order to maintain the formal columnar shape.

However, if you have two or more trees planted close together and wish the branches to mingle to form a tall hedge or screen, guide your pruning accordingly.

Plant for Varied Effects

One of the special delights of these little columnar trees is that you can utilize them in so many decorative ways around your home.

Planted as two gate posts at the entrance to your home, or at the top of a walk, you'll have two unusual flowering, fruiting sentinels to greet guests.

For a sizable expenditure, you can get enough of these decorative beauties to form a gorgeous hedge, by planting them about three feet apart and letting the branches intermingle as they grow.

And, of course, you can use single trees to spot about your property, at the corners of your lawn, to add a graceful formal note against a bare wall of your house—use your own judgment as a landscape artist.

Just be sure that each tree has full sunlight, and that you plant at least two apple or pear trees as they require cross-pollination to bear the luscious fruit you want to pick.

This modern development, in tune with smaller property areas for modern living, can bring you much pleasure. And you sure will surprise admiring visitors!

Fun-to-grow Quintuplet Fruit Trees!

Great fun and good eating too are yours with the modern quintuplet apple trees. Imagine picking from one tree as many as five different varieties of red, yellow and striped apples! And the varieties ripen in succession so that you have fruit starting in summer and carrying through to winter.

While more a novelty than a practical fruit tree, the quintuplet apple does bear delicious edible fruit. Plant for full sun, fertilize and spray like other fruit trees. One species available now gives you red delicious, yellow delicious, red Jonathan, yellow transparent and Anoka apples.

Since this species is self-pollinating, you don't have to plant more than one tree. In fact, if you want just a single fruit tree, and your taste has a wide range, this may be exactly the tree for you!

Pick Quadruplet Peaches

Peach trees are available too, producing two, three and four different varieties on one tree, bearing fruit in succession over a period of months.

The art of grafting different varieties of the same fruit on one tree actually has practically no bounds. Horticulturists point to records of trees on which they've grafted over fifty different varieties on a single tree, with two dozen different kinds of apples produced from the tree in a single year!

Next scientific marvel . . . a fruit bowl tree bearing the ingredients for an entire fruit salad?

Luscious New English-inspired Apple

A superdelicious new apple will have the doctor coming to your house, if he's a friend and a gourmet. Because at last you can serve and enjoy a new apple variety—new to the United States, that is, but one that friends who've visited England have raved about to me for years.

You've probably also seen people drooling as they told you about the delicious special flavor of Cox's orange pippin which they relished in England. I've heard so often, "It's the world's finest eating apple, bar none!" But it's a very perishable fruit, so couldn't be shipped well.

While breeders haven't had much success in growing Cox's orange pippin here, they finally have combined it with America's famous McIntosh. The variety introduced by the New York State Experiment Station has been dubbed "Barry."

I haven't munched on a Barry myself, but they tell me that the flavor is exceptional and exquisite, and that the light golden color inside adds exciting eye appeal to taste appeal.

If you're enterprising, try to get a couple of trees now so that eventually you can pick and serve this rare and reputedly marvelous treat.

Radiant Red-red-red Peach Trees!

If you like to "see red," you can now enjoy a triple-feature, triple-red little peach tree that's a delightful new decorative novelty. It never grows taller than ten feet, and has dramatic, graceful, ruby beauty.

In spring, the foliage is a bright glowing red. At the same time, the tree develops an abundance of deep rose blossoms—an enchanting picture. The blossoms then turn into perfectly round little peaches which ripen into dark red spheres, about 1½ inches in diameter.

When you bite into these juicy little peaches, you'll find the insides luscious white, with a sweet delicious flavor.

This red-leaf peach tree is a delightful addition to your home. It requires no more than the usual care of dwarf fruit trees in respect to planting in full sun, fertilizing and spraying.

However, don't think that the fruit will begin to match the huge luscious peaches that are grown on regular trees. Consider this ornamental flowering beauty primarily as a decorative asset, with a special bonus of small but satisfying peach gems.

As such, it's a little masterpiece of fruitful color!

New Enthusiasm Over Espaliered Plants!

More and more gardeners are enjoying the training and growth of espaliered plants and small trees—a type of gardening that has been very popular in the great formal estates of Europe. Espaliered plants are simply those that are trained to grow flat against walls, fences, trellises, screens or any such upright surface—in severe formal patterns like a huge candelabra, or in loose informal designs.

Why not try one or more espaliered plants against the garage or house wall? It's fun and creative as you "sculpture" with Nature's aid.

I've seen a particularly effective use of espaliering in a home where a lovely little fruit tree was trained against an open

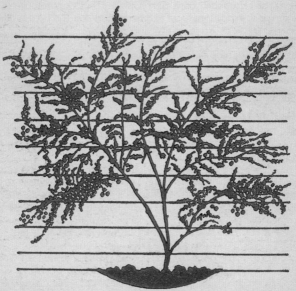

Train dwarf tree to form graceful branching design.

wire screen which separated the terrace from the back entrance to the house. It provided a "living partition" of lively growing green to make the terrace more of a separate outdoor room, especially attractive for barbecue dining.

How to grow espaliered plants and trees? It's not difficult if you keep after the plants with regular care so that they stay within bounds and don't get out of hand. Here are a few basic guides:

Prune, Prune and Prune Some More

1. Dwarf fruit trees are good examples for instruction. Select a healthy specimen that has three or more strong upright stems; the best bet is to buy trees which have already been started and trained for espaliering. Cut back canes and shoots that will mar the desired formation—right to the main stems. Prune side growth back, but leave a few inches on each, to promote more fruit spurs.

2. Plant according to normal directions given on other pages, in plenty of rich, fertile, well-drained soil, a foot away

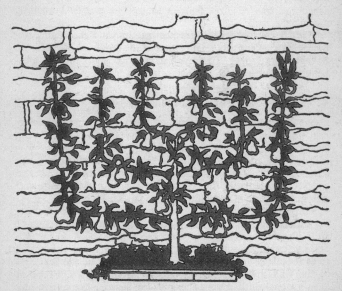

Espaliered dwarf pear tree in lovely candelabrum shape.

from the wall or fence. Fruit trees must have at least five hours a day of full, direct sunlight. Evergreens should be planted to face north.

3. Tie the branches to the wall, after you've determined the pattern you want your tree to follow—whether it's a candelabra effect, branches growing like the widespread fingers of a hand, forming many outspread horizontals, or an informal fan effect—you decide, you're the artist!

Make sure the nails or screw-eyes are well anchored on the surface you choose, and use strong tie-backs of flat wire or plastic so as not to cut into the supported stems or branches.

4. Proper pruning is very important and decisive in your espaliering success. Your heavy corrective pruning should be done in early spring and in winter, before fast growth begins. Cut out crossing and competing stems ruthlessly. Prune side growth into the planned shape. If the tree has reached the maximum height for your purposes, cut back the terminal shoots.

Use sharp pruning shears, not heavy hedge shears. Clean, sharp cuts help keep the plant healthy.

You must also trim back outward growth that stands out too far from the wall, because the beauty and symmetry of an espaliered tree requires flatness as well as proper branching against the wall.

With flowering shrubs, correct pruning and shortening are done very effectively right after full flowering, when the flowers start fading. Thus, you encourage and promote most beautiful future buds.

Excitement in Design

You have increasing fun as you learn more about espaliering, just as an artist learns and improves with each painting he completes.

You can train the beautiful firethorn, a semievergreen shrub with gorgeous red and orange autumn berries, against a drab fence so that the foliage sprays out and appears as a rich green fountain sparkling with color accents.

You might decide to play tricks with a number of flowering quince trees, and form a blooming and repeating design of large blossoming triangles against the garage wall—an intriguing, eye-catching conversation piece. Simply space the young trees about two feet apart when you plant, and tie the branches to the wall in triangular formations as they grow. Prune at least every month during the growing season, to remove any growth that spoils your design.

Eat your designs, as well as enjoying the sight of them, with pretrained espaliered dwarf fruit trees. Most popular is the candelabra shape, with two main branchings from each side of the trunk. On a vertical branch, you keep cutting back new side shoots each month during summer to about four inches. You cut back shoots on horizontal branches to about six inches. This promotes bearing fruit spurs, so you can grow and pick the maximum in apples, pears, peaches, plums, cherries—whatever you plant.

Many Varieties Invite Espaliering

Choose your own favorites from the many beautiful shrubs and trees that respond graciously to espaliering. Forsythia is very amenable, also flowering quince, winter jasmine, abelia, many roses and others.

Among evergreens, yew, holly of many types, and other varieties thrive and form decorative patterns gracefully.

Most dwarf fruits take to espaliering excellently, also currant and gooseberry bushes, and others.

Treat your espaliered plantings well, with plenty of fertilization and watering, and they'll respond by delighting you with their exquisite formations and grace.

4-Way Speed Boost for Shade Trees

With modern methods and materials, you can speed up growth of shade trees so you can enjoy their beauty and practical aid to your property *years earlier* than if you just let the tree grow on its own. Here are four basic check points that many tree scientists recommend to you:

1. Don't skimp when planting a good shade tree. Dig a little wider than you'd ordinarily be minded to, so you can put more loose soil around the root-ball and give the roots a better chance to spread rapidly. Mix in to the loose soil a top quality peat moss or some other good composting material. The extra cost, time and labor you put in at this point pays off in establishing the tree faster, and in much speedier growth over the first year especially.

2. Feed the tree generously twice a year, using dry or liquid plant food with high nitrogen content. Applying some of the recently developed ureaform plant foods which feed the tree nitrogen over a long period of time is very effective.

3. Water thoroughly! A deep soaking at least every two weeks during the dry season is a must. That means soaking the water in deep—not inches deep, but a couple of feet deep. Probably the greatest "miracle" boost you can give a young

shade tree is this deep, deep soaking in hot, dry weather with Nature's own wonder-worker—*water*.

4. Prune the tree each year, but better prune too little than too much. Simply clip off a few of the lowest branches. A recommended rule with shade trees under twenty feet in height is to confine pruning so that at least three fourths of the tree is top with branches and foliage—and only one fourth trunk.

Puts You Years Ahead!

These extra hours each year, and the little extra money for fertilizer, pay off astonishingly. Your trees will actually attain useful height—so that they perform their graceful shading function *as much as two years earlier* than without this modern four-step care.

And you'll have beautiful flourishing trees that, with proper care, will add considerably to the value of your property—and can outlast the house itself!

Transplanting Trees, Watch the Growth Line!

You can go to a lot of expense and trouble planting a tree, and lose out on the glorious flourishing results you long for, if you disregard these reminders. In actually setting the tree in the ground, *make sure it stands at the same grade, as exactly as you possibly can, as it grew in its original spot* (at the nursery or elsewhere). Determine this by the easy-to-see growth line on the trunk. With this precaution, your tree is ready, set—grow!

You've made certain, of course, to prepare your planting pit properly. Don't make the mistake of paying a lot for the tree, and then skimping on the soil—you'd actually be better off the other way round.

Your best insurance of top results is to dig your pit *oversized*. Particularly with small trees, make your pit a minimum of two feet wider than the widest root spread. Make sure the pit will drain properly, is not blocked by some obstacle like a rock or ledge, and that it's generously back-filled with good topsoil. Or, use the original subsoil, mixed with some humous material such as spagnum peat moss (readily available at stores and nurseries).

Apply a good fertilizer, containing plenty of nitrogen for a good growth boost. Cultivate the surrounding areas deeply. With these precautions, you'll prove to others that, in spite of the popular Joyce Kilmer poem, *man can* make a tree . . . grow better!

Trunks—Handle with Care!

After you plant a young tree, be sure to wrap the tender trunk with burlap or heavy manila paper. This will help prevent abuse from sun, wind, harsh weather and to some degree from harmful insects.

You can now get heavy kraft paper especially prepared for this purpose. And the strong new household foils are also good and effective, but expensive; however, the foils have the advantage of clinging to the tree trunk once you press them on, saving you the time and trouble of tying with cord.

Yes, wrapping until the tree is well established may well prevent wrecking from exposure to the elements!

"Living Circle Guide" for Fertilizing Trees

You'll get excellent results in fertilizing small trees particularly with regular applications of a good complete water-soluble plant food. But follow this tip for quickest and best results.

If you apply the fertilizer right next to the trunk of the tree, you're not getting directly to the "living circle," that is, where most of the root tips lie. That's where the tree absorbs nourishment more effectively.

The "living circle" can be measured with your eye, just about where the ends of the branches are. Follow this circle with your hose or sprinkling can as you water in a balanced liquid fertilizer that's complete with valuable trace elements.

You'll revitalize the growth of your tree in a hurry!

Measure Your Miracles, on Young Trees

Just as you stand young children up against the wall every few months and check their growth in height, you'll enjoy measuring the growth of young trees—and it's also a valuable guide to their state of health.

You don't have to measure all the branches on each tree. Just measure a few shoots and keep a record of the average length. Then compare their growth with the following averages:

Young apple, pear and cherry trees should grow at least eight to ten inches each year.

Other, faster-growing fruit trees—peaches, plums and apricots—should grow anywhere from twelve to twenty inches yearly.

Slower, sturdier trees like oaks and elms should produce eight inches or more of new growth.

Speedier-growing common varieties like poplars and willows should grow twelve inches or more in a year.

Granted that there's sufficient rain, your trees should do as well or better than these averages. If so, keep doing what you're doing—you're on the right track.

But if your trees are below average growth, they need feeding. Especially toward fall, apply a good dry- or water-soluble fertilizer as directed on the package—and repeat regularly as instructed. Also, be sure the trees get plenty of water during the year.

With this checkup, and proper care and attention, you'll have healthy, vigorous trees whose beauty will give you increasing pleasure each year.

Use Hormones to Prevent Unwanted Fruit Growth!

It's amazing but true that while hormone chemicals will work wonders in increasing fruit growth and production, they can also be used to stop growth of unwanted fruits!

You may wish to prevent growth of some fruit such as some crabapples that you have for beauty of foliage but not for fruit.

Also, horse chestnuts are frequently undesirable if they invite invasions of small boys and ruination of the nearby lawn.

Pick tempting apples and pears from columnar trees.

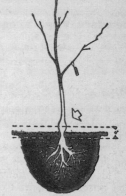

Set graft point above soil level on dwarf fruit trees.

With some mulberries, gardeners frequently prefer that fruit-production be checked to prevent staining of adjacent walks.

In such cases, you can buy corrective hormone products for these preventive purposes. Follow instructions in spraying the blossoms, usually in heavy dosages, but only as directed. Properly used for prevention of fruiting, such spraying will assure you of lovely, healthy trees and foliage but without the undesirable fruits.

And, where you've applied the spray properly to thin out some of the fruit on a tree, you'll have a wonderful increase in the size and quality of the fruits that do grow. Isn't it gratifying to have such miracles at your fingertips now?

Hormones Keep Apples from Dropping Off!

A friend used to say to me sadly, "I have some lovely apple trees, but so many of the apples drop off prematurely, ahead of proper picking time, that the loss depresses me every season."

That needn't happen to you any more. Another hormone "miracle" will keep your apples on the tree so they won't drop off before they're ripe to be picked. You can get these hormone products now at your garden supply dealer . . . look for labels instructing on *drop-off prevention for apples.*

Application is simple. Just make the solution to the concentration directed on the label, and spray as instructed.

One vital caution is essential: better watch those apples carefully and pick them as soon as they reach ripeness and maturity. Otherwise, because of the hormone application, those apples may hang onto the tree until they're way overripe and not usable at all!

Again, as with most of science's "miracle" products, you and your intelligence are highly important ingredients.

Miraculous Spray Thinning of Apples

More and more commercial fruit growers are using amazing new sprays for thinning out apples and other fruits. That's a late report by no less than the U. S. Department of Agriculture. You too can get better fruit crops by using these thinning sprays if your trees bear too heavily.

This exciting new thinning technique results in many benefits: better-looking fruit of larger size; more uniform, better-tasting fruit. Most remarkable, some species which ordinarily have produced biennial crops *actually bear fruit annually* with proper spray thinning!

If you buy a fruit thinning spray, be sure to apply exactly as instructed with the product you use, and you'll have better crops "automatically"—eliminating tiresome and less effective hand thinning.

Miracle "P" Protects Peach Trees

Here's a very simple and miraculously effective way to protect your precious peach trees against borers. These pests are much too prevalent and only very good luck will keep your peach trees from being harmed and even ruined by borers at some time, unless you do something about it.

It's as easy as this. Get a package of magical crystals of *paradi-chlorobenzene* at a garden supply store or nursery. Spread a circular band, about two inches wide, of the crystals around the tree, but about four inches away from the tree in order not to make contact with the trunk.

Then cover the band of crystals with a light dusting of soil. The purpose is twofold—for a more natural look, and primarily to help keep the fumes from the crystals in the soil for greatest effectiveness.

With this quick treatment, you can forget about the nasty borers and remember the luscious peaches you're going to pick.

How to Win Victories with Vines!

One decorative touch that many people overlook is the beauty that a flowering vine can give to a flat, drab wall, fence or other uninteresting surface. Think of adding this extra dimension of foliage enchantment to your gardening.

You can choose from a marvelous variety of vines these days, which will give you much pleasure over a large or small area, using practically no room on the ground!

See how simple it is to get exceptionally fine returns from a small area by planting a vine.

Easy Planting Suggestions

Spade up an area close to the wall or fence where you'll set your vine, allowing several inches of space all around the outspread roots. Crumble the soil well for better drainage, and mix in some peat moss and a complete plant food.

Set the collar of the plant about two inches below the surface of the earth. Fill in the soil, watering as you fill, then firm the earth well. That's all—your vine is set to go and grow!

Tips on Caring for the Vine

After the vine has emerged and is growing well, help keep it cool and moist during the summer by applying a mulch of peat moss or whatever material you have handy. Keep the vine watered well. Fertilize well at least twice a year, and more, with a complete liquid or dry plant food. You can apply a good water-soluble fertilizer right on the foliage itself!

Train the vine along the surface, as you wish it to climb. Help support the growth with flat plant-tie bands, or flat loops of leather or plastic which won't cut into the stems. Special hooked screws or nails are also good, so long as surfaces aren't sharp and injurious.

A graceful trellis of wood or aluminum or other material that suits the surface is a fine help.

Prune the vine's healthy growth only if you want to reduce its growing speed. Otherwise, prune each year to remove thin, spindly or dead wood. A mulch of leaves or straw or peat moss is helpful protection as winter sets in.

Watch out for vines strangling themselves. Some varieties wrap stems and tendrils around other growth, the plant choking and strangling itself or other plantings adjacent. A checkup every few months will enable you to prune away any such murderous tendrils; cut away as tenderly and carefully as a surgeon performing a delicate operation.

Protection Against Infestation

Keep checking your vines for insect or disease damage, just as you do other plants. Then apply the miracle chemicals recommended elsewhere in this book. For fungus troubles, such as black rot disease, the new fungicides, ferbam or captan, are usually very effective.

As a class, vines are extremely hardy and won't give much trouble usually, with regular inspection and action.

Choose from Many Varieties of Vines

Make your own selection from a good supplier, according to what you like best, and ready availability. Here are some varieties that are generalliy obtainable in vigorous, improved species, and can be grown beautifully in most areas:

Pink anemone clematis provides lovely flowers in spring, and a screen of decorative foliage all through season. You can also get magnificent giant clematis with huge spectacular flowers up to eight inches across! The blooms are large enough to use as cut flowers which last over a week indoors.

Boston ivy is a favorite with its beautiful small leaves. Other varieties of ivy, developed for improvement in recent years, are hardy and decorative.

Purple wisteria opens into lovely large lavender clusters of fragrant flowers. When the long flower clusters finish blooming, thousands of attractive green leaves appear. This hardy vine grows high and drapes along a surface beautifully.

Silver lace is an amazingly fast-growing species. It can grow fifteen feet or more in one season. In August, it cloaks your wall with hundreds of tiny white flowers, and continues right up to frost. Looks delicate, but it's really a vigorous, sturdy beauty.

Wintercreeper, one of the sturdiest of the evergreen vines, is versatile in that it either trails along a low fence or climbs with your help. Foliage is very attractive glossy green.

Everblooming honeysuckle thrives in sun or partial shade and will enhance your home with hundreds of colorful flowers, deliciously fragrant especially toward evening—a delightful "welcome home" after a day away at work.

The vines listed are just to give you a small start in making your selection. There are dozens more for your choice and pleasure, including the very popular decorative and edible grape vines, of course.

Keep the vine in mind as a "plus" gardening feature, as an extra "miracle" of green glory enriching your premises.

Landscaping Flavor Sensation— Seedless Grapes

Wherever you can use a decorative vine in a sunny area—on walls, trellises, fences, porches—consider a lovely grape vine. Now you can get and grow delicious rich golden yellow seedless grapes, as well as blue concord, golden muscat and other purple, white and golden varieties.

Grape vines don't require much more than average vine care, yet they grow gracefully and enrich your home with their lovely green leaves. The fruit you pick is a special welcome bonus.

Tips for Best Results

Plant grape vines with the same care, and following the same instructions as given for planting tree roses.

Fertilize your vines well with a dry complete fertilizer, and with several boosts on foliage and roots each season with a complete water-soluble plant food.

Your grapes will mature more quickly if you plant the vines in a warm spot, with plenty of sun, as against the side of a building or on a flat fence of boards or tight poles.

Use the miracle sprays against disease. Ferbam and captan fungicides work wonders in preventing and eliminating black rot which may attack your grapes. As a whole, the vines are hardy and disease resistant—when you buy top-quality plants.

Plant New Seedless Beauties

Your family will enjoy the beauty of the vines, the privacy of grape vines if used as a shield, and particularly the fruit of the comparatively new seedless varieties.

Get well-matured plants. Three-year-old seedless grape vines may bear some fruit the very first year in your garden, as much as six lbs. per vine the second year, and up to twenty-five lbs. from a single vine the third season!

The grapes are medium size, very juicy and deliciously sweet. The flesh is golden yellow, firm, meaty and crisp. And this fruiting marvel matures as much as a month before many other types of grapes.

You've never tasted grapes at their best until you pick them off your own vines, wash briskly and then pop them into your mouth. Good eating and good health!

HOUSE PLANTS

---

5 Important Pointers to Indoor Plant Growth

"Let joy be confined!" the poet might have said in respect to growing plants indoors. Of course millions of us know the tremendous pleasures to be derived from bringing Nature's radiant colors and beauties inside our homes.

But, for the thriving results you want, you must realize one basic truth: bringing Nature's wonders indoors is definitely a matter of growing plants under unnatural conditions. The key to success is to try to duplicate a natural environment just as much as possible.

Aside from trying to duplicate natural conditions with your own greenhouse or special setup, here are the major valuable guides to success with house plants, granted that you start with healthy plants and good fertile soil, and that you protect them when necessary against insects and disease.

1. LIGHT: The proof that many plants simply won't survive without light is that your choicest specimens won't thrive in a dark cellar or continuously darkened room, no matter how much water and fertilization you give them.

Most plants, including callas, geraniums, African violets and many other popular indoor varieties, won't flourish without some full sun. So keep the plants where they'll get most sunlight. If they're becoming pale, shine a 100-watt bulb on them, fairly close-up—but not so close as to burn, of course—for a couple of hours as twilight sets in. The green will usually come back in a hurry.

And, remember that your plants are *heliotropic*. No, that's not a dread disease, it merely means that they grow toward the sun. So, set a day at the end of each week to turn the plants halfway around, or else they may grow heavily one-sided and you'll have a curious collection of leaning towers of Pisa.

For most fern varieties, the plants prefer no sun. Others, including some begonias, caladium and fuchsia need only a little sunlight.

2. WATER: Water your plants every few days, and learn to judge just how much water they need, depending on how they respond, whether water collects and appears swampy. Use your own good sense as a guide, for you'll get to know your plants as good friends. Too much water may sometimes be almost as harmful as too little, although you're better off watering too much than letting plants go dry.

If you're in an area where the water from your tap is heavily treated with chemicals, watch for ill effects on your plants. You may wish to collect rain water, or melt down snow although this isn't often necessary.

And here's something very few people stop to think about. The rains that fall from above during best growing seasons are never icy cold. So don't ever use icy cold water on your indoor plants or you may shock them out of growth. It's easy enough to run water that's room temperature. How would you react to having your feet drenched suddenly with icy cold water?

3. HUMIDITY: Excessive dryness indoors is even worse for your plants than for yourself. Moisture in the air is necessary to vigorous plant life and radiant foliage, just like water in the earth that feeds the plant's roots. Moisture in the air keeps natural starches in plants from drying out, helps prevent leaves from going dry and brittle.

An easy method of humidifying, which is better for your health as well as for your plants, is to keep water trays on or behind radiators.

Another good method is to place the plant in a saucer or tray of some sort, keeping some water in the tray and elevating the pot or other container above the level of the water, with stones or rods, so that moisture rises around the plant. This is particularly desirable if you keep your plants on a hot radiator.

4. AIR: The foliage of plants separates carbon dioxide from the air by an intricate natural process. If common undesirable fumes, such as gas or fresh paint fumes are in the

air, or if the air is heavy and stale continuously, this delicate process breaks down. Your plants will become weak and sickly.

Better make sure your plants get fresh air daily, but be guided sensibly by how you bring air indoors for yourself. Never, never keep your plants in a draft, or open windows so that a blast of cold air shocks the plants' normally warm stems and foliage. Opening windows slightly from the top, or a narrow opening in casement windows, or simply opening windows, not too wide, in the next room, will keep the atmosphere airy and your plants cheery.

5. DUST: As further proof that most of gardening, indoors or outdoors, is just good sense, think a second about the dust problem. Outdoors, there's always enough breeze, even if you're not aware of it, to keep dust and dirt from settling on plants. But indoors, with little movement of the air, dust collects on the plants—although not always visible to the eye.

When dust settles on foliage, the leaf pores become clogged. The plant has trouble absorbing carbon dioxide from the air. The miraculous process of photosynthesis is impaired, and the plant stops manufacturing starches for energy and growth. Sounds terrible, doesn't it?

But it's so easy to keep plants sufficiently dust-free with a very soft brush or cloth or, better yet, with refreshing light spraying every couple of days. However, never spray and go away leaving drops of moisture if sun is shining directly on the foliage. The drops of water act like a magnifying glass, concentrating the sun and sometimes causing brown spots from burns.

All this may sound complicated but it's really very easy, won't take you more than a few minutes a day at most, unless you enjoy dawdling over your plants and admiring them, as most gardeners do. Beyond all, you constantly have the beauty of nature about you and your loved ones, enriching your lives.

As for recommended varieties of house plants, the range is almost limitless. So many of your outdoors favorites can be brought indoors, and there are many special indoors beauties. Make your choice according to your own tastes in flowers, foliage and size. You'll enjoy most those that you personally select for your home.

Points on Repotting House Plants

Some experts sum up the best advice about repotting house plants in one word: *don't!* That is, don't repot a plant unless you're certain it has outgrown its present pot. Actually it's more difficult for a plant to thrive and grow best in a pot that's too large than one that's just a little too small.

But when your plant has grown to the point where roots are starting to come through the bottom of the pot, it's time to give it a new home. Choose a pot that's only a little larger, scrub it out clean, and you're ready for repotting.

Steps for "Miracle" Results

1. Place a few chunks of broken clay pot, or some small stones at the bottom of the new pot, for proper drainage.

2. Have some rich potting soil handy; fill in a layer over the stones or chunks at the bottom of the pot.

3. Turn the old pot upside down, with your hand gently cradling the plant and top soil. Tap the pot on the side of a bench or other object, and the complete plant and soil will slide into your hand.

4. Center the plant carefully in the new pot, keeping the root mass intact. Fill in the new soil around the sides, pressing in firmly, but avoid a cementlike texture.

5. The plant should now be firmly centered in the new pot, an inch below the top rim. Water in well with a good water-soluble fertilizer (I get excellent results with a packaged 15-30-15).

Your plant will now have the best restart in life in its new home. Happy growing!

Wick Watering Wizardry for House Plants

Many gardeners who are wizards at growing magnificent house plants claim that the best possible way to give the plants plenty of the right kind of moisture is through wick watering. They state that only this ingenious method provides proper and uniform moisture.

To add to your gardening ease, now you can buy excellent, long-lasting wicks made of spun glass material. Or, you can use homemade wicks that you fashion yourself out of ordinary heavy burlap.

How to Make Wicks

If you're a do-it-yourselfer, here's a simple lesson in wick-making. Cut a burlap strip about 5″ long and 5″ wide. Cut a slit down the center about 1½″ long. Bunch the remaining length and tie with cord fairly tight in three places, about an inch apart. Your wick is ready for use.

In the empty pot, push the tied end down through the hole

at the bottom of the pot. Then spread out the flat, slitted cloth in opposite directions, lining the inside bottom of the pot. Put in your soil or sand and the plant, without using any pebbles or pieces of pot at the bottom.

Now place the pot in a larger, deep saucer or low pan of any material that will hold water, with the tied end of the wick resting in the saucer. If the pot doesn't balance, even it out in the saucer with a few bits of wood, metal washers or such.

You simply fill the saucer with water, and keep filling with water as often as necessary. Your homemade wick acts like a lamp wick, pulling the water up into the soil as needed.

If you've used burlap for the wick, it's best to change to a new one every few months, as the porous material tends to rot somewhat.

Two types of good make-'em-yourself wicks for house plants.

Special "Miracle" Tip

Every few weeks, instead of filling the saucer with plain water, fill with a solution of water-soluble fertilizer, in proportion as recommended on the package. If a spray is handy, wet the foliage also with the solution.

You'll be surprised and delighted with the exceptional growth and beauty of blooms with this liquid fertilizer boost. If you're in a mood to see for yourself, give this treatment to one plant, and leave another plant like it untreated. That's the best convincer I know, and an enjoyable revelation for you and any skeptical friends!

Plastic Is New House Plant "Baby Sitter"

I've seen women almost weep about leaving their house plants when going off for a week or two on a vacation or trip. Will the neighbor actually remember to come in and water the beloved plants every day? What to do?

Now plastic film offers a miraculous solution, will act as "baby sitter" keeping your house plants in good condition until you return. And the only "baby sitter" fee you pay is the cost of the plastic film which you can use over again later if you handle it with care.

Here's how the plastic film takes care of your house plants while you vacation elsewhere happily. Buy thin, transparent polyethylene film for gardening at a store or nursery. Then wrap the film snugly around the plant, *after you've watered the plant thoroughly*.

Be sure the plant is "packaged" by the film, like a head of lettuce at the market—firmly holding to the plant, but not so tight that it presses hard against leaves or branches. See that the film is as airtight as possible around the pot.

That plastic "packaging" will keep moisture in, enough for up to two weeks. The transparency will let necessary light get to the plant. And the film has many tiny perforations which enable the plant to "breathe."

When you return from your vacation, simply unwrap the plastic covering, water the plant and care for it as usual.

Now your worries are over, and your carefree vacation is wrapped up happily by this plastic miracle!

Spray Extra Beauty on House Plants

With a touch of your fingertip, now you can spray extra beauty on the leaves of your philodendron, ivies and other hard-surfaced foliage plants!

A handy new product that comes in a pressure can sprays a plastic-type of coating on the leaves and gives them a long-lasting lustrous shine that adds to the plant's beauty.

In addition, the spray gives the leaves extra resistance against dust, which doesn't stay on the shiny surface. The amazing coating has an elasticity so that it "grows" with the leaves.

Just one spraying helps to beautify the hard-surfaced leaves and keep them more beautiful for a long, long time.

Killing "Springtails" on House Plants

That chemical marvel, *lindane,* comes to your rescue quickly if you find your house plants invaded by tiny white jumping insects. These rather cheery looking little fellows are named "springtails." You may see them dashing about on the soil when you water your plants, and in the moist saucers or bottoms of plants.

If your soil is rich and fertile, springtails prefer to feed on these nutrients, and generally won't harm the plants. But if they can't find the organic matter they want in the soil, they'll then start feasting on the roots of your plants and weakening them.

You and science to the rescue! Mix a solution of 25 per cent wettable lindane powder, one tablespoonful per gallon of water. Then water the plants thoroughly.

If those springy springtails are still in evidence about a week later, another application of the lindane solution to the plants will usually make them disappear completely.

3 Ways to Avoid Pot-withering

If you're a gardener who loves indoor plants as well as outdoor (and most do!), you don't take much pride in having a green thumb if the lower leaves of your African violets and many other plants show damage, withering and finally drop off. The reason in most cases is that the leaves are killed by contact with the rims of clay pots in which soil chemicals have inevitably collected.

Here are three simple ways you can prevent such ugly damage. Use a glazed pot . . . or dip the upper rim of a clay pot in paraffin to provide a glossy, noncollecting surface . . . or cover the pot rim decoratively with tin foil.

Your plants will reward you with prideful beauty from top to bottom leaves!

More Fun—Garden Under Lights!

When the wintry weather drives you indoors, you can bring your gardening enjoyment in with you by setting up a very simple light-nurtured garden in your cellar or attic or a spare room. Just choose a location where the temperature won't go too low or too high. An average of 65° to 70° is best for success with most average varieties.

Your setup can be as simple as a "table" made of boards placed on a few wooden sawhorses. On top of this, you can set some watertight flat pans, to hold many little pots or flats of plants—the species you enjoy most.

Above it all, install dependable cool, strong light. One of the most satisfactory sources of light is a double 85-watt fluorescent fixture, placed about fifteen inches above the plants, but adjustable to varying heights as plants grow. The size of your garden will determine the length of the fixture, or vice versa.

An automatic timer is necessary for the fixture, as the lights should be on about fourteen hours out of each twenty-four, and you shouldn't make your plants take chances with your own handling of the switch.

Tend the plants like other indoor plantings, in regard to proper watering, fertilization, protective and corrective spraying, air and humidity.

I must warn that once you start gardening under lights, you're likely to keep adding more tables, more fixtures, until you're even spreading out into other rooms. In fact, the wife of one of my business associates tells me that since her husband started gardening under lights, she can't even drive him outdoors during the summer!

Think of how much he saves in sun-tan lotion!

AFRICAN VIOLETS

How to Grow "Miracle" African Violets!

If you're not growing African violets in your home already, you're going to, sooner or later! So you'd better grow them sooner and according to the best methods, in order to get the greatest pleasure from these exquisite plants—in the quickest possible time.

If you're not too familiar with African violets, the first shock will be that they're not even "violets" at all, as most people know traditional violets. They're a beautiful species in their own right, and many people state flatly that they're as close as you can come to perfection in house plants.

In any case, you can derive much pleasure and beauty from African violets. They're small enough to decorate most any room. Contrary to some propaganda, they're easy to grow. All you have to do is know how: a few simple basic rules suffice, along with some special "booster" tips, and you'll be enjoying their lovely blooms and rich green foliage all year 'round.

Added Pleasure in Joining
The African Violet Society of America

So fiercely devoted are African violet fans that many of them are joined in a society that helps them get more enjoyment out of growing their favorite species, and out of life.

You too may derive added pleasure from joining this group. If you're interested, write to the African Violet Society of America through your favorite garden magazine.

Many Gorgeous Varieties for Your Choice

In the first place, you don't have to limit your growing of African violets to the standard purples. Before you choose your first plants, realize that you can select just those colors that suit your taste and thus will give you most pleasure. So don't just begin with any plant offered you, or be satisfied if the choice available is limited. Seek another supplier.

Make your selection from this check list of colors: blue, purple, pink, reds, lavender, white, and a wide variety of bi-colored blooms, blue-and-white, Burgundy-and-white, purple-and-white, and lots more.

Also, you can grow the popular single varieties, others that produce blooms with ruffled edges, or dramatic double flowers. An almost limitless field of enchantment is open to you!

Potting Your Plants

You don't need or want tremendous pots for your African violets. Pots up to six inches in diameter are usually adequate. Avoid very high pots since the African violet is a low-growing plant, and shows off best in a low planter.

Most any favorite pot or planter will do, but I lean toward the newer plastic planters since they don't absorb any water from the plants, so you don't have to water as often. Also, the plastic and glazed pots don't harm foliage on contact.

You'll avoid troubles if you sterilize the pot before planting. It's usually enough to scrub with soap and very hot water. Even better, wash out with a handy household disinfectant, then rinse in hot water. Don't worry that the African violet is supersensitive—it's not. It's just safer to sterilize the pot, for the very best results; it's quite likely you won't have trouble even if you skip this sterilizing step.

For soil, it pays to buy specially packaged African violet soil, making sure it's marked "sterilized"—as most such packaged soils are. This is a modern advance that pays off in far better growth. Here again, if you wish to use what you have available—you may get satisfactory results with a soil you put together yourself—mix about a third of good fertile earth, a third of vermiculite and a third of peat moss. You'll be better off if you bake that mixture in a moderate oven for about an hour in order to sterilize it. (No, don't plant in the hot soil, unless you want baked African violets!)

Now, on to the potting. Place some stones or pieces of pot (very clean or sterile) in the bottom of the pot, as with other indoor plants, for drainage. (You can also use wicks in the pot, as explained elsewhere in this book.) Fill with the special African violet soil so that the crown of the plant is exactly level with the top of the earth, not below the earth.

Leave about a half inch of space between the soil and top of the planter. The soil should be snug and dense in the pot, but not too tight or compact. Just "caress" the soil into pleasant firmness as you fill.

Water in the plant gently. As an extra growth boost, use a mild solution of liquid plant food to help the plant get started vigorously.

For repotting with fresh soil, or moving plants to larger pots, follow the same simple procedure.

Feeding for Glorious Growth

Just as mothers have their pet formulas for babies, there are many pet ideas about feeding, among African violet fans. Some go all out for *liquid manure,* but nothing I've ever seen has convinced me that results are better than with an excellent modern water-soluble plant food, easy and pleasant to handle (not smelly), and formulized by scientific methods to provide not only the major nutrients, but also vital trace elements that will help your African violets to beam with full vitality.

For most vigorous, healthful growth, feed with water-soluble plant food—in the solution recommended on the package you buy—every two weeks during spring and fall, fastest-growing seasons, and every three to four weeks the balance of the year.

Be Wise in Watering

Here's where your personal sense of "loving care" comes in. According to atmospheric conditions in your home, learn how much or how little to water your plants. General rule: keep the soil moist but not flooded.

Use a long-nosed watering can so you place the water on the soil, not on the foliage. African violets are in a special class in that respect, as water-spotting on foliage can be quite harmful. Especially don't let water accumulate on the foliage in the sun or under lights, lest those watery "magnifying glasses" act to burn the leaves.

As with other indoor plants, apply water at room temperature or slightly warm, in order not to risk giving the plants the shivers and shock.

Light on Your Subjects

One thing that African violets can't live without is plenty of light. Without it, you won't get flowers—at any rate, not the "miracle" flowers you want. It's easy to fool yourself, because often the plants will produce rich green leaves even with insufficient light, but if those plants don't bloom, a lack of light is usually the reason.

For best results, see that the plants get up to four hours a day of sunlight on the average, preferably during the early morning or late afternoon hours, not in the strong midday sun.

African violets also love modern fluorescent lighting. Best recommendation is to use two-tube 40-watt fluorescent lights, set about a foot above the tops of the plants, turned on from twelve to sixteen hours a day. You can get planters now complete with fluorescent lighting, and very attractive for most any room.

A third method is to shed light for several hours a day on your African violets under a lamp with a 100-watt bulb. Just be sure that the bulb is at least 1½ feet from the top of the plant.

Of course, it's bad to "overheat" your plants with too much artificial light, or even overexposure to sunlight. Your tipoff on this score is when leaves turn pale green and assume a generally withered look. Correct your lighting and your African violet will usually respond and return to its normal green beauty fast.

One more tip: as with all indoor plants, keep turning the pots every few days if next to a window or other light concentrated from one direction, otherwise they'll grow lopsided toward the light.

See the difference gibberellins make on African violets.

Good Housecleaning Helps

As soon as flowers start fading, nip them off—to keep the plant looking proud and beautiful. Do the same with leaves that look less than healthfully perfect, as they'll be replaced soon.

Brush very gently, or spray with a fine mist every few days to clean dirt away from the dust-collecting leaves. But never spray under bright light or sunlight.

If bottom leaves that may touch the rim of a clay pot turn brown and withered, pluck them off. Then cover the rim with aluminum foil so that the clay can't contaminate the leaves by direct contact. It's helpful to wipe the rim of any pot, even glazed or plastic, with a damp cloth every few weeks anyhow, to keep the surface clean of any residue that might collect and harm the foliage.

Such good housecleaning means healthier plants of any variety!

Modern Protection Pays

To help prevent insect troubles before they begin, it's wise to spray your African violets every few weeks with a good general indoor insecticide. Those containing wonder-working *malathion* are particularly effective. Such spraying—so simple with the new aerosol cans—will prevent and control most harmful insects that may attack African violets.

Beware of Mites

If your plant starts looking sickly, and the leaves turn yellowish and dull green, mites have probably attacked. First, move that plant at least a foot away from healthy plants, so that the mites can't spread. Then, use the malathion spray, repeating as directed on the product you buy—if necessary. Usually such sprays work with amazing speed to kill the mites and help your plant recover beautifully.

If Crown Rot Develops

Sure sign is when a plant droops in spite of sufficient watering. Remove the plant from the pot and examine the roots. If rot has attacked them, remove the infected roots completely, dusting the unimpaired portions of the roots with a *fermate* powder. Then repot in a new container with new soil. Water with liquid plant food and the African violet will usually bounce back and thrive. Crown rot is quite uncommon, fortunately, and is usually the fault of too much watering, or watering into the foliage rather than directly on the soil, as recommended.

Begin . . . Add . . . Enjoy

African violet fever is catching. And it's wonderful! Once you start with a single plant or a few, chances are you'll want more colors, more varieties. The reason is that the rich foliage and enchanting blooms are so rewarding in their grace and beauty.

Just start and tend them well, as suggested here. Keep African violets out of drafts . . . see that there's plenty of humidity in the air, temperatures from 60° to 75°. Practically any place indoors, or in your own greenhouse, the lovely blooms will delight you week in, week out.

Reproduction by Mail Leaves!

That's not a misspelling—"mail" leaves is correct, not "male" leaves, in this instance. African violet fans are actually helping friends hundreds and even thousands of miles away to enjoy reproductions of their own favorite plants.

If you wish to befriend a friend who's also an African violet enthusiast, mail him or her one or more leaves from your most beautiful plants, with at least 1½ inches of stem on the leaf.

Just wrap the leaf carefully, flat and snug in polyethylene film. Protect it with a piece of firm cardboard and slip into an ordinary envelope. Shoot it out airmail if that speeds delivery. As soon as your friend receives it, he can place it in water or vermiculite, as instructed on these pages.

In a short time perhaps you'll even receive a snapshot of your "mail" offspring, happily thriving and spreading pleasure and beauty in a home far away. No letter ever conveyed a sweeter message!

HERBS

Extra Happiness in Growing Healthful Herbs

If you've never grown herbs, by all means set aside a section of your garden, or borders along a path, or a little area not too far from your kitchen door for this happy kind of gardening that rewards all your senses!

You'll love the scent of spicy herbs as you walk and work in your garden. You and your family will rave about the delicious extra flavorings your home-grown, fresh-picked herbs add to foods. And your eyes will be delighted by the sight of perky, softly colorful herb plants about your home.

Each herb is, in itself, a little flavor "miracle" of nature. Just look and follow these simple tips on how to start growing herbs at their best. You can go on from there to become more and more "herb-happy" each season.

Herb Plantings Multiply Your Pleasures

Most herbs are very easy to grow, and as you pick, they multiply rapidly. The more flavorful leaves you pick, the more flavor the plants seem to want to give you. Soon you'll find you have plenty of extra plants which you can give to friends and neighbors as you thin or confine the growth.

You don't have to go wild and grow every herb you've ever heard of. No matter how many you grow (or how many I list here), some grumpy gourmet is going to say, "What, you had the nerve to leave out the wonderful Whatchamacallit?" So, start with a few of your favorite flavors, and expand later, if you like.

You can start herbs from seeds, or grow your own seedlings indoors before the outdoors season begins. Many gardeners, especially at the beginning, prefer to use young plants available from nearby nurseries. You can usually get a fine variety of species which are quite inexpensive.

Planting Herbs for Top Results

Most herbs don't require too rich or too specialized a soil. They'll ordinarily thrive most anywhere in your garden where they get full sun.

Set the plants into moist soil, well fertilized, preferably with a somewhat sandy consistency. Since the area isn't large, it's easy to mix a little sand in if you have a clayey soil.

Just be sure that the earth is loose and drains normally. Water plentifully. A good water-soluble plant food is a great growth booster, giving your herb plants extra vitality and vigor, with resultant superior flavor.

With young plants, shade them a bit for the first week until they become well established—if planted during hot sun season. With seeds—perfectly satisfactory in most species, except that they just take a little longer—follow package directions, and keep watering plentifully.

Many Delicious Varieties

Most herbs will grow in most climates, with just the ordinary attention required by most of your other plants. And what a thrilling range of flavors to grow! Here are just a few.

Sweet marjoram grows about twelve inches tall. It has pale lavender blossoms and little rounded leaves. Many good cooks use the fresh-picked leaves (and later, dried) in chicken soups and stuffings, in peas, potatoes, and even tender young string beans.

Sweet basil grows beautifully as a light green plant a couple of feet high. After flower buds form, keep picking the foliage and using it fresh with tomatoes particularly, also with meats and in soups. Excellent dried, too, the fresh leaves have an especially tempting tang. There I go drooling into my typewriter again!

Appetizing anise grows dainty and delicate, about a foot and a half high, gracing the garden and providing unique flavoring for cookies and cooking.

Summer Savory produces little pointed leaves and lovely

purple blooms, branching low in the garden. Sprinkled over many of the tasty vegetables of the cabbage family, for example, it adds an entrancing extra touch of tingling flavor.

Lacy dill sprouts a couple of feet high, its delicate foliage and flowers waving in the slightest breeze. Used sparingly in salads, soups and on meats, it provides special delectable flavor —at its very best fresh picked from your herb garden.

Summer savory is a rewarding herb.

Robust borage reveals heavenly blue little flowers to delight the sight, and is a flavor favorite with many who consider it indispensable for salads, pickling, and even as a titillating touch in fresh fruit drinks.

Chives . . . parsley . . . caraway . . . thyme . . . sage . . . spearmint and peppermint (which thrive lustily in semishaded locations particularly) *. . . rosemary . . . lemon-verbena . . . rose geranium . . .* and many, many more are yours to enjoy, just for the planting and only a little pampering and continuous picking.

And if you have a cat, by all means grow a little catnip: the plants are decorative, and your furry friend will pronounce this phase of gardening *purrfect!*

Continue Outdoor Herbs Indoors

With many of the varieties like parsley which are so flavorful in the fresh green leaf, you'll want to bring plants indoors before frost. Just transplant them into pots or windowboxes, and many varieties will thrive well in a cool room where they get plenty of window sunshine.

Follow the rules given for most indoor plants. Use a rich, porous soil, water regularly, feed with liquid plant food, provide plenty of sun and air, but protect against drafts. Mint, basil, rosemary, chives, parsley—they're just a few of the luscious herbs that will grow happily indoors.

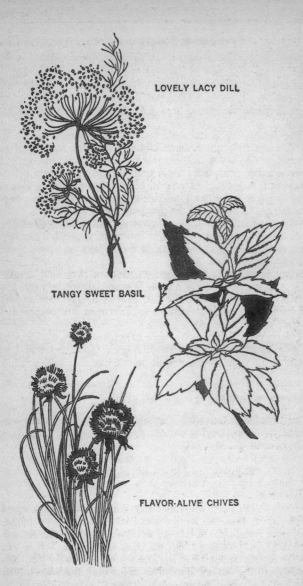

LOVELY LACY DILL

TANGY SWEET BASIL

FLAVOR-ALIVE CHIVES

Herbs are "flavor miracles" of nature.

Preserve Your Herbs, Too

While herbs are at their peak of flavor when picked fresh from the garden, they're also excellent when dried, seasoning your foods deliciously through all the seasons. And you'll find that you usually have an abundance for drying, as well as using fresh, because the plants and foliage multiply so enthusiastically.

The processing is quite simple. Pick the leaves on a hot, dry day just before the plants bloom. Leave the leaves out in full sun until they wilt. Then take them indoors and spread them in a dry, fairly cool place until they're thoroughly dried.

Just crumble a leaf in your fingers as a test. Put the leaves away in paper boxes, well identified, in a place where no moisture can get to them, lest the precious leaves mold.

With seeded herbs such as caraway and anise, gather the seeds just when the pods seem at the bursting point. Then dry them thoroughly, which only takes a few days, and pack them in small, airtight jars.

Some talented gardeners make their own potpourri combinations of herbs, then place them in small labeled jars and use them as gifts for favored friends. There's hardly another gift that brings such exclamations of joy, or is more truly expressive of your personal regard!

Yes, in every way, there's more happiness in life for gardeners who grow herbs—and it's such good taste, any way you regard it, in your garden and at your table.

Chives Alive!

A "miracle" taste touch for salads, vegetables, sauces and many other foods is a flavoring with fresh chives, kept alive right on your kitchen window sill.

You can usually pick up decorative little clay pots of young chives at your grocer, at garden stores, or even from a neighbor. But it's up to you to keep them at their greenest, freshest and tastiest!

Here's how. Keep the soil fairly moist with a little water every day or two, but never drenched. Avoid much sunlight, as chives love light but not an excess of sun. Watch out for browned tips, pinching them off right at the tips. When you use the chives at the table or in cooking, which will be surprisingly often, cut off the leaves right near the base of the plant.

They'll be all yours, right at your fingertips—flavor-alive, thriving chives!

ROCK GARDENING AND GROUND COVERS

For a Rock Garden that Wins Special "Hoorahs"

There are two different excellent reasons for growing a rock garden, and either or both will give you tremendous pleasure and a rare kind of special beauty to enjoy.

One reason is to solve difficult landscaping problems, where you have a nest of rocks, or a large boulder that you can't remove easily or don't want to do without because of its robust allure.

The other reason is that you simply want to enjoy the particularly entrancing contrast of rugged rocks and Nature's soft, colorful foliage and growth—and that you want the delight of growing some of the small and low plant specimens that don't fit into the regular garden plan.

Whatever the reason, a good, thriving rock garden has a special grandeur that will enrich your days with rich bloom at least three quarters of the year. Here's how to go about building a particularly efficient rock garden that will assure you the "miracle" growth you want:

Preparing Your Ravishing Rock Garden

1. Choose a slight sloping area preferably, or you can also use level ground—the swelling slope simply adds graceful contour, but doesn't promote extra growth particularly. Sunshine is needed in any situation.

Don't choose an area around the base of a tree, because the garden will look artificial and awkward. Also, the plants will have to fight the tree roots for nutrients, and may succumb to the shade thrown by the tree. Growth is most likely to be stunted and comparatively drab.

Don't just scatter rocks, regularly or irregularly, in the middle of your lawn or in an unseemly part of your garden. Choose a place where rocks will seem a natural, expected part of the landscaping. And don't set in too many rocks; a good rule is that it's better to place too few stones than to crowd in too many, for your plants need space to develop vigorous root growth and support.

Now, go to work carefully—you'll enjoy this phase if you take it slowly and easily, even though it involves considerable labor. Your results will be worth it!

2. Dig down into the earth for a depth of about a foot (dig around any rocks already in place). Fill the area about six inches deep with a layer of coarse gravel. Now fill in a couple of inches of partly rotted leaves or humus.

At this point, place your rocks, varying in size, shape and color, and fitting in naturally, not in any set pattern. Use your good taste and judgment, co-ordinating the rock spacing and placement to the surroundings, to avoid a man-made look. Bury the rocks about half to two-thirds in the soil, building up soil underneath where necessary.

3. Fill in soil around the rocks, using a mixture of one-third peat moss, one-third fertile soil, and one-third sand. You can use other good soil mixtures, of course, if more convenient for you, such as a combination of small gravel with the sand. The main object is to have a mixture airy enough to retain moisture and yet to drain well.

4. This is an important "plus" to accelerate growth and keep down weeds, to give you exceptional results. Place a mulch over the soil, about an inch deep, of medium gravel or granite chips—applied loosely and not packed down. This mulch adds lovely background beauty also to your plantings, and helps blend rocks and growth in an effect artistic and pleasing to the eye.

Now you're all set to plant, according to your personal selections (tips on these pages), very much according to proper planting procedures in your general garden. When you set in the plants, water well with a liquid plant food, and you'll get rich, flourishing, beautiful growth, with the rugged loveliness that only a rock garden can provide!

Planting Your Rock Garden Most Beautifully

Plan your plantings with this important color guide in mind. Combine dwarf evergreen growth with colorful small flowering plants—then you'll have an entrancing contrast of bright yellows and reds and whites against the subtle green, gray and bluish backgrounds of evergreen foliage, all blended beautifully by the deep gray and whitish, darkish tones of the rocks!

In your rock garden, even more than in your other gardening, let yourself be influenced by your personal taste in planning floral coloring and foliage shapes. Choose varieties that are particular hardy favorites in your area, then experiment later.

Here are some suggestions to help you, including newly improved plants that are especially hardy and beautiful:

Small Spring-flowering Bulbs

By setting in small varieties of bulbs in the fall, you'll have color in your rock garden starting in February and running through the early spring months. Select from low-growing better-than-ever favorites: crocus, snowdrops, winter aconite, small iris, dwarf hyacinths, glory of the snow and others. Scatter a rainbow of early color throughout the area, preferably in small clumps.

Other Flowering Beauties

For later spring, and through the summer and fall, you'll get vigorous growth and enchanting color from dwarf varieties of alyssum in white and lavender, phlox, lovely creeping veronicas, dianthus in a wide palette of glorious shades, small geraniums, cardinals, and many many more for your choice from seeds, nurseries and colorful catalogs.

Feature Some Unique Specimens

Hardy cactus plants are sprightly and unusual, making bright conversation pieces as they poke out of your rock garden. Choose spots with plenty of sun, planting in moist, sandy soil. When the plants are well established, popular varieties will produce exotic little golden flowers, followed by rich orange fruits—quite dazzling against the contrasting rocks.

"Live forever" plants, more prosaically known as sempervivum, are not only decorative but also thrive sturdily, with great resistance to any attacks by pests or disease. (The same

miracle chemicals you use in the rest of your garden will help control infestation in your rock garden too.)

These succulent plants, with tropical type of foliage, hug the stones, dig into crevices with their shallow roots so that sometimes they seem almost to be living on air. With their spreading graceful petal formations, looking somewhat like artichokes, they're very decorative and cheerful to view.

Stringy snowcrop sedum is one of the very popular varieties of this fleshy succulent plant. Its airy low growth seeks out places to spread its graceful foliage, softening the contours of hard rock. A very hardy species, you can root many cuttings in moist, sandy soil when you wish to multiply plantings throughout the rock garden.

These are just a few of the unique and delightful plants especially suited to your rock garden. Find other "rock enthusiasts," and you'll have extra pleasure comparing and exchanging your combined unusual species.

The Covering Tips on Ground Cover Plants

Granted that good grass is the most beautiful green carpeting for most sizable areas, let's face one big fault. Grass just won't grow adequately in certain places such as in deep shade, under dense trees and shrubs, and on steep banks. Yet you want rich green growth. What's to do about it?

Your best solution is to plant one of the hardy ground cover varieties, one that provides thick, compact and attractive growth. You'll preserve and enhance the beauty of your landscaping. However, if you're covering a wide area, remember that you can't walk over these covers as you can on grass.

On the other hand, you won't have to mow the hardy ground covers as you do grass. And there's much less need for fertilizing and watering. I said *less* need; you still must provide proper preparation of the soil, at least annual fertilization, some weeding, some watering—just not as much. And you won't have crabgrass nightmares about these areas!

Varieties Continually Improved

Like most everything else in gardening, the popular ground cover plants are being improved right along as a species. By going to reputable suppliers, you can get more vigorous varieties of ivy, for example, which will hold their beauty and color far better through the winter.

There are actually hundreds of different ground covers from which you can choose. Primarily you want those that will be most attractive in your area all year round. You can get ever-greens, types of plants that produce flowers or berries, and very low as well as higher kinds. If possible, try to see the species growing first under similar conditions to yours.

Plant with Care, for Endurance

You want your ground cover plants to live with you a long long time (they're perennials, of course!), so build their permanent home properly, pretty much the way you prepare a lawn right.

Dig up the area about ten inches deep. Mix in peat moss or compost for good drainage and aeration. Add plant food and rake in thoroughly.

Space out the plants as specified for the particular species you choose. Staggering the rows provides better coverage.

Firm the soil around the plants well, but don't "cement" them in. Water plentifully, the first time particularly, so that the roots will reach down deep and not grow just along the surface.

Usually it will take one or two growing seasons for your plants to spread and combine to provide the dense covering you want. During this period, you'll have to keep the beds relatively weed-free—preferably by hand because weed-killers may injure the young plants. But when the plants have merged, their shade will prevent most weeds from growing.

Care and Propagation

Fertilize your ground covers at least once a season. A water-soluble plant food is particularly practical and effective because you can feed right on the foliage with safety, whereas a dry fertilizer may burn the plants if not applied with extreme care. If you use a liquid fertilizer, repeat feedings several times a season, because its effect, while quicker, is not as long-lasting as dry fertilizer.

With most ground covers, pruning helps in the early spring preferably. Cut out all dead growth. Use your judgment in removing some of the top growth, to encourage the development of sturdy, bushier plants.

When plants have matured and are well established, many gardeners like to develop new plants from cuttings. Follow directions recommended for rooting cuttings elsewhere in this book. Especially if you have large areas to cover about your house, you may wish to develop cuttings to avoid the expense of buying lots of new plants.

Replant any spots that may have failed to grow and are
sparse or barren. Otherwise, weeds may seize the opportunity
to grow and steal nutrition from adjacent plants. Here too
cuttings will come in handy for renovating any trouble spots.

Some Choice Ground Covers Recommended For Shade

Epimedium, Bishop's Hat. This lovely ground cover produces many exquisite little flowers in spring, about an inch
wide, and shaped like tiny bishop's hats, hence the name. The
flowers are combinations of red, violet and white, and show
up beautifully against dense green foliage.

Leaves turn rich bronze during the fall and often retain that
lustrous color into the winter months. This evergreen grows
about nine inches high. Start with rich soil, keep moist and
well fertilized. Set in plants about ten to twelve inches apart.
Grown at its best, this and other varieties of epimediums make
a rewarding showing of color and texture in a mass.

Hedera Helix, Ivy. Seek out the newest varieties of this
English ivy when you plant, since they're hardier and keep their
color better through the winter. Growing six to eight inches
high, this strong evergreen is available in various sizes of
leaves, to your choice.

Set plants 1½ to two feet apart, as this species spreads rapidly. It thrives best in a fairly rich soil, and should be kept
rather moist but not too wet. Avoid exposing this shade-lover
to much sun.

Wild Ginger, Asarum caudatum. This evergreen, available
in several variations of the same family, produces very attractive, gleaming dark foliage. In late spring it is dotted with
small purplish flowers which aren't very evident. It's not really
ginger, but the rootstocks are said to be aromatic (I don't recommend chewing on them).

This rich species spreads slowly, so plant only about nine
inches apart, in fertile soil. Keep watering well. Grows to height
of about seven inches, loves the shade, and beautifies those
hard-to-cover areas wonderfully.

For Shade or Sun

Pachysandra terminalis. By any name, this is still "good old
pachysandra," now better than ever in hardy improved varieties. It grows about six inches high, and produces small white
flowers in spring, but they don't show up too well as they're
frequently hidden in the dense foliage.

Set plants about six inches apart for a good, dense cover. Pinch or cut back the tops of plants very early in spring before real growth starts. You'll promote thicker, bushier plants. Just don't cut down too far or you'll inhibit growth.

Only fair soil is required, medium watering, and regular fertilization. But don't expose to full sun. This is a very fine, uniform green cover for steep banks as well as flat areas.

Vinca Minor. This name is much classier than "myrtle," which some people call this dark and lustrous evergreen. It will delight you with the beauty of its white and blue flowers in spring, sparkling against the rich green background of lovely leaves, growing about six inches high.

Sturdy one- or two-year-old plants spread rapidly, so set them about a foot apart. Excellent on steep banks too because this beauty really digs in with its roots and holds on.

Vinca minor is a great favorite, and deserves it. Consider it very seriously for your ground cover problems in shade or sun.

For Sun

Sedum Stonecrop. There are many cousins in this big sedum evergreen family. Perhaps the most beautiful is sedum acre, also dubbed goldmoss stonecrop. This gem has little pointed, light green leaves that hug the ground and form a mat about two inches high. Plants spread swiftly.

While it is hardy and stands some abuse, it's not advisable to walk on sedum because its somewhat succulent foliage breaks down and mashes out. It is dotted with lovely tiny yellow flowers in late spring. Plant in good soil, fertilize regularly, water moderately—for a lush light green carpeting of cover.

Juniperus horizontalis, creeping juniper. This is just one of the juniper ground covers, all with imposing horicultural names which fortunately don't inhibit their ready growth.

This attractive variety grows from twelve to eighteen inches high. Foliage is exquisite blue-green to green, spreads rapidly and forms a dense, though rather high, covering. Plant as far as two to three feet apart, in average well-drained soil.

If you choose a juniper, investigate several other popular varieties available, some with steely blue foliage which turns colorful purple in fall and winter. Make sure to plant for plenty of sun.

There's no question that ground covers are grand for enriching problem spots and selective areas. They'll flourish for you beautifully if you give them the adequate care suggested.

The trouble some gardeners have with ground covers is that they plant and forget tending them. But you must realize that, like all of nature's worthy growth, these fine plants require and respond to care in planting, watering and fertilizing. Do your part, and you'll enjoy their luxurious beauty thoroughly!

HOME GREENHOUSE

Explore the World in a Greenhouse!

Yes, the whole world is yours when you have your own home greenhouse! There's hardly a plant in the world that you can't grow when you can control the climate by regulating the heat, light and moisture with push-button precision.

You'll be able to live in your "garden" twelve months of the year. You can show admiring friends exotic blooms in midwinter, varieties you never dreamed you could grow. With today's "miracle" fertilizers, insecticides and appliances, you can grow prize-winning specimens of rare or common plants, in such size and beauty as never produced before!

All that and more is the big lure for most gardeners. That's why, sooner or later, you'll probably get around to having some kind of greenhouse setup. Fortunately, modern construction methods and advances make it possible for you to buy a prefabricated greenhouse for under $200 today! Or, you can build one yourself.

Prefabricated Greenhouses Easy to Assemble

With just a few ordinary tools, most anyone who has fewer than twelve thumbs can usually assemble a prefabricated greenhouse in several hours or half a day. *But,* suppose it even takes you a day or two to set up your greenhouse right? What's the difference, you're going to get a lifetime of pleasure out of it.

The new aluminum greenhouses are more costly than wood, but they'll probably last lots longer without repairs or renovation. And with aluminum, you won't have to paint both outside and inside regularly. You'll have to make your own decision, according to your own feeling about these materials, and also taking into consideration how much you wish to pay.

You can get lean-to models which attach directly to your home or to the garage, either on the wide side of the greenhouse or the narrow end. You can choose from a variety of ready-made sizes, as small as seven by ten feet, and upwards—just about as large as your pocketbook can stretch.

Your best bet is to get a batch of catalogs from the many good companies now making prefabricated greenhouses. Select according to your personal needs and desires. But let me warn you that once you buy a greenhouse, you're hooked. You'll be absorbed in one of the most exciting and rewarding hobbies on earth. It's great!

Choosing the Right Type

Your choice of a greenhouse will be as personal as your selection of a home. Before you buy the smallest size, keep in mind that you'll keep wanting to expand your plantings, so I advise you to buy as large a house as you can, rather than the smallest. Like a woman buying a refrigerator, within a couple of days she's usually wishing she'd purchased the larger size!

Check the materials carefully before you buy. If you choose wood, it should be specially prepared redwood, not just ordinary wood which may rot and go out of shape in a hurry. Glass should be double strength, not ordinary quality. If the windows are plastic, make certain that the quality has been proved right in use—for efficiency and endurance as well as appearance. Some of the new plastic materials are excellent, but others sag in a hurry and have other flaws.

Special features such as weathertight, tough plastic channels for the glass, instead of putty, are very desirable. The little details will make a big difference in your results and enjoyment. Bear in mind that the lean-to type may have big advantages for you in respect to piping in electricity, heat and water from an adjacent room. You might even want to make your lean-to greenhouse an extra family room, a cheerful living "solarium."

On the other hand, the separate greenhouse has special merits in privacy, and completely isolated control of heating and temperature.

Tips on Heating

Is it costly to heat a greenhouse? Not according to most owners. Many report that it averages out to about $6 a month. Of course it all depends on where you live, and what kind of heating system you install. Contrary to general belief, even tropical plants don't require more than 60° to 65° at night.

If your greenhouse is attached to your house, you may be able to pipe a radiator right to your regular home heating system. Manufacturers of prefabricated greenhouses usually give instructions on doing it yourself, although I advise consulting a plumber.

Often it's more practical to have a small individual heating unit, operated by electricity, by bottled or natural gas, or by oil or coal. The most important point is to make sure that whatever heating system you have is regulated by automatic thermostat control. If not, you'll wear yourself out trotting in and out of the greenhouse checking the heat, or else you're likely to have frozen or roasted plants.

New Automatic Ventilation

Now you can get simple automatic controls which open and close roof ventilation during the daytime hours. This may not seem important, but it is. Success or failure in growing the "miracle" blooms you want will often depend on proper ventilation. Temperature and air are two vital keys to excellent greenhouse growth. Usually it's enough to have just one or two vents controlled automatically, to cut down your investment.

Hints on Humidity and Watering

Another helpful but not essential "plus" is to install automatic humidification in your greenhouse. This isn't absolutely necessary usually, as you can maintain good humidity balance without constant observation.

My advice is to pass up installing automatic humidity controls until you've had the greenhouse for a while and learned the ropes. That'll be plenty of time to decide, unless you don't mind the investment, in which case it's definitely desirable.

It's just about a "must" to have running water in your greenhouse, usually fairly simple to install. In addition to the need for water on the spot for your plants, it's most helpful for the washing and cleaning up chores you'll have.

If you fill your greenhouse with a wide range of plants, with different appetites, you'll have to take particular care to water "by prescription" rather than giving the same amount to all. For example, you may drown cacti and succulent plants unless you take care.

An excellent tip from greenhouse experts is to have a waterproof pan or pans a few inches deep. Fill the pan with vermiculite mixed with some peat moss, or just sand, and keep moist. Set a number of pots of water-loving plants into this mixture. They'll thrive on the extra humidity and won't require such frequent watering.

Of course potting your plants in mixtures containing peat moss, vermiculite and other moisture-holding materials will require less frequent watering. And naturally, you'll leave as much as an inch space between the soil and top of the pot, so you'll have room to fill and soak in plenty of water on your rounds.

Light, Shading and Infestation Control

Because some plants require more light than others, and some varieties thrive best with considerable shade, you'll have to learn this control also. Follow the instructions provided with your prefabricated greenhouse.

Look into new plastic sheetings which can be very helpful. You'll learn how to place some plants under benches to furnish extra shade. It all adds up to a fascinating scientific adventure.

For control of insects, harmful fungus and disease, the same wonder chemicals available for your outdoor garden will be a tremendous and essential help. The main tip is to watch constantly for any trouble, and then spray or dust at once.

Variety Is the Spice of Greenhouse Life

Because you can grow most anything in a greenhouse, except a giant redwood tree, there's a great temptation to fill it too fast and with too many different kinds of plants. It's best to take it easy, because even with restraint your spaces will be filled too quickly, and you'll be faced with the unhappy decision regarding which of your favorites to discard!

No one can tell you just what you should grow—that's your own happy choice. Here are some greenhouse favorites as a guide to start you thinking.

Orchids are a delight in the greenhouse, and not nearly so difficult to grow as you might expect.

Amaryllis responds beautifully, with some showy blooms lasting over a month in those perfect growing conditions.

Annuals of all kinds thrive wonderfully, of course. And the greenhouse will help you start many of your favorites ahead of time so that they go into the garden with greater development and vigor, for quick growth and resplendent bloom.

Camellias are a greenhouse sensation in colder areas, exquisite in foliage and spectacular in bloom. Your corsages will be a highlight at social events!

Bulbs, especially rare and delicate varieties, can be brought to bloom during winter months, making it truly June in January.

Cacti . . . *calendulas* . . . *chrysanthemums* . . . *cyclamen* . . . *cypripediums* . . . the list of greenhouse glory is endless, right through the glamorous alphabet of Nature's lushest growth.

And the list of greenhouse wonderment is endless too. Vines and hanging baskets offer you extra beauty. You can change the calendar at will. You can even pick your own fresh strawberries during a snowstorm. Imagine having cut flowers of your own daily selection and picking, all through winter!

Before you start a greenhouse, bear in mind that it will require time and regular attention. You can spend a lot or a little buying marvelous new equipment such as electric spray guns, stainless-steel instruments, or you can make do for the most part with what you already own.

But one thing is certain, once you experience the deep and exciting enjoyment of such controlled indoor gardening, you'll wonder how you ever lived without it.

Good luck to your greenhouse thumb!

CUT FLOWERS

Cutting Flowers for Lasting Beauty

1. You'll keep your cut flowers longer, and looking fresher, if you gather them late in the afternoon after the sun has gone. That's when the blooms are at their peak of vigor.

2. Choose blooms just as they're about to open from the bud, and soon after they've opened. Tight buds may never open in the vase. Mature blooms won't have much rich beauty left in them, once cut.

3. Use care in cutting so that you keep the plant looking graceful and ornamental outdoors, as well as decorating your home indoors. Space out your selection from a number of plants, if possible.

4. If at all practicable, carry a pail or other water container with you. Plunge the flowers into the water just as soon as you've cut them, with very few exceptions. You can even leave them there until ready to go into the vase. A few minutes of exposure to air eliminated at this point can mean many more hours of radiant beauty indoors.

Miracle Chemicals Keep Cut Flowers Longer!

When you pick your loveliest specimen flowers, or armfuls of lilacs or mums or whatnots (my favorite species!) from your garden, of course you want them to reflect their radiance indoors as long as possible. Here's how.

Just as new miracle chemicals and fertilizers can help you grow the most beautiful blooms, others help them live longer in the vase. So don't just dump the flowers in water; drop one of the life-extenders into the fluid and you'll actually enjoy the gorgeous colors looking fresh and alive *days longer*.

You can buy a number of good "cut flower foods" or "life prolongers" at garden supply counters, in tablet or powder form. Use them as directed, and exactly as directed, for far greater enjoyment of vases glowing with floral glory in your home, in the living room, in bedrooms—all over the place. For more delight each passing hour, bring indoors Nature's inspiring outdoors beauty.

Important Pointers

Here are some more basic tips to give you "miracle results" with your cut flowers.

1. Be sure that the glass vase or other container is clean. Dirt and bacteria in the container at the start tend to stuff and block the tubes in the stems which carry the life-preserving water to the flowers. Without this free supply, the blooms wilt faster.

2. When you cut the stems from the plant, always use a sharp blade, whether razor blade, knife or garden shears. Here

RIGHT

WRONG

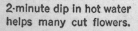

2-minute dip in hot water helps many cut flowers.

Cut flower stem at slant; exposes more area to water.

again, a fresh, sharp cut helps the stem to absorb water more readily. Fuzzy, ragged edges tend to block free flow of water.

3. This is something few people know, yet it's important in helping to keep blooms alive longer. Remove all leaves and foliage below water in the container. The reason is that the water-logged leaves decay; the result is that the flowers fade faster.

4. Most people plunge cut flowers into cold water, just run furiously from the tap. Don't you make that mistake. The flowers like it much better when placed in warm water, about the temperature of a nice, warm bath, or room temperature. That's because the stem absorbs the warm water much more freely, easily and speedily than when the water is cold. And you'll be rewarded by seeing the flowers perk up faster and stay alive-looking longer.

5. Finally, don't place the flowers over a radiator or close to the source of heat in a room. The heat acts to make the water evaporate faster than the flowers can absorb it. The same thing happens when you place flowers in a draft; the moving air removes water rapidly, preventing the flowers from absorbing water most efficiently.

Actually it's so simple for you to follow these tips, and add so much to your enjoyment of living color and beauty in your home. Just a few seconds of extra care perform miracles in adding hours and days to the inspiring radiance of your cut flowers.

Handling Cut Flowers for Best Results

1. The first tip about handling cut flowers is to handle them as little as possible. Hold by the stems, never by the blooms. As much as possible, prevent blooms from rubbing against one another or from contact with table or other surfaces.

2. Keep stem ends always in water, of course. Length of stem hasn't much effect on long-lasting quality. Deep water is better than shallow, for longer life. It's best to change the water every couple of days; if you're using chemical preservatives, add more to the fresh water.

3. A light, refreshing spray of water on blooms and foliage frequently helps preserve the fresh look. But don't drench the flowers—use either a fine spray or none at all.

4. Avoid narrow-necked containers which tend to squeeze and congest the stems. Wide-necked containers, most any rustproof material, are best. You don't function at your best either in a too-tight collar, do you?

Flower arranging is too broad a subject to cover here, but all the activities now concerned with flower arrangements, and the personal enjoyment and compliments involved, can add a great deal to your joy from gardening! You might well look into this exciting subject.

Hot-water Energizer

A two-minute hot-water immersion of stems works wonders in lengthening the life of two classes of cut flowers:

. . . Woody plants—this includes varieties such as roses, chrysanthemums, hydrangea, orchids, rhododendron.

. . . Bleeding varieties—such as poppies, dahlias, hollyhocks.

First, wrap the flowers and foliage in newspaper or other paper, snugly at the bottom, leaving only a couple of inches of bottom stems exposed.

Place the stems in hot water, and leave about two minutes.

Unwrap the bunch and place in room-temperature water.

The lovely, longer-lasting blooms appreciate this hot "foot bath."

Pump water and longer life into hollow-stemmed species.

"Pump Treatment" for Hollow-stemmed Blooms

For special arrangements of most spring bulbs and succulent plants—tulips, water lilies, calla lilies and such—it helps tremendously, in fact it's practically a "must," to pump water into the hollow stems beforehand.

First, stand the flowers in a deep vessel filled with room-temperature water. Leave them up to a half hour to give plenty of time for absorption.

Now, with a small pump for that purpose, pump fresh water directly into each stem, one at a time.

The blooms will stay vigorous and beautiful much longer with this custom-tailored inoculation. Another trick is to spray the flowers frequently with water, after you've completed your lovely arrangements.

Try the Charcoal Trick

You'll be surprised and impressed with the way plain, ordinary charcoal can often help prolong the life of your lovely cut flowers. Try it in one vase, and leave it out of a similar vase nearby—just as an interesting test.

Simply drop a few chunks of thoroughly prerinsed charcoal in the container. This very absorbent material helps keep the water free from odor and cloudiness.

If you have crystal clear containers, and find the charcoal unattractive, by all means leave it out—it's not that important to your blooms.

Spare the Aspirin

I don't know who started the rumor that an aspirin tablet dropped in the water would keep cut flowers lasting longer. Could it have been the manufacturers of aspirin? I doubt it. At any rate, horticultural scientists can't seem to find any benefits from the use of aspirin this way.

Better save the aspirin for your headaches—which are also eased by the sight of exquisite flowers, especially those beauties you grow yourself.

EQUIPMENT

More Power in Power Equipment

You'll get tremendous help from the modern power tools. But choose carefully on the basis of the size of your property, your pocketbook and your personal viewpoint as to the amount of time and labor you want to put into tending your lawn and garden.

You can get so many different types of power clippers, mowers and other tools that I can't even begin to list them here. Furthermore, new models come out every month. For instance, you can get inexpensive little power mowers or streamlined beauties with "vacuum" attachments that suck up grass clippings, leaves and debris as a swift rotary blade cuts the grass.

Best advice is for you to visit *several* reputable dealers before you make your final selection. Don't be overpowered by the magnificence and gadgetry of some models. Buy according-ing to your personal requirements, not for a property ten times the size.

On the other hand, beware of alluring "bargains" on the basis of low price alone. Just use your wisdom as a shopper— look, look elsewhere, *think it over for a few days*, then buy and enjoy the marvelous new equipment to the utmost.

Good Equipment Deserves Good Care

Even the best mechanisms need adequate attention. Keep moving parts clean and well lubricated. Remove rust spots before they spread, and protect for winter storage. Drain gas tanks before putting power tools away for long periods. Clean up spark plugs and other vital parts, and have repairs made *before spring*.

Thus, you help prevent troubles before they happen. You'll find that power tools leave you much more time for the enjoyment of gardening. Treat these modern aids well, and they'll serve you wonderfully.

Modern Season-beater—
Aluminum Cold Frame

For years many gardeners have enjoyed the advantages of a good cold frame for beating the season—getting seeds and plants started before spring weather opens up, by keeping out frost and maintaining higher temperatures in the framed area. And now, better modern materials help you get the benefits more easily and efficiently than ever before.

In practically no time at all, you can put together a garden cold frame of lightweight aluminum and plastic that will serve you year after year without rusting, rotting or need for painting. With the plastic materials used, there's no more worry about glass breakage.

The new frames have many fascinating features such as aluminum rain gutters which admit ventilation for your seedlings without letting the downpour flood them, and lids that slip away when you work in the cold frame.

Modern aid—lightweight "lifetime" aluminum cold frame.

Easy to Set Up

Least costly way is to buy a prefabricated aluminum cold frame that you put together yourself. You don't have to be a mechanic!

A popular size available is about three by four feet, with transparent plastic top "windows" that lift or slide—easy to handle because they weigh very little.

In some good models, the plastic sheeting is reinforced underneath with aluminum wire. The special new plastic materials have exceptional insulating qualities to keep cold out and heat in. These magical materials make the most of sunshine, gathering helpful ultraviolet rays for plant life.

Starts Fine Variety of Plant Life

Just pick a convenient corner of your property and set your new cold frame there, where it won't intrude on the garden. You prepare the earth, plant and fertilize as recommended for a good planting bed. In early spring, before outdoor gardening weather begins, you start bulbs, seeds and seedlings so they're far advanced for planting in your garden as soon as the weather is warm enough.

Your garden will be glowing with beautiful foliage and gay color weeks ahead of your neighbors' who don't get an early start with a cold frame. And while the cost of the modern aluminum cold frame may seem lots more at the beginning than the old wood and glass frames, upkeep in work, time and money is practically nil.

A good cold frame will certainly warm up your gardening enthusiasm and results considerably ahead of ordinary planting season!

Wonderful Featherweight Trellises

Marvelous aluminum is now made for trellises that add immensely to the ease and pleasure of modern gardening. Available in a variety of decorative shapes, they're so lightweight that the material is a cinch to handle.

You cut to size quickly and neatly, and attach with aluminum nails or rustproof wire or other material to the surface you wish to cover.

If you decide to change the trellis to another spot next season, it's easy to move and attach. We gardeners enjoy being fickle and changeable, and the new miracle materials certainly help us to indulge our temperament.

While an aluminum trellis may seem a little more costly, remember that it will last year after year and doesn't require painting and repainting.

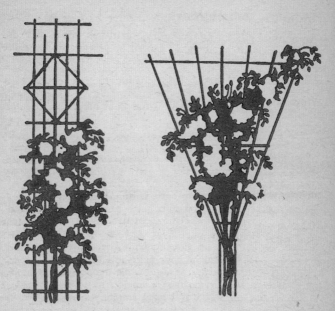

New lightweight aluminum trellises don't rust.

Moisture-measuring Gadgets

"How dry I am!" That's what plants and grass often complain about, not by voice but by exhibiting their drying and drooping foliage. To take the guesswork out of moisture measurement, modern manufacturers now offer attractive, compact instruments for the gadget-minded gardener.

Of course you can measure the depth of moisture in soil in a general way simply by digging down with a slim trowel or special soil-testing rod. But, to be more exact and scientific about it, you can now buy a soil moisture recorder which will help you to measure quickly and easily the moisture content of the earth in many places in your lawn and garden.

Some of these gadgets are topped with dials for easy reading. Far from a necessity, this is a nice item to own. And, here's a tip for the birthday of the gardener who "has everything," one of these attractive instruments makes a different and exciting gift.

Indelible Plant Marker

An unusual gift for an enthusiastic gardener who goes in for a big variety of plantings in garden or greenhouse is an impressive new metal strip embosser. Looks something like a large hand stapler.

Simply feed in a roll strip of metal, turn an alphabet wheel, press down, and letter by letter the plant name appears on the thin flat metal strip. Snips off cleanly, and there's the plant name embossed on metal indelibly and permanently. You can use the name strip again and again on successive plants.

It's rather costly, but as an "important" gift, it'll make a big hit and, with refills available, lasts a gardening lifetime.

Two-legged Wonder-winder

This comes under the department of why-didn't-I-think-of-that. A very simple winding device is now available to help you wind up garden hose, rope that you've used to protect lawn or hedge, long tape, or for any such winding job.

This ingenious product looks like a simple metal rack, with only two legs, and a drum reel in the center. You just push the two spikes right into the ground (like pitchfork prongs) wherever you want to do the winding job.

Then you attach the hose or rope to the reel, grab the handle, and wind away quickly and easily.

The two legs in the ground hold the frame firm, and as you wind you still have one hand free to help guide the rope or hose, or even to scratch your head while you think of the cold refreshing drink you're going to enjoy after finishing in the garden.

Handy Canvas Carrier for the Garden

There's a clever new canvas contraption which helps around the garden wonderfully at any cleanup time. It's a sheet of strong white duck cloth with a cotton rope drawstring worked into its construction.

When you're raking the lawn after cutting the grass, gathering leaves, cutting hedges, planting a new shrub—or any such tasks—protect the lawn and lighten your work by spreading out this flat canvas first. Pile the debris and leaves in it.

Then, simply pull the drawstring, and the canvas forms a large pouch which you tote away easily.

Also, you can pile up waste material on the canvas while working in one spot, drag it over easily to the next place where you're going to work, and accumulate the trash. This system will save you plenty of steps from constant round trips.

Keep a Corer Handy

One of the handiest "tools" in my garden kit isn't even a tool at all. It's a simple, inexpensive old apple corer, one of those long, hollowed-out metal tubes with one scalloped edge, and a handle.

I use it for digging out some tough lawn and garden weeds and getting them out roots and all, for transplanting seedlings, scooping out quick deep holes, etc.

Try it! You'll find that this commonplace household gadget goes right to the "core" of many little garden tasks. Hmm.

Use plain old apple corer as a gardening aid.

Quick Trick Preserves Garden Tools

When gardening season is unhappily over, and you put away your garden tools, there's a tendency just to walk away and let them weather the winter unprotected in a garage or shed. Then, when you pick up the tools in spring, they're tarnished or rusted, unpleasant to sight and touch.

Yet, just a few minutes of application will keep the tools clean and help protect them against rust and corrosion!

You don't need any special materials; just take out one of the excellent modern paste waxes that you undoubtedly have around for household or auto use. Rub the wax on the metal parts of the tools and leave them.

This quick waxing will not only save you money in preserving garden tools, but will also be a spur to more pleasurable gardening in a hurry when the first whiff of spring beckons you out to work in the good earth.

Warning Tip . . . Separate Your Sprayers

This tip can save you many dollars through the years in preventing loss of valuable plants. For the little money a sprayer costs, it will pay you many times over to have separate sprayers for your strong weed killers, and for milder insecticides that you apply directly to plants.

If you wash out a sprayer completely after applying a violent weed-killer solution, you can use the same device for your milder insecticides and other sprays. But we humans at our best are apt to be careless at times. Or perhaps Husband thinks that Wife cleaned the weed killer out of the sprayer when she finished using it, but maybe the roast started burning and she rushed into the house without washing out the sprayer thoroughly. (Or vice versa when Husband left his gardening to take an important phone call.)

As a result of such accidents, you next fill the sprayer with a comparatively mild insecticide which you spray on prized rose bushes. Then you wonder why the roses and foliage turn black or growth is stunted.

My tip is that you own two sprayers. Paint a large "W" on one to denote that it's to be used for weed killers only. And use the unmarked sprayer for milder insecticides and other chemicals. Clean each sprayer thoroughly after each use anyhow.

With this extra separate-sprayer caution, you're bound to avoid some costly destruction of beautiful plants, foliage and blooms.

Gardens That Merrily Roll Along

New aluminum gardens on wheels are available for you now, extremely decorative and very practical.

In various sizes and shapes, you can buy these sturdy and attractive garden carriers in two, three or more tiers. The aluminum construction makes them lightweight and easy to move about.

Benefits are double. In line with the new trend toward changing decorative room arrangements from time to time, or for different occasions, it enables you to switch your indoor garden from corner to corner and room to room as it pleases you.

Secondly, you can move plants around easily in seconds to get more good window light as the sun shifts, or to move temperamental plants like African violets away from too-strong sunlight pouring in through a window.

For indoor usage, fluorescent lights are available, built right into the lightweight aluminum construction. Watertight trays are another helpful feature.

As the seasons change, move your garden on wheels out to the terrace, to the front porch, and then indoors again. It's another modern aid to more pleasure from gardening, around the clock and through the year.

New gardens on wheels.   Use long-nosed waterer.

ODDS AND END

_____

Garden and Grow Slim!

While gardening won't guarantee to make you thin, or give you a figure sure to win beauty contests, it can work miracles in trimming off some inches, flattening your abdomen and rewarding you with better posture.

Here's the one most important tip for a better figure and physique through gardening, whether you're male or female. This pointer is much better for the health of your back also, helps avoid those sacroiliac's-got-me screams. It's simply this.

You do a lot of bending when working in your garden, so train yourself to bend this way. Don't stand stiff-legged, breaking your body in half bending from the hips, rounding your shoulders and bending your head downward. That doesn't do you much good.

Instead, bend your knees, and lower yourself that way, keeping your back relatively straight, bending forward from your hips. Don't let your shoulders round forward. Don't let your head bend more than necessary.

Then, when you get up, still keep your back straight, your shoulders back, and thrust your body erect with your thighs. Don't just get up, thrust up with your thighs!

It's really easy once you get the habit. Practice going down that way, bending your knees, stay down a few seconds, then thrust your body up, as described. Keep it in mind, and soon you'll be doing it naturally as you work in the garden, without even thinking about it.

You'll gain in improvement in your figure and posture, and you'll find that working this way is less tiring.

Another quick tip is to hold your abdomen in as you work, bend, reach out to pick flowers, stretch up as in trimming a high shrub or picking fruit from a tree.

At first you'll have to keep reminding yourself, "Abdomen IN . . . abdomen IN"—or simply, "AbdomIN!"

But soon it'll became natural to you, part of your new improved posture. And you'll be delighted when the tape measure proves to you that gardening has trimmed actual inches from your abdomIN.

What about Organic Gardening?

Organic gardening, stating it most briefly, is gardening without the use of any chemicals. This interesting phase of gardening is covered in detail in many books, and in its own monthly magazine.

There's no question that organic gardeners produce some wonderful growth results—and, just as certainly, marvelous growth of every kind is obtained by gardeners using the "miracle" chemical products developed by science.

From a strictly nonpartisan viewpoint, I have never seen any evidence that organic gardening can produce better results than gardening with chemicals. From examination of hundreds upon hundreds of tests, there's also no question that modern scientific methods of gardening, and farming, outproduce strictly organic gardening—by enormous margins.

Whichever type of gardening you choose, or if—as many wise and able gardeners do—you combine both, you'll gain much in pleasure and rewarding results.

Calling All Men . . . as Well as Women

Garden clubs are wonderful for women, of course, but they're not for the ladies only. You men can get an extra measure of gardening pleasure, and a help in producing better results from your garden, if you join with other fine gardeners across the nation in the Men's Garden Clubs of America.

Chances are there's a branch convenient to you, just for the asking and looking. Lectures, demonstrations and productive community work are part of their helpful activities, in addition to just plain getting more fun out of gardening.

It's up to you, of course—just a tip about another door you can open if you wish, to another path through the wonderful world of gardening!

More Pleasure in Plant Societies

Are you a chrysanthemum cheerer? An iris enthusiast? A rose raver? Passionate about peonies? Dizzy over day lilies or delphiniums? If you have one real flower favorite, you'll get extra joy out of growing and pampering them for perfection if you belong to a society dedicated to that particular variety.

Belonging to a group with that common bond will help give you friends and correspondents from coast to coast. And you'll gain valuable information and news of interest from the society's publications and bulletins.

Each of the plants listed above, and others, has its own dedicated society. If you're interested in joining, you can learn the address of the nearest branch from your favorite garden magazine, or probably at your local library.

Of course it hardly needs saying that you can get great benefit and enjoyment also from joining your local garden club. If these lines spur or inspire you to join a plant society or garden club, then I'll be thrilled, for I will have added to your pleasure in living.

It's so true—gardeners have more fun than people!

Secret of Happiness

Somewhere I read the translation of a Chinese proverb; many of you have already found it to be true, or you'll discover it to be so:

"If you want to be happy for a few hours, drink wine until your head spins gaily.

"If you want to be happy for a weekend, get married and hide away.

"If you want to be happy for a week, kill a tender pig and eat it.

"If you want to be happy all your life long . . . *become a gardener!*"

You—the Greatest Garden Miracle of All!

As you read on these pages about all the wonders that new miracle products and established top-gardening procedures can produce, remember: don't ever get the idea that you can just sit by and watch "miracles" happen in your garden.

No. You, the gardener, are still the greatest miracle of all. Unless you use your effort and intelligence in tending your garden, and applying the many fine products and procedures available, you'll never have the "miracle garden" you want or the magnificent results that will give you the deep thrill of pride and accomplishment.

So, a sweeping bow to you and your work and interest and constant application! And, keep in mind that those fine people devoted to gardening and agriculture and the problems of growth from the soil, never stop seeking new and better products and ways to grow more and better plants and crops.

Keep trying and looking and learning—not only from today's availabilities but from tomorrow's miracles. We'll never reach the ultimate, but we'll get as close to it as possible.

Garden progress has been wonderful. *But you ain't seen nothin' yet!*

An Apology

If I've left out word about any of your garden favorites, or haven't completely covered instructions you require, I apologize. It pains me to neglect so many marvelous plants and variations of gardening.

My excuse is simply that while there are no limitations to the "miracles" that take place in Nature's gardens, there is a limit to the number of pages in a book.

Please understand, and accept my most sincere wishes for good luck and happy gardening!